MASS-MEDIATED TERRORISM

MASS-MEDIATED TERRORISM

Mainstream and Digital Media
in Terrorism and Counterterrorism

Third Edition

Brigitte L. Nacos

ROWMAN & LITTLEFIELD PUBLISHERS, INC.
Lanham • Boulder • New York • Toronto • Plymouth, UK

ROWMAN & LITTLEFIELD PUBLISHERS, INC.

Published in the United States of America
by Rowman & Littlefield Publishers, Inc.
A wholly owned subsidary of The Rowman & Littlefield Publishing Group, Inc.
4501 Forbes Boulevard, Suite 200, Lanham, Maryland 20706
www.rowmanlittlefield.com

Estover Road, Plymouth PL6 7PY, United Kingdom

British Library Cataloguing in Publication Information Available

Library of Congress Cataloging-in-Publication Data
Nacos, Brigitte Lebens.
Mass-mediated terrorism : the central role of the media in terrorism and counterterrorism / Brigitte L. Nacos.-3rd ed.
    p. cm.
Includes bibliographical references and index.
ISBN (cloth): 978-1-4422-4760-4
ISBN (paper): 978-1-4422-4761-1
eISBN: 978-1-4422-4762-8
1. Terrorism-Press coverage-United States. 2. Terrorism in mass media. 3. Terrorism and mass media--United States. I. Title. PN4784.T45N35 2007
303.6'25--dc22

2006101217

Printed in the United States of America

♾™ The paper used in this publication meets the minimum requirements of American National Standard for Information Sciences—Permanence of Paper for Printed Library Materials, ANSI/NISO Z39.48-1992.

Contents

Introduction to the First Edition

A s I ARRIVED at the Brussels airport from New York last year, nervous security agents asked me to open a small gift-wrapped package that had raised their suspicion as my handbag moved through the x-ray machine. The package contained golf balls. A few months later, as I went through a security check at London's Heathrow Airport to catch a flight to New York, a security agent unpacked my cosmetic bag and opened a powder compact. In all of my domestic travels and flights to overseas destinations, the security personnel at U.S. airports never took a second look at my carry-on luggage. Even before the simultaneous hijackings of four commercial airliners and the kamikaze attacks on New York and Washington on September 11, 2001 (referred to ever since as "the events of 9/11," or simply "9/11"), most frequent air travelers were aware of the lax airport security in the United States. Now we know that terrorists notice, too.

Experts in the fields of terrorism, antiterrorism, and counterterrorism had long feared and expected more lethal, international terror on American soil. But few were prepared for the unprecedented attacks on the World Trade Center Towers in New York, the Pentagon in Washington, and the failed attempt on a third target in Washington, most likely the U.S. Capitol, the seat of the Congress. But neither intelligence officers nor terrorism scholars should have been all that surprised. Based on our knowledge of insufficient airport security and of persuasive intelligence that the architect of the first World Trade Center bombing in 1993, the infamous Ramzi Yousef, and some of his fellow terrorists had planned the simultaneous hijackings of American airliners as early as 1995, and that some of these terrorist circles intended to fly a plane into the CIA headquarters near Washington, government officials should have anticipated this sort of super-terrorism.

A few of them actually did. William S. Cohen, then U.S. Secretary of Defense, warned in 1999 of the very real threat that "weapons [of mass destruction] will find their way into the hands of individuals and independent groups—fanatical terrorists and religious zealots beyond our borders, brooding loners and self-proclaimed apocalyptic prophets at home." Moreover, he cautioned that in "the past year dozens of threats to use chemical and ideological weapons in the United States have turned out to be hoaxes. Someday, one will be real."[1] Although appearing in an op-ed piece in the *Washington Post*, the startling statements did not alarm the news media. Neither television news nor the leading print media picked up on or explored the secretary of defense's dire prediction. Leslie H. Gelb, President of the Council of Foreign Affairs, commented that he was "astonished" because "none of the television networks and none of the elite press even mentioned it."[2]

While over-covering terrorist incidents, highlighting routine warnings of more devastating terrorism to come, and occasionally pointing to flaws in the counterterrorist preparedness programs, the media did not follow up on serious signs and warnings of the looming terrorist threat as outlined by William S. Cohen's carefully chosen words. After the attacks of 9/11, few in the news media recognized their neglectfulness in this respect. The columnist Richard Cohen was an exception when he wrote:

> I know a guy—never mind his name—who was on one of those government terrorism commissions—never mind which one—and used to say I ought to talk to him. I never did. I was too busy, not just with Bill and Monica but with other things as well, some of them very important. Anyway, I never wrote about the terrorist threat to this country. I was negligent.[3]

This kind of self-examination was scarce and came too late. Nevertheless, as public officials struggled to respond to the attacks on New York and Washington and the plane crash near Philadelphia, the anthrax threat, and the hunt for the perpetrator(s), the media proved indispensable. Television, telephones, radio, newspapers, newsmagazines, and the Internet amounted to a communications network that, at its best, created virtual public meeting places and, at its worst, exploited highlight replays of human evil's most horrific images of destruction.

I began to work on this book long before Osama bin Laden, al-Qaeda, and their associates in terror cells in Europe, the United States, and elsewhere wrote a new chapter in the annals of terrorism on September 11, 2001. Although at the time the most lethal terrorist acts ever, neither the events of 9/11 nor the subsequent anthrax attacks changed my understanding of the mass media's central role in the terrorist scheme. To be sure, these perpetrators exploited the media more shrewdly than other terrorists, but their deeds affirmed my thesis of the media's centrality in the calculus of terrorism, regardless of whether the violent deeds are major or minor in size. Historically, terrorists vied for publicity (having to settle for mouth-to-mouth reporting before the invention of the printing press); now they can exploit far-reaching, instant, and global media networks and information highways to carry the news of their violence along with what has been called "propaganda of the deed."[4] Indeed, as the weeks following the attacks on the World Trade Center and the Pentagon and the U.S. counterattacks on targets in Afghanistan made utterly clear, relatively weak terrorists such as Osama bin Laden and his al-Qaeda terrorist organizations can be formidable players against powerful nations—even the United States, the world's only remaining superpower—in a propaganda campaign triggered by violence.

A Short Outline for This Book

As it happened, nearly a year before terrorists struck hard inside American borders, the United States suffered a major terrorist attack abroad and the United Kingdom sustained a stunning, if far less harmful terrorist attack in the midst of London. Both of these instances demonstrated the effectiveness of terrorism as far as its perpetrators' publicity goals were concerned. Marking these events in the first year of the twenty-first century as starting points, chapter 1 explains the concept of mass-mediated terrorism and describes how it works in actual terrorist incidents. Although I am aware of the fundamental disagreements over the definition of terrorism, I undertake a new effort to solve this dilemma by suggesting a terminology that links the understanding of terrorism to its perpetrators' deliberate goal—to acquire publicity in the form of media coverage. When the Cold War ended, many foreign policy experts expected less anti-American and anti-Western terrorism in what they envisioned as the "new world order," offering ample opportunities for global cooperation. In order to give the reader a better understanding of the post–Cold War terrorist threat, the chapter traces the developments and reasons for the emergence of more and more lethal terrorism, beginning with the fall of the Soviet Union and the disintegration of the communist bloc.

Never was the news about acts of terrorism as bad and dramatic as it was on September 11, 2001, and thereafter. Chapter 2, although not planned when I began writing the book, examines how the mass media figured into the impact of the 9/11 terrorist events and how the news media reported this unfolding drama and the following anthrax letter scare. In times of major natural and man-made catastrophes, the public depends on the news, especially television and radio reports, for information about the crisis at hand and for instructions about what to do and what not to do. To be sure, much of the information was provided by public officials or members of the business community, but the news media provided generous access to people involved in managing the crisis and/or used these officials as news sources. While it is important to know whether the news served the public interest in this particular respect, one is equally as curious about a host of other questions and issues, such as the reporting patterns during the most acute stages of the crisis and thereafter, whether news organizations became unwittingly the instruments of terrorist propaganda, or whether the media suspended its traditional watchdog role vis-à-vis government in the face of an extraordinary emergency. While some of the most obvious questions and issues of the media coverage were actually raised by critics as the terrorism crisis unfolded, my second chapter provides a comprehensive examination of the news of September 11 and thereafter.

Chapter 3 demonstrates that political violence for the sake of publicity succeeds even when terrorists stage rather modest acts of terrorism. As long as terrorists offer visuals and sound bites, drama, threats, and human interest tales, the news media will report—and actually over-report—on their actions and causes at the expense of other and more important news. Terrorism fits into the infotainment mold that the news media increasingly prefers and offers villains and heroes the promise to attract new audiences and keep existing ones. Here the news is not different from the entertainment industry, which thrives on villains and heroes in its search for box-office hits. Moreover, in our celebrity culture, whenever possible at all, terrorists receive celebrity treatment. News reporting made the names of earlier terrorists household words in their immediate target countries, and sometimes beyond. Carlos the Jackal, Andreas Baader and Ulrike Meinhof of the Red Army Faction, or Arafat in the PLO's terrorist phase come to mind. But more recent terrorists, such as Osama bin Laden and Timothy McVeigh, were treated like legitimate celebrities in the news—in the case of bin Laden, actually before the events of and after 9/11. Because the term terrorism has negative connotations, perpetrators of political violence do not like to be called terrorists. As chapter 3 demonstrates, the news media uses the t-word to describe some political violence but avoids the term when reporting on similar incidents of violence for political ends.

A decade ago, when Charles Kegley Jr. wrote, "all terrorism is international" (Kegley 1990), I was not persuaded. Today, if only because of the global nature of the new media, Kegley's earlier conclusion seems far more plausible and convincing. Chapter 4 explores mass-mediated terrorism on the premise that the new means of information and communication in particular offer groups and individuals with violent agendas and messages of hate unlimited, unchecked, and inexpensive opportunities to reach audiences around the globe. In the late twentieth and early twenty-first centuries, groups with terrorist designs communicated with members and supporters via satellite phones, e-mail, and Internet sites while still depending a great deal on the traditional news media to report their violent activities and the causes behind those acts. In addition, the stronger radical movements were able to establish their own radio and television stations and networks. Finally, the relatively easy access to these new means of communication developed into a convenient tool for the recruitment of members or followers and for the solicitation of donations.

Chapter 5 examines how the mass media cover anti- and counterterrorist policies in the American context and how this news figures into decision making regarding the prevention and the countering of terrorism. Because military retaliation and prevention acts are the only responses that are competitive with terrorist acts in terms of reaping publicity, chapter 5 presents case studies of American military strikes in response to terrorism, from the 1983 bombing of Libya to the attacks on al-Qaeda and Taliban targets in Afghanistan following the September 11, 2001, kamikaze attacks in the United States. Since the three cases prior to the retaliatory strikes against Afghanistan were minor, this chapter concentrates on the media's portrayal of this first phase in "the war against terrorism" and on reactions at home and abroad. Moreover, content analyses reveal how the crisis-managing President Bush, who was relentless in his efforts to appeal to the domestic public, to the political elite in Washington, to the international community, and to the world's most prominent terrorist Osama bin Laden (who was in hiding), fared in the news.

As the fears and predictions of mass destruction terrorism grew in the last decade of the twentieth and early years of the twenty-first century, federal, state, and local governments in the United States intensified their efforts to create and/or beef up permanent emergency response agencies. Moreover, programs were established, conferences organized, and emergency simulations and exercises conducted to prepare emergency response professionals from law enforcement, fire departments, emergency medical services, National Guard, etc. for dealing with worst-case terrorist attack scenarios. Not surprisingly, in this context, questions were asked about effective public information in the midst of terrorist crises, and the handling of the news media was discussed. When terrorists strike, one of the most important tasks of crisis managers, in particular, and of leaders in the community of emergency response professionals, in general, is that of informing the public and, for this purpose, of dealing with the news media. Based on my studies of media coverage in terrorist and other foreign and domestic crises (Nacos 1990, 1994a, 1996b) and discussions with emergency response professionals, I wrote chapter 6 as a blueprint for effective public information and media relations during terrorist crises. The flip side of the chapter's recommendations could serve as a guide for ethical news coverage in the case of major terrorist incidents.

Finally, the short concluding chapter weighs the positive and negative features of the inevitable links between the mass media, on the one hand, and terrorism as well as counterterrorism, on the other.

Notes

1. William S. Cohen, "Preparing for a Grave New World," *Washington Post*, July 26, 1999, A19.

2. Gelb is quoted here from Joe Klein, "Closework: Why We Couldn't See What Was in Front of Us," *The New Yorker*, October 1, 2001, 45.

3. Richard Cohen, "The Terrorism Story—And How We Blew It," *Washington Post*, October 4, 2001, A31.

4. Nineteenth-century anarchists and social revolutionaries understood their political violence as "propaganda of the deed" in that they considered their terrorist acts a means of sending messages to both governments and the general public. See Schmid and de Graaf (1982, 11–14).

Introduction to the Second Edition

SINCE I FINISHED THE MANUSCRIPT for the first edition of this volume in early 2002, about six months after 9/11, many more major acts of terrorism were perpetrated and many more innocent people were killed and injured. As I write this introduction, the United States has not been struck again, but many other countries have been attacked by terrorists, among them Morocco, Russia, Indonesia, Spain, the United Kingdom, Egypt, India, Pakistan, Sri Lanka, Iraq, Israel, and Jordan. During the same period, equally, or even more, deadly counterterrorism measures were undertaken, most notably the invasion and subsequent occupation of Iraq by a military coalition that was mostly composed of U.S. and UK troops. In the last five years, hardly a newscast was aired and a newspaper printed without containing reports on terrorism and counterterrorism. Terrorism and the threat of terrorism put deep imprints on American politics and policies to an extent unimaginable before 9/11 and even in the months immediately following the attacks on the World Trade Center and the Pentagon. Effective and sensible anti- and counterterrorism policies, along with controversial policies allegedly pursued in the name of counterterrorism, took center stage in the United States and other countries as well.

The post–9/11 years tested the American news media's willingness to cover, but not over-cover, actual acts of terrorism abroad, the numerous terrorism threats issued by terrorists themselves, the frequent elevations of the Bush administration's color-coded terror alerts, and the revelations about foiled terrorist strikes against American targets. But just as news organizations hyped this news before the 9/11 attacks and in the immediate aftermath of those events, this tendency did not subside. On the contrary, terrorism, threat warnings, and military responses to terrorism were over-covered and magnified, while the relaxation of official terrorism alerts and the incremental successes of traditional intelligence and law enforcement work at home and abroad were under-covered and minimized. And in the years after 9/11, most of America's news organizations slanted their coverage heavily in favor the administration's arguments.

When sophisticated terrorists like Osama bin Laden and his al-Qaeda associates, as well as like-minded individuals and cells strike, they want the whole world to know about their deeds. In the last few years, more global television networks joined the existing ones and offered international terrorists ever more opportunities to spread their propaganda. The Arab satellite network Al-Jazeera in particular became a truly international player because of its reporting from Afghanistan before and after American-led coalition forces drove the Taliban and al-Qaeda leadership out of that country. Al-Arabiya was the most prominent newcomer on the worldwide television networks scene, and the Lebanese Hezbollah's al-Manar is probably the best example of a local television station growing into a global satellite TV network with large audiences around the world. Finally, the Internet became far more important as a means of communication and source of information. This edition of *Mass-Mediated Terrorism* examines the new developments and how they figure into the terrorist and counterterrorist communication objectives.

As I updated the second edition, I drew heavily on the constructive comments of several instructors who used the first edition in their courses and were kind enough to suggest changes and additions.

Besides updating chapter 1 in several places, I added a section that spells out the four distinct media-centered objectives of terrorists and a passage on terrorists' ability to teach their deadly craft by having their deeds showcased in the media and by publicizing their most gruesome acts on their own or friendly Internet sites.

I made only minor changes in the second chapter because I believe that its thorough examination of the 9/11 news coverage remains relevant. The same is true for chapter 3 ("Political Violence as Media Event"), which deals with the media-terrorism connections in general terms. One journal review complained that media events had a particular meaning in communication research since Daniel Dayan and Elihu Katz (1992) defined them as being televised "live," ceremonial, and preplanned, such as the funeral of President Kennedy, a royal wedding, or the Olympic Games. I saw no reason to change the chapter's title. After all, terrorists, too, put a great deal of preparation into staging media events—albeit without letting TV networks in on their planning.

I rewrote the beginning of chapter 4 ("E-Terrorism and the Web of Hate") to address the expanded use of Internet and other media by terrorists, such as DVDs, video games, and terror rap music. In many cases, the material is either advertised on the Internet or offered as downloads. By multiplying their websites and by establishing online television and radio programs, terrorists become increasingly independent of the traditional news media. Whereas actual radio and television transmitters can be silenced by bombs, as the Israeli Defense Force demonstrated by targeting Hamas's radio station in Gaza, virtual radio and television may lose their websites—but only for as long as it takes to find alternative sites.

Significant revisions in chapter 5 ("The Mass Media and U.S. Anti- and Counterterrorism") were particularly necessary with respect to the Iraq War. I deleted some material, in particular the section about the mass-mediated debate on civil liberties and military responses to 9/11, in order to write extensively on the failure of the U.S. news media's reporting during the build-up to the war, the coverage of war protests, and the "embedded press" scheme during the invasion phase.

As suggested by a number of colleagues who used the text in their courses, I added a chapter (now chapter 6) on terrorism, counterterrorism, and the public. Since we know a great deal about various media effects on public attitudes, we assume that the news content affects the public's feelings about terrorism and measures to prevent further attacks as well. After presenting pertinent public opinion trends, the chapter links television coverage of terrorist threats and official alerts issued by the U.S. administration to the public's threat perceptions and to presidential approval ratings.

Chapter 6 of the first edition ("Responding to Terrorist Crises: Dealing with the Mass Media") is now chapter 7, but is otherwise unchanged. The original short conclusion, now chapter 8, remains in place. I added a few thoughts as an "Addendum to the Second Edition."

Introduction to the Third Edition

> Terrorist groups like al Qaeda and ISIL deliberately target their propaganda in the hopes of reaching and brainwashing young Muslims, especially those who may be disillusioned or wrestling with their identity. That's the truth. The high-quality videos, the online magazines, the use of social media, terrorist Twitter accounts—it's all designed to target today's young people online, in cyberspace.
>
> —President Barack Obama, 2015

The citation above reveals that President Obama underscored the importance of social media for the effectiveness of contemporary jihadist organizations' propaganda dissemination, when he addressed the White House Summit on Countering Violent Extremism. A decade earlier, when I wrote the second edition of this volume, the various digital means of mass self-communication that Obama mentioned did not yet exist. Facebook was in its infancy; YouTube and Twitter and other social media networks were not yet born. Some terrorist groups had websites and discussion forums. There was plenty of room on the World Wide Web for the preachers of hate and violence. But the traditional media, television, print, and radio were by far the dominant players in the local, national, and global media landscapes. No wonder that terrorist publicity and propaganda objectives could only be realized by receiving coverage by traditional news organizations. This has changed rather dramatically during the last decade or so with the rise of blogs, social media networks, and mobile phone apps—all potent communication weapons for the most sophisticated media operations of terrorist organizations but for less sophisticated small cells and lone wolves as well.

Given these changes and my recent research interests in other areas of media, terrorism, and counterterrorism, I wrote several completely new chapters and rewrote others. The only chapters left mostly in their original form are chapter 6, formerly chapter 2, and chapter 11, chapter 7 in the previous edition. Instead of devoting a separate chapter to terrorism, counterterrorism, and the public, as was the case in the previous edition, I included more public polling material in various chapters, especially in chapter 10. I decided on several new chapters and topics in reaction to the comments and requests of colleagues who used the earlier editions and in response to comments and questions by my students, fellow instructors, terrorism/counterterrorism experts, and emergency responders to my presentations at conferences, workshops, and teachings at home and abroad.

So, here is the chapter line-up of the heavily revised third edition:

Given the centrality of media in terrorism, chapter 1 provides an explanation of the temporary communication landscape, a discussion of the definition of terrorism and whether 9/11 was the advent of a completely "new" terrorism, and finally an assessment of the terrorist threat in the twenty-first century. Chapter 2 details why and for what purposes communication is so central in the calculus of terrorism. While significantly revised, these first two chapters retain material from chapter 1 in the previous editions, especially the "triangles of political communication and terrorism" models.

Completely new are the following three chapters, with chapter 3 providing a history of terrorists' use of alternative media starting with nineteenth-century anarchists. Yes, the media experts of the Islamic State or ISIS have unprecedented alternative media that they control at their disposal but earlier terrorists used the newest media technologies as well to self-publicize their messages. The new chapter 4 examines computer-assisted terrorism, chapter 5 the role of the traditional news media in terrorism and in the dissemination of the virus of terrorist contagion.

Chapter 6 is a detailed case study of mainstream media 9/11 news as presented in the first two editions of this book. Since the attacks on the World Trade Center and the Pentagon were as of this writing the most lethal, most shocking, most spectacular terrorist strikes, I believe that this account remains relevant and interesting.

The next three chapters, again, are new additions to the volume. Chapter 7 explores gender stereotypes in the media as they relate to terrorists. Since research reveals that media consumers do not sharply distinguish between news and entertainment media, Chapter 8 takes a look at entertainment as it figures into both terrorism and counterterrorism. Chapter 9 is devoted to terrorism and counterterrorism and freedom of expression issues that arise from both terrorists' efforts to exploit the media and governments' efforts to curb terrorist communications and/or terrorism or counterterrorism news. Chapter 10 is a heavily revised and updated version of chapter 5 in the second edition that describes how the traditional news media cover counterterrorism.

Chapter 11 presents a guide for crisis managers, political leaders, and emergency response professionals on what to do (and not to do) in terms of public communication and how to handle the news media in the wake of terrorist strikes or other emergencies. With the exception of being updated, this is mostly the same text as presented in the first two editions. This chapter was well received, especially by the emergency response community, students of criminal justice, as well as domestic and foreign officials in the counterterrorism communities, but less so by colleagues in academia who did not see scholarly merit in such a practical how-to approach. I still believe that this is a useful model for effective, mass-mediated crisis management.

1

Media and Terrorism in the Twenty-First Century

In 2007, during a speech at Kansas State University then Secretary of Defense Robert M. Gates made a remarkable admission. "Public relations was invented in the United States," he said, "yet we are miserable at communicating to the rest of the world what we are about as a society and a culture, about freedom and democracy, about our policies and our goals. It is just plain embarrassing that al-Qaeda is better at communicating its message on the internet than America. As one foreign diplomat asked a couple of years ago, 'How has one man in a cave managed to out-communicate the world's greatest communication society?' Speed, agility, and cultural relevance are not terms that come readily to mind when discussing U.S. strategic communications."[1]

Without mentioning Osama bin Laden's name, Gates credited the al-Qaeda leader and his lieutenants with beating America in the propaganda war—although at the time social media sites were in their infancy and a far cry from playing the starring roles in global communication that they were in the years to come. Osama bin Laden could not dare to personally access the Internet and prominent social media networks from his hiding place in Pakistan for fear of being discovered. However, others among al-Qaeda Central's leaders, such as American-born Adam Gadahn (also called Azzam, the American) and the man who would replace bin Laden after his death, Ayman al-Zawahiri, exploited social media for propaganda and recruitment purposes without the United States or other Western governments seeming capable of effectively countering their campaigns or those of other terrorist movements and groups. But they never came close to the more recent, stunning communication strategy and tactics of the self-proclaimed Islamic State (also called ISIS or ISIL).

When I wrote the previous edition of this book, TV networks, major news-papers, leading news magazines, and the most important wire services were still the predominant sources of news. Internet sites and blogs were not as widespread as today, and, most importantly, there was no social media as we know it now. While Facebook existed as limited social media—first for students at Harvard and then for college students elsewhere, YouTube, Twitter, and other now popular online networks were in their infancy or did not yet exist. The dramatic advances in information and communication technology that we have witnessed in the last decade or so affected most, if not all, people in all parts of the world either directly or indirectly. Because terrorism thrives on communication, publicity, and propaganda, contemporary terrorists have exploited literally all features of the Internet, especially social media net-works—just as their predecessors utilized the newest communication forms of their particular eras. This centrality of media and communication in ter-rorism is reason enough to begin this volume with a few observations about the digital revolution and the information and communication features that media-savvy terrorists have been eager to exploit. Following that, there is a detailed discussion about the definition of terrorism.

More than half a century ago, Marshall McLuhan (1994 [1964]) predicted vast advances in communication technology and envisioned a global village where information moved instantaneously from one place in the world to any other. While McLuhan did not foresee a unified, tranquil, conflict-free global village, others assumed that people from different cultures, races, religions, etc., and geographic locations would learn about each other—and perhaps understand each other better. Writing several decades later, Benjamin Barber (1995) did not describe harmonious information societies and a more like-minded global community; instead he warned that global media along with widely promoted and distributed consumer goods—originating mostly in the West and especially the United States—would alienate people and commu-nities with deep roots in their cultural traditions and values whether living abroad or at home in America.

Never before has there been more information available to more people, more speedily, and more affordably than it is today. But the same spoken word, the same TV image, and the same film narrative can be and are per-ceived differently by different people. Media content can unite and divide.

Looking at the domestic realm, suppose the U.S. president speaks at a me-morial service for the victims of a mass shooting in a shopping mall (whether a horrific crime or act of terrorism) and calls for more thorough background checks before anyone can buy an automatic assault weapon. While many Americans would agree in the hope that lives could be saved, many others would vehemently resent the presidential initiative as an attack on their Second

Amendment right. Taking an example from the international setting, think of political leaders in the United States of America speaking of the "war on terrorism" in the post–9/11 years when many Americans associated the phrase with efforts of the military and law enforcement communities to fight organizations like al-Qaeda and the self-proclaimed Islamic State abroad and prevent foreign terrorists from striking again within the United States. But many Muslims around the globe as well as a substantial number of Muslim Americans believe that the war on terrorism is in reality a war against Islam. Similarly, whereas visuals documenting the beheadings of Western hostages by an ISIS executioner were cheered by fellow jihadists and their sympathizers, the same gruesome videos were condemned by most people around the world.

The offending speech, image, film, and cartoon that are tolerated in liberal democracies in the name of freedom of expression and press freedom can be perceived as libel, blasphemy, and punishable by audiences in countries with different forms of government, different cultures, religions, and values. Just think of the consequences of the amateurish film "Innocence of Muslims" that degrades Islam and the Prophet Mohammad. Two trailer versions of the film, produced by an Egyptian American allegedly in support of Coptic Christians in Egypt, were uploaded on YouTube in the summer of 2012. Once the videos were dubbed in Arabic and posted on Internet sites, violent demonstrations and deadly riots broke out in several Muslim countries around the time of the eleventh anniversary of the 9/11 attacks. Many Americans and Westerners were highly critical of the offensive movie but understood that freedom of expression allows both the good and the bad, the wrong and the right words and images to be publicized. Or think of the blatant attack on the Paris offices of the satirical publication *Charlie Hebdo* in early 2015, when jihadist gunmen killed a dozen people and injured several more in revenge for the weekly's satirical depiction of the Prophet Mohammad, Islam, and sharia law. During the carnage, the gunmen screamed, "We have avenged the prophet" and "Allahu akbar" (God is the Greatest). French President Francois Hollande called the attack an assault on freedom of the press. Indeed, the terrorists were killing and maiming people for exercising their civil liberties, the most esteemed rights in liberal democracies.

Although people have access to more information, more news sources, and more means of communication than ever, they do not necessarily survey the diversity of information and opinions available in the marketplace of ideas but rely solely or mostly on those sources that fit their own views, including opinions on public affairs issues and religious matters. They retreat to TV, radio, Internet sites, blogs, social media posts, and links that narrowcast to insular slices of the total audience pie. This breeds resentment, disunity, even extremism and fanaticism; the result is a widening of the perceived "us" versus "them" divide, between in-group and out-group(s). Thus, instead of the digital town hall where people with different views deliberate and find some commonality and agreement, there is a digital Tower of Babel with different tribes speaking in different ideological, partisan, religious, ethnic, racial, and regional tongues. At its most extreme, this can result in political violence—war and/or terrorism.

To be sure, communication technology is value free; it can be used for the good and for the bad. Whereas terrorists themselves believe that they use media and communication for the good, those who reject their violence believe otherwise. Such opposing views indicate that the same terrorist act can be considered as either justifiable or despicable, as either the rightful act of freedom fighters or the evil deed of ruthless outlaws. The slogan "one person's terrorist is another person's freedom fighter" captures these contrasting value judgments—reason enough to explain up front what is meant by the term *terrorism* in the context of this volume.

What is Terrorism?

Trying to define terrorism is easier said than done and often results in heated discussions. Many articles and even books have been written about the perennial efforts to find a widely accepted definition but to this day there is not one universally accepted version. Aware of controversies surrounding the definition of terrorism, Martha Crenshaw (1995, 7) explained,

> It is clear from surveying the literature of terrorism, as well as the public debate, that what one calls things matters. There are few neutral terms in politics, because political language affects the perceptions of protagonists and audiences, and such effect acquires a greater urgency in the drama of terrorism.

When Ramzi Yousef, the mastermind of the first World Trade Center bombing in 1993, was tried in a New York courtroom, he told the judge defiantly, "Yes, I am a terrorist, and I'm proud of it."[2] Some nineteenth-century anarchists and revolutionaries, too, did not reject the t-word for terrorist. After the Russian revolutionary Vera Zasulich shot and wounded the dictatorial governor of St. Petersburg, Fydor Trepov in 1878, she dropped her gun instead of using it to avoid her arrest. "I am a terrorist not a murderer," she explained. However, as James Forest (2012, 171) concluded, the Zasulich case "represents one of relatively few examples in which the term 'terrorist' was embraced by the perpetrators of the violence." The reason is obvious: In modern times, the terms *terrorism* and *terrorist(s)* have negative connotations. As Richard E. Rubenstein (1987, 18) put it, "To call an act of political violence terrorist is not merely to describe it but to judge it . . . terrorism is what the other side is up to."

Mindful of the value judgments tied to the term terrorism and aware as well of divergent views about particular kinds of political violence, the mass media seem uncertain when to call an obviously political act of violence "terrorism," when to label it "crime," and when to use still other descriptions. (I will discuss this in more detail in chapter 5.) The result is an inconsistent use of terms to describe the perpetrators of political violence (terrorist, criminal, attacker, bomber, guerrilla, militant, etc.) and their actions (terrorism, crime, bombing, kidnapping, assassination, etc.). What would explain that the news media called the bombing in an Atlanta park during the 1996 Olympic Games "terrorism" but the attack on an abortion clinic in the Atlanta suburb Sandy Springs several months later a "crime?"[3] Surveying a multitude of news articles and transcripts about politically motivated violence does not provide a satisfactory answer, nor does the content of speeches by domestic and foreign leaders. Not the perpetrators, not the severity of an attack, not its venue determine what language is chosen. In view of these definitional inconsistencies, one observer concluded, "In a real sense, terrorism is like pornography: You know it when you see it, but it is impossible to come up with a universally agreed definition" (Kegley 1990, 11).

The U.S. Department of State, with jurisdictions in the area of international terrorism but not in the domestic realm, adopted a terminology that is close to *the* official U.S. government definition because it is contained in Title 22 of the *United States Code*, Section 2656f (d), a federal statute, which requires the State Department to provide Congress with annual reports on terrorist groups and countries that sponsor terrorism. According to this statute's and the Department of State's definitions,

- "Terrorism" means premeditated, politically motivated violence perpetrated against noncombatant targets by subnational groups or clandestine agents, and is usually intended to influence an audience.
- "International terrorism" means terrorism involving citizens or the territory of more than one country.
- "Terrorist group" means any group practicing, or that has significant subgroups that practice, international terrorism.

The first part of this definition in particular delineates the following and in some parts the most important and most controversial characterizations of terrorism that deserve further discussion:

Terrorism Is Political. Political and/or social grievances, real or imagined, when not resolved in domestic or international politics, lead in extreme cases to violence. Secular terrorists tend to be motivated by political principles and ideologies. Nationalists like the Algerian National Front and the Provisional Irish Republican Army insisted on the universal right of self-determination; New Left secular groups like Germany's Red Army Faction and the Italian Red Brigades were driven by Marxist ideology. The political nature of terrorism is widely agreed upon. Religious terrorism, too, has political ends but is mostly explained, promoted, and justified as dictated by religious doctrine. But in spite of all the religious symbolism and explanations, at the core of these alleged religious groups and movements are political grievances and objectives. Bin Laden's al-Qaeda called for the overthrow of the ruling House of Saud in his birthplace of Saudi Arabia, the destruction of Israel, and the removal of Western troops and influence in the Muslim world. ISIS has revealed even more ambitious political designs, namely, the reestablishment of the Caliphate with the rough outlines of the Ottoman Empire. Just as seemingly religious terrorists pursue political objectives, secular terrorism often has religious components as well. As Mark Sedgwick (2004, 808) observed,

> Just as religious terrorism turns out to have important political elements, "secular" terrorism also has important religious elements. Many nationals have spoken of their cause as "sacred" and it is not hard to conceive of a leftist speaking of the cause of the opposed masses. A Russian terrorist of the first wave wrote of terrorism as "uniting the two sublimities of human nature, the martyr and the hero."

The Targets are Civilians (or Non-Combatants). By definition, terrorists target civilians; they target their victims intentionally; and often seemingly randomly. Thus, we assume that the victims of terrorism are in the wrong place at the wrong time, for example, standing near the finish line of the Boston Marathon in the spring of 2013, when the Tsarnaev brothers Tamerlan and Dzhokhar ignited their homemade, lethal bombs. Looking at the big picture, though, the targeting of victims is not always at random. Targeted people are selected because of their nationality, religion, race, ethnicity, or other group associations. The cartoonists, writers, and editors of the satirical French magazine *Charlie Hebdo* were expressly targeted because jihadists considered their satirical depictions of Islam as blasphemy that needed to be avenged. White Supremacists target Jews, African Americans, Asians, and Hispanics; members of the anti-abortion extremist group "Army of God" seek out physicians and other providers of legal abortions; jihadists in Muslim countries target Christians, members of other non-Islamic religions; Sunni extremists target Shi'ites and vice versa. Some definitions of terrorism equate non-combatants and civilians. If one agrees with the inclusion of non-combatants in the "civilian" category, the devastating truck bombing of the U.S. Marine barracks near Beirut in 1983 that killed 241 would qualify as terrorism as would the 2000 attack on the USS *Cole* during a fueling stop in the Yemini port of Aden that resulted in seventeen deaths and three dozen injured sailors. In both cases, the targeted members of the U.S. Marine Corps and U.S. Navy were not involved in combat. But their inclusion in the "civilian" category is controversial and certainly rejected by all kinds of terrorists.

Speaking of innocents or innocent bystanders is another way for observers to describe the victims of terrorist attacks. For most terrorists, there are no innocents and no neutral bystanders; there are comrades or supporters on the one hand and the enemy on the other hand. Therefore, especially for modern-day terrorists the distinction between civilians, non-combatants, and active members of the military does not matter at all when they justify the selection of their targets. In a fatwa or religious edict that Osama bin Laden and Islamic clerics released jointly in 1998, the al-Qaeda leader wrote,

> The ruling to kill the Americans and their allies—*civilians and military* [emphasis added]—is an individual duty for every Muslim who can do it in any country in which it is possible to do it, in order to liberate the al-Aqsa Mosque and the holy mosque [Mecca] from their grip, and in order for their armies to move out of all the lands of Islam, defeated and unable to threaten any Muslim. This is in accordance with the words of Almighty God, "and fight the pagans all together as they fight you all together," and "fight them until there is no more tumult or oppression, and there prevail justice and faith in God."[4]

Similarly, the influential imam Anwar Al-Awlaki, a Yemini and American national, used his sermons, interviews, and e-mail exchanges to urge his followers to kill all Americans, soldiers and civilians alike. In a 2010 sermon he said, "Don't consult with anybody in killing the Americans. . . . Fighting the devil doesn't require consultation or prayers seeking divine guidance. They are the party of the devils. . . . It is either us or them."[5]

The Perpetrators of Terrorism Are Non-State Actors. While the U.S. Department of State and the FBI identify subnational groups and individuals or agents as perpetrators of terrorism, some experts have discounted individuals as terrorists. One question arising in this context is whether individuals that commit political violence but do not belong to a group should be considered terrorists. In the past some terrorism experts argued that to be a terrorist required association with a group. Bruce Hoffman (1998, 43), for example, observed that "terrorism is conducted by an organization with an identifiable chain of command or conspiratorial cell structure." But after the number of so-called lone wolves as perpetrators of terrorism increased dramatically, Hoffman and other scholars changed their minds and sided with those who all along considered individuals without formal ties to groups as terrorists if they struck civilians for political ends. Consider for a moment U.S. Army psychiatrist Dr. Nidal Hassan, who in 2009 killed thirteen persons and injured thirty others in a shooting spree at Fort Hood, Texas. Hassan listened to the above-mentioned Anwar al-Awlaki's sermons, exchanged e-mails with him, and followed the imam's advice to kill American soldiers. In an interview with Al Jazeera, Awlaki, a prominent leader of al-Qaeda in the Arabian Peninsula (AQAP) branch, explained his violent, anti-Western ideology. "The United States is a tyrant, and tyrants across history have all had terrible ends. I believe the West does not want to realize this universal fact," he said. "Muslims in Europe and America are watching what is happening to Muslims in Palestine, Iraq and Afghanistan, and they will take revenge for all Muslims across the globe."[6] The Anti-Defamation League documented one and a half dozen known cases in which al-Awlaki inspired followers in the United States and in the United Kingdom to plan and carry out terrorist attacks in their respective countries.[7] Not all of those plots succeeded. The would-be underwear bomber Umar Farouk Abdulmutallab, a young Nigerian who planned but failed to blow up an airliner on a transatlantic flight from Amsterdam to Detroit on Christmas Day 2009, had met and was a devotee of al-Awlaki. Faisal Shahzad, a Pakistani American, was affected by al-Awlaki's Internet sermons when he tried but failed to explode a car bomb at Times Square on May 1, 2010. Recognizing that a large number of participants in terrorist plots were easier to detect and foil by the enemy, al-Qaeda and ISIS appealed to "lone wolves" and tiny cells in the West to strike the infidels. This was summarized in the following appeal published in ISIS's online magazine *Dabiq*:

> It is very important that attacks take place in every country that has entered into the alliance against the Islamic State, especially the US, UK, France, Australia, and Germany. Rather, the citizens of crusader nations should be targeted wherever they can be found. . . . Every Muslim should get out of his house, find a crusader, and kill him. It is important that the killing becomes attributed to patrons of the Islamic State who have obeyed its leadership. This can easily be done with anonymity. Otherwise, crusader media makes such attacks appear to be random killings. Secrecy should be followed when planning and executing any attack. The smaller the numbers of those involved and the less the discussion beforehand, the more likely it will be carried out without problems. One should not complicate the attacks by involving other parties, purchasing complex materials, or communicating with weak-hearted individuals.[8]

State and Non-State Actors: Why Differentiate?

The greatest definitional disagreement concerns the inclusion or exclusion of those who carry out political violence that deliberately targets civilians. The issue is whether to distinguish between non-state actors on the one side and state actors or governments on the other side. When one defines terrorism as political violence that is deliberately targeting civilians, this definition would certainly cover the 9/11 attacks or the Oklahoma City Bombing but also the unthinkable acts of "state terrorism" committed in Germany under the rule of Adolf Hitler or in the Soviet Union under the rule of Joseph Stalin. There are different views on the U.S. air strikes on targets in Afghanistan following the terrorism of September 11, 2001, the bombings of sites in Sudan and Afghanistan in response to the attacks on U.S. embassies in East Africa in 1998, or NATO's air raids on Serbian targets during the conflicts in Bosnia and Kosovo in the 1990s. For some, the civilians killed in those strikes were not deliberately targeted but fell into the "collateral damage" category; thus these were not examples of terrorism. For others, these strikes were ill advised because it was likely or even certain that they would kill and maim civilians; thus, these were examples of state terrorism.

However dissatisfying it may be, one terrorism expert has argued, "political language divides along the fault line separating mass violence from individual or small-group violence" (Rubenstein 1987, 17). While this distinction in the terminology of violence seems to be the case most of the time, there are those who do not accept that government violence tends to be exempted from the unwelcome t-word. Writing before the demise of the Soviet Union, Herman and O'Sullivan (1989) tied many of the definitional incongruities to the Cold War biases of Western governments, Western terrorism experts, and Western media that looked upon the West as the sole victim of terrorist activities. More importantly, they argued that "the Western establishment has defined terrorism so as to exclude governments, which allows it to attend closely to the Baader-Meinhof gang and Red Brigades and to play down the more severely intimidating actions of governments" (ibid., 214). In the first case, the authors pointed out that nongovernmental actors were called terrorists; in the second case, the governments were "said to be merely violating 'human rights,' not engaging in 'terrorism.'"

Besides those perceived linguistic biases, the meaning of the term *terrorism* has changed greatly over time. In its original definition in the eighteenth century, it meant violent actions from above, by the state, such as those during the Reign of Terror in the wake of the French Revolution, when *terrorism* meant the mass guillotining of the aristocracy and other real or perceived enemies of the state. During the nineteenth century, the definition of *terrorism* expanded to include violence from below, such as the assassinations of prominent politicians by anarchists. In the twentieth century, *terrorism* came to mean mostly political violence perpetrated by non-state actors, regardless whether autonomous, state-sponsored groups, or individuals (Vetter and

Perlstein 1991); and this definition remains dominant in the early twenty-first century.

Since it is unlikely that there ever will be a universally accepted definition of terrorism, I suggest a solution that can at least bridge the definitional controversies concerning the quite common division between state and non-state actors. The starting point is the notion of mass-mediated terrorism and its definition as political violence against civilians and non-combatants committed *with the intention to publicize the deed, to gain publicity and thereby public and government attention.* This characterization is compatible with definitions put forth by many experts in the field, for example, Louise Richardson (1999, 209) who defines terrorism as "politically motivated violence directed against noncombatants or symbolic targets which is designed to communicate a message to a broader audience." The importance of communication in the terrorist design is also implicit in Crenshaw's (1995, 4) observation that terrorism "targets a few in a way that claims the attention of many."

Governments are usually not interested in advertising violence that targets civilians in their own countries or abroad. In sharp contrast to terrorists, governments, especially in democracies, tend to speak of collateral damage inflicted unwittingly on civilians or innocent bystanders as regrettable consequences of war—and if possible, they keep silent. One instructive example concerns an incident during the Vietnam War, when former U.S. Senator Bob Kerrey and his squad of Navy SEALs, while on one of their search missions for Vietcong leaders, encountered and killed more than a dozen unarmed Vietnamese civilians, most of them women and children. It took thirty-two years and the persistent questioning of an investigative reporter before Kerrey publicly acknowledged the tragic incident in the village of Thanh Phong.[9] Neither the young Americans who committed this political violence nor the U.S. government officials who sent them into war wanted to publicize the incident then or any time thereafter. Was it an act of political violence or terrorism? Yes. Was it an act of *mass-mediated* terrorism? No.

This is different, when governments act in the name of counterterrorism, when they claim to respond to terrorism or threats thereof by fighting terrorist organizations within or outside their borders or state sponsors of terrorism. Then, decision makers—especially in a democracy—will go public to enlist popular support, most of all, if military deployment is involved. In the post–9/11 era, for example, when President George W. Bush declared and launched the "war against terrorism," the administration and its supporters engaged in a massive publicity campaign to enlist support for military actions in Afghanistan and thereafter the invasion of Iraq. In such cases, I suggest, one can speak of *mass-mediated counterterrorism.*

This would also apply if a government admits publicly that its intelligence community and/or military have assassinated the leader or an important member of a terrorist organization or warns openly that terrorists are targeted for assassination. In such cases, publicity may be considered helpful in a government's efforts to (1) spread anxiety among leading terrorists and (2) satisfy a fearful public that demands protection. In late 2000, for example, Israeli officials acknowledged "publicly, explicitly, and even proudly" (Sontag 2000) that their military was targeting and killing individual Palestinians accused of actual attacks on Israeli citizens or of planning such deeds. While Palestinians spoke of "state terrorism" and "assassinations," a highly placed government official in Israel defended these acts as countermeasures and said that the "most effective and just way to deal with terror is the elimination or incarceration of the people who lead these organizations" (ibid.). After a particular incident that targeted an alleged mastermind behind anti-Israeli terrorism but killed eight Palestinians—among them two boys—Foreign Minister Shimon Peres reacted angrily when an interviewer used the term *assassination* to characterize the action. "Suicide bombers cannot be threatened by death," he argued. "The only way to stop them is to intercept those who sent them."[10] And Prime Minister Ariel Sharon made clear that "actions to prevent the killing of Jews" would continue.[11] Similarly, after Anwar Al-Awlaki was assassinated in an American drone attack in September 2011, President Barack Obama declared,

> Earlier this morning, Anwar al-Awlaki—a leader of al Qaeda in the Arabian Peninsula—was killed in Yemen. The death of Awlaki is a major blow to al Qaeda's most active operational affiliate. Awlaki was the leader of external operations for al Qaeda in the Arabian Peninsula. In that role, he took the lead in planning and directing efforts to murder innocent Americans. . . . The death of al-Awlaki marks another significant milestone in the broader effort to defeat al Qaeda and its affiliates. Furthermore, this success is a tribute to our intelligence community, and to the efforts of Yemen and its security forces, who have worked closely with the United States over the course of several years.[12]

In the same statement, the president issued a warning to other terrorists, when he said, "we will be determined, we will be deliberate, we will be relentless, we will be resolute in our commitment to destroy terrorist networks that aim to kill Americans, and to build a world in which people everywhere can live in greater peace, prosperity and security."[13]

But nothing resulted in more publicity than the killing of the most wanted and most intensively hunted terrorist ever, Osama bin Laden. Neither the George W. Bush nor the Barack Obama administrations made a secret of their determination to hunt down the al-Qaeda leader to bring him to justice one way or the other. Four days after 9/11, President George W. Bush was asked during a short exchange with reporters, whether he was convinced that Osama bin Laden was "at least a kingpin" of the unprecedented terrorist attack. "There is no question he is what we would call a prime suspect," Bush answered. "And if he thinks he can hide and run from the United States and our allies, he will be sorely mistaken."[14] The al-Qaeda chief remained high on the agenda of both the Bush and Obama administrations, the media, and the public. In mid-December 2001, when the U.S. and its allies fought al-Qaeda and the Taliban in Afghanistan, there was another exchange between the White House press corps and President Bush as the following exchange illustrates:

Ron Fournier, Associated Press. Sir, two things. Is Usama bin Laden cornered? And when you weigh the pros and cons of either option, would you rather take him alive so you can question him or dead so you don't have to deal with him?

The President. I don't care. Dead or alive, either way. I mean, I—it doesn't matter to me. Secondly, I don't know whether we're going to get him tomorrow, or a month from now, or a year from now. I really don't know. But we're going to get him. And I—the American people must understand.[15]

Using the dead-or-alive slogan well known from old Wild West wanted posters, President Bush left no doubt that there was no priority of getting the al-Qaeda boss alive. And it was not President Obama's priority either to get bin Laden alive. On May 2, 2011, Osama bin Laden, the founder and head of al-Qaeda, was killed in a daring commando raid by the U.S. Navy's SEAL Team Six in his hideout in Abbottabad, Pakistan. Most Americans were glad that the man responsible for a wave of deadly terrorist spectaculars against their country and its citizens was dead and did not question whether he was killed in a fight with the SEAL team or assassinated without resisting. The following excerpts are from a speech to the nation that President Obama gave shortly after bin Laden's demise:

Good evening. Tonight, I can report to the American people and to the world that the United States has conducted an operation that killed Osama bin Laden, the leader of al-Qaeda, and a terrorist who's responsible for the murder of thousands of innocent men, women, and children.

Today, at my direction, the United States launched a targeted operation against that compound in Abbottabad, Pakistan. A small team of Americans carried out the operation with extraordinary courage and capability. No Americans were harmed. They took care to avoid civilian casualties. After a firefight, they killed Osama bin Laden and took custody of his body.

For over two decades, bin Laden has been al-Qaeda's leader and symbol, and has continued to plot attacks against our country and our friends and allies. The death of bin Laden marks the most significant achievement to date in our nation's effort to defeat al-Qaeda. Yet his death does not mark the end of our effort. There's no doubt that al-Qaeda will continue to pursue attacks against us. We must—and we will—remain vigilant at home and abroad.[16]

Defining State Terror and Non-State Terrorism

At this point, we need to return once more to the discussion of mass-mediated terrorism. If one understands this term as relating to violence for political ends against civilians and non-combatants or innocents, one collides with the above-mentioned arguments of those who insist that states are far greater perpetrators of terrorism than are non-state actors. But as noted above, there is the profound difference between terrorists who want publicity and those in charge of states or their agents who do not want to publicize political violence they perpetrate deliberately against civilians. As Crenshaw (1995, 4) points out, political violence carried out by states "is usually carefully concealed in order to avoid public attribution of responsibility." When committed by governments, violence against civilians can be and has been in many instances equally as brutal and lethal as the actions of non-state actors and often far more cruel and causing the death of far more people. For this sort of state violence, there are a number of appropriate pejorative terms, such as *war crimes, crimes against humanity, human rights violations, genocide, atrocities*—and *terror*. As the linguist Geoffrey Nunberg (2004, 7) has noted, "Unlike 'terrorism,' 'terror' can be applied to states as well as to insurgent groups." Bruce Hoffman (1995, 25), too, points to the distinction between *terror* to characterize state violence "mostly against domestic populations" and *terrorism* to describe violence by "non-state entities."

Post–World War I Germany can serve as an example here. Beginning in the 1920s, well-organized, violent squads of Adolf Hitler's followers, most notably his storm troopers (Sturm Abteilung or abbreviated S.A.) or Brown Shirts, attacked political opponents and stirred the political instability that brought him to power in 1933. But equally, or more important, was the massive propaganda campaign that the movement waged relentlessly—even when it entered the legitimate political process and participated in elections. Clearly, this was a case of mass-mediated, political violence deliberately carried out against civilians. In other words, it was terrorism. Once Hitler and the Nazi Party were in power, they institutionalized the mass killing of civilians, mostly Jews, who were the victims of genocide, and also against other "undesirable elements," such as communists, socialists, and gypsies. During

Hitler's reign of terror, more than ten million innocent civilians were brutally tortured and killed in the implementation of government policies. This was unspeakable state terror, as were the imprisonment and killing of many millions of people in the Soviet Union during Joseph Stalin's rule. More recently, totalitarian regimes in various parts of the world oppressed, persecuted, tortured, and killed thousands, hundreds of thousands, and millions of people within their borders—in Argentina, Cambodia, Rwanda, and many other places. No case of non-state political violence comes close to the enormity of these atrocities. To characterize this kind of political violence committed by the power-holders in states as "terrorism" would actually minimize the enormity of systematic political violence and mass killings of civilians by those in control of governments.

So, given the enormity of political violence against civilians deliberately perpetrated by governments and their agents, I call this *state terror*. Following this chapter's discussion, this, then, is my definition of terrorism (and mass-mediated terrorism) in the context of this book:

> Terrorism is violence by non-state actors that deliberately targets civilians to further political objectives and aims for publicity.

The "Old" versus "New" Terrorism Debate

Changes in communication technology are among several reasons why some terrorism experts argue that more recently a *new terrorism* emerged that is fundamentally different from the old variety. Even before the attacks of 9/11, there was a growing perception that terrorism was changing, or had already changed, and that the "new" terrorism was more lethal, more likely to inflict catastrophic harm on target societies, and more often the work of religious or pseudo-religious groups or individuals. Following the 1995 nerve gas attack in the Tokyo subway by a doomsday cult (Aum Shinrikyo) that killed twelve persons and sickened thousands of commuters, experts concluded that the release of the gas would have killed far more people had members of the Aum cult handled the poison differently. Pointing to the Japanese group's ability to develop a weapon of mass destruction (WMD) and know-how to build other kinds of WMD from sources in Australia, the United States, Russia, and elsewhere, then U.S. Senator Sam Nunn concluded that the Japanese case signaled the beginning of "a new era" in terrorism. He warned that weapons of mass destruction could spread indiscriminately and fall into the hands of terrorists (Drew 1995, 1). After the events of 9/11, the notion of a "new" and far more dangerous type of terrorism gained momentum among terrorism experts and public officials alike. But a few scholars did not subscribe to the idea of a new type of terrorism. Martha Crenshaw, a leading terrorism scholar long before the attacks of 9/11, cautioned that "today's terrorism is not a fundamentally or qualitatively 'new' phenomenon but grounded in an evolving historical context. Much of what we see now is familiar and the differences are of degree rather than kind" (Crenshaw 2006, 2).

Following the simultaneous bombings of the U.S. embassies in Kenya and Tanzania in 1998, then Secretary of State Madeleine Albright explained, "What is new is the emergence of terrorist coalitions that do not answer fully to any government, that operate across national borders and have access to advanced technology" (Rose 1999, 1). Concluding that the "new terrorism differs fundamentally from the more familiar politically motivated terrorism," Steven Simon and Daniel Benjamin (2001, 5, 6) identified the "absence of a plausible political agenda" and "the absence of constraints on violence" as particular characteristics of new terrorist organizations and al-Qaeda and its leader Osama bin Laden as the prototype of this new phenomenon. Pointing to a number of differences between the "old" and "new" terrorism, Walter Laqueur (2003, 9) observed that contrary to the old terrorism, the new type is "indiscriminate in the choice of its victims" and aims at inflicting "maximum destruction." According to Bruce Hoffman (1999, 9), the "new terrorist organizations embrace far more amorphous religious and millenarian aims, and wrap themselves in less-cohesive organizational entities, with more diffuse structure and membership." And for Ian Lesser (1999, 2) the organizational and other changes inside terrorist organizations are so profound that "all of this renders much previous analysis of terrorism based on established groups obsolete."

But others have questioned the arguments of the "new" terrorism school. Rejecting Secretary of State Albright's above-cited explanation of a "new" terrorism, Gideon Rose (1999, 5) wrote for example, "The secretary's words would have been accurate had they been uttered a century earlier, when a loose-knit transnational movement quite literally devoted to the promotion of anarchy wreaked havoc across the globe." He recalled correctly that "some anarchists showed no scruples in inflicting large numbers of civilian casualties" (ibid., 5). Similarly, Niall Ferguson compared contemporary terrorism a la al-Qaeda's 9/11 attack and earlier examples of catastrophic terror. "On reflection," he wrote in a post–9/11 essay, "there are precedents for nearly all the elements of the attacks of September 11; the only real novelty was their *combination*" (ibid., 117). Questioning the alleged shift from the "old" to a "new" terrorism and its "potential of being misleading," especially with respect to countering the "new" terrorism, Alexander Spencer (2006, 25) suggested the abandonment of the term "new terrorism" and, perhaps, its replacement with terms such as "terrorism of today" or, to signal the evolution of this sort of violence use the plural: "terrorisms." For Crenshaw (2006, 26), rejecting our accumulated knowledge of terrorism by dismissing it as "obsolete" is dangerous in that it "could lead to mistakes of prediction and policy as grave as those attributed to lack of recognition of the threat." To be sure, for a new generation of post–9/11 terrorism scholars the task of studying terrorism and assessing terrorists was to be much easier without learning about and dealing with the long history of this kind of political violence and its perpetrators.

In questioning the idea of a "new" terrorism, Spencer (2006, 25) asked, "Can we really expect terrorists to remain as they were in an isolated state of inertia, separated from the evolving world around them? If this was the case we would have to call most things new every single day." And Crenshaw (2006, 26) concluded that "differences among groups and differences in patterns of terrorism over time do exist, but many of these shifts are due to a changing environment, largely associated with what is termed globalization."

I argue that terrorism itself has not fundamentally changed with respect to objectives, methods, targets, propaganda, and so on, but that today's practitioners of non-state political violence against civilians or non-combatants operate in a different environment than their predecessors. For the most part, the altered circumstances have been brought about by changed geopolitical conditions after the end of the Cold War, the accelerated processes of globalization in the sense of interdependence and interconnectivity in economics, transportation, culture, politics, migration, and most of all by the digital communication revolution. Understanding these changes will help us to assess contemporary terrorism and how global media and communication networks figure into that threat.

The Terrorist Threat in the Twenty-First Century

Although this book is about the centrality of communication in the scheme of terrorism, the mass media's obsession with spectacular terrorist incidents, and the reactions of the general public and governmental decision makers, it is important to examine and explain at the outset how the end of the Cold War and related and unrelated geopolitical changes figure into contemporary terrorism and, probably, future terrorist threats as well. After all, a fresh look at political violence as a means to communicate powerful messages is especially urgent, when terrorism is likely to remain a very serious threat in the years and perhaps decades to come.

Actually, no one should have been surprised that the twenty-first century recorded a large number of terrorist incidents in many parts of the world. Numerous experts in the field and government officials, from President Bill Clinton to President George W. Bush and CIA Director George Tenet warned of the unprecedented dangers in the "new era of terrorism," as former U.S. Senator Sam Nunn put it.[17] President George W. Bush and his national security team recognized terrorism among the major threats to America's national security. In support of the establishment of a National Missile Defense System, Secretary of Defense Donald Rumsfeld said, "We must develop the capabilities to defend against missiles, terrorism and newer threats against our space and information systems."[18] Government officials and scholars pointed to the proliferation of weapons of mass destruction after the disintegration of the Soviet Union, when they made their gloomy predictions as to future terrorist threats. And in an assessment of the post–Cold War threats to the United States' national security, Vice President Richard Cheney summarized these concerns before 9/11 the following way:

I think we have to be more concerned than we ever have about so-called homeland defense, the vulnerability of our system to different kinds of attacks. Some of it homegrown, like Oklahoma City. Some inspired by terrorists external to the United States—the World Trade towers bombing, in New York [the first bombing in 1993]. The threat of terrorist attacks against the U.S., eventually, potentially, with weapons of mass destruction—bugs or gas, biological, or chemical agents, potentially even, someday, nuclear weapons. The threat of so-called cyberterrorism attacks on our infrastructure. (Lemann 2001, 59)

The United States received its first bitter taste of biological terrorism in the form of anthrax spores a few weeks after the terrorist attacks on the World Trade Center and the Pentagon in 2001. But the potential for more lethal and, indeed, catastrophic terrorist violence was only part of the alarming story. As the end of the twentieth and the beginning of the twenty-first century demonstrated, most terrorist incidents were orchestrated by groups and individuals who used the same or similar methods as their predecessors in the 1970s, 1980s, and 1990s—hijackings, hostage-takings, bombings, suicide missions, assassinations, and facility assaults. The perpetrators of the attacks on New York and Washington on September 11, 2001, used conventional means—i.e., the hijacking of airlines—and turned them into instruments of mass destruction.

When the United States and other Western democracies were still primary targets of terrorism in the 1970s and 1980s, some experts argued persuasively that this kind of political violence was merely a nuisance rather that a serious problem for these target countries (Laqueur 1987). Others warned that the world should brace for a more violent chapter in the long history of terrorism and described eerie scenarios of major terrorist actions that would cause mass disruption and even mass destruction (Kupperman and Kamen 1989). For a short time, the collapse of the Soviet Union and the end of the Cold War fueled hopes of a drastic reduction in terrorism, but this optimism was soon dashed by a wave of major terrorist attacks. The first World Trade Center bombing in 1993, the Oklahoma City bombing in 1995, and the sarin gas attack in Tokyo's subway system that same year were the opening shots in a salvo of lethal terrorist spectaculars that continued with the bombings of the U.S. embassies in Kenya and Tanzania in 1998, the suicide attack on the USS *Cole* in 2000, and the kamikaze attacks on the World Trade Center and Pentagon in 2001. And 9/11 was followed by a host of terrorist spectaculars, especially in Europe and Asia. There are several reasons why terrorism has become a far more serious problem in the post–Cold War world than during the long East-West conflict.

First, the collapse of communism and the end of the bipolar world order resulted in the dismantling of a mechanism that, in a strange way, kept terrorism within a manageable range. Before the Iron Curtain fell, the United States, its western European allies, Japan, and assorted regimes in Latin America were frequently the targets of leftist terrorists who fought against the capitalist and imperialist world—especially the United States. During these years, the American superpower was also the primary target of secular and religious groups who opposed Washington's Middle East policies and involvement in the region—particularly in support of Israel. In those years, terrorism made strange bedfellows. The German Red Army Faction, for example, teamed up with Palestinian nationalist and Islamic fundamentalists; terrorism sponsor Muammar Gadhafi of Libya and Palestinian groups lent support to the Irish Republican Army; and secular Latin American terrorists cooperated with religious Arabs and left-wing extremists in western Europe. All the while, anti-American and anti-Western terrorists enjoyed significant support from Eastern bloc countries in the form of arms, training facilities, and safe havens. However, the fact that this web of terrorism extended deep into the Soviet bloc and fostered political violence against the West provided, at the same time, a mechanism of restraint: The Soviet Union could use its influence over Eastern bloc countries, such as East Germany, and client states, such as Libya, to keep anti-Western and anti-American terrorism beneath a certain threshold so as to minimize the risk of a confrontation between the superpowers.

During this period, leftist terrorists (i.e., the Italian Red Brigades or the German Red Army Faction) and nationalist and religiously motivated groups (i.e., various secular Palestinian and Islamic groups in the Middle East) preferred to target influential persons from the political, business, or military realm rather than innocent victims. When innocent bystanders were targeted, the inflicted harm was not as extreme as in many more recent incidents. As the Soviet bloc disintegrated and Moscow's power decreased, the restraining mechanism vanished. The few surviving and newly emerging movements and groups, poised to use political violence for their causes, were far more autonomous than they were during the previous decades.

Moreover, the Cold War world order limited the likelihood of disproportional counterterrorist strikes by Western states, most of all the United States. Washington did not want to upset the balance-of-power arrangement. With this in mind, the Carter administration decided against punitive military strikes against Iran during the Iran hostage crisis at a time when the Soviet Union had invaded Iran's neighbor, Afghanistan. When the Reagan administration saw the need to strike back at terrorism, its officials did not choose Iran, then considered the most flagrant sponsor of anti-American terrorism, but the comparably weak Libya as the target of U.S. retaliatory strikes. No doubt, American decision makers were well aware that the North African state was far less important in Moscow's geopolitical interests than Iran and that an attack on Libya would not risk a military clash with the Soviet Union. To this end, the 2001 U.S. air strikes against targets in Afghanistan in the hunt for Osama bin Laden and the Taliban leadership would have been inconceivable during the Cold War because of the Soviet Union's proximity to this country.

The second reason why terrorism became a serious problem is that the end of the old world order unleashed nationalist and religious frictions that were suppressed in the past. The breakup of the Soviet Union into more than a dozen independent states did not end the historic ethnic and religious conflicts within and between those new republics but, rather, allowed them to explode. The conflict between Russia and separatists in the province of Chechnya as well as the ethnic hostilities in Bosnia and Kosovo were cases in point. From the outset, terrorist threats and actual violence figured prominently in the Chechen struggle for independence. Aware of their own weakness in comparison to Moscow's military force, rebel leaders warned as early as 1992 that they would bomb Moscow's subway system and attack nuclear plants (McMullan 1993). Given that terrorism is the weapon of the weak, it was hardly surprising that the continuing conflict between Chechen separatists and the Russian army led to terrorist acts against Russian targets both in the Chechen province and elsewhere in Russia. Similarly, terrorism was part of the ethnic conflicts in Bosnia and Kosovo. The Muslims in Chechnya and Bosnia felt abandoned by the West. In the early 1990s, Sefir Halilovic, the then commander in chief of the Bosnian Army, threatened that terrorists would put "European capitals ablaze" unless the West supported Bosnian Muslims (Ranstorp and Xhudo 1994, 210). Andrei Dudayev, a Chechen rebel leader, threatened terrorist attacks against western Europe, charging that the West supported Russia's aggression against Chechnya (*New York Times* 1996, A6).

To be sure, militant Muslims were not the only ones preaching, threatening, and committing political violence in these regions. On the contrary, Bosnian Serbs, for example, were the first party to resort to international terrorism in the Bosnian conflict when they seized French members of the UN peacekeeping contingent as hostages in order to prevent NATO air strikes. In this particular incident, media considerations played prominent roles in the calculations of both sides. The Serb hostage holders allowed television crews to film their captives with the expectation that the French government would not be able to remain firm once the French people saw the faces of their scared countrymen on their television screens. Fearing the impact of these kinds of visual images on the public, decision makers in Paris asked French television networks to obscure the faces of the hostages electronically.

The mobilization and increased activities of religious and pseudo-religious movements and groups increased the likelihood of a type of terrorism that causes far more deaths, injuries, and damages than secular political violence. And the religiously motivated perpetrators of political violence were increasingly celebrated like heroes, like martyrs, as this description attests:

> At a "martyr's wedding"—a ceremony honoring two Palestinian boys who died fighting the Israelis—at Martyr's Square in the Gaza strip banners and signs congratulated Ahmed and Ibrahim "for dying in the service of God." Ahmed's mother chanted, "I am proud. . . . Thanks be to God." (Finkel 2000, 50)

This scene, witnessed by a reporter in the fall of 2000, was not an unusual one. Just like their fathers, uncles, and older brothers, young boys fought and died in the Palestinian intifada for the glory of god. Whether Christian identity adherents in the United States and Canada, militant Jewish fundamentalists in Israel, Muslim jihadists in the Middle East, Africa, South Asia, and elsewhere, or bizarre sects like the Aum Shinrikyo in Japan, in these cases "violence first and foremost is a sacramental act or divine duty executed in direct response to some theological demand or imperative" (Hoffman 1995, 272).

Those who consider themselves God's soldiers in a holy war are not bound by the moral limitations of secular terrorists of the past. In that light, it is hardly surprising that the most shocking acts of terror in the recent past were the work of groups that tied their political objectives to their particular faith— from the first World Trade Center bombing to the Tokyo nerve gas attack, from the deadly attack on Palestinians worshiping in a mosque at Hebron to the suicide attacks on the World Trade Center and the Pentagon. Khadar abu Hoshar, convicted of plotting to bomb tourist sites in Jordan and awaiting his execution in a Jordanian prison, showed no regret but affirmed his decision to devote his life "to the cause of jihad, or holy war, in hopes of bringing to power governments that follow the strict code of Islamic law."[19] For the same reason, suicide missions have been far more common among religious or pseudo-religious terrorists, rather than secular ones, as are plots designed to cause the greatest possible harm. As one expert sees it,

> The combination of religion and terrorism can be cited as one of the main reasons for terrorism's increased lethality. The fact that for the religious terrorist violence inevitably assumes a transcendent purpose and therefore becomes a sacramental or divine duty, arguably results in a significant loosening of the constraints on the commission of mass murder." (Hoffman 1995, 280)

Suicide terrorism is not a new phenomenon. In 1983, for example, explosive-laden trucks, driven by suicide bombers, plowed into the U.S. embassy in Beirut, Lebanon, and into the U.S. Marine barracks near Beirut, killing many Americans. But altogether, suicide terrorism was rare at that time. This changed in the following decades. Beginning in the mid-1990s, suicide terrorism took on epidemic proportions in the Middle East, when Palestinian terrorists mounted a series of lethal attacks in which they died along with hundreds of victims. The Palestinian terrorists were typically in their early twenties, indoctrinated in fundamentalist mosques and schools and eager to become *shadinin* or martyrs in the *jihad* or holy war against the Jewish state.

Probably inspired by the perceived success of the attacks on New York and Washington and the Hamas-sponsored suicide missions against Israelis, a secular Palestinian group, Al Fatah's military branch Al-Aqsa Martyrs Brigade, began to target Israeli civilians with "human bombs" in late 2001 and intensified this campaign in the spring of 2002. This was, to be sure, not the first time that secular terrorists had been chosen by their leaders or volunteered to kill themselves in order to kill others. Members of the Kurdish Workers Party, for example, undertook suicide missions earlier. But in the case of the Al-Aqsa Martyrs Brigade the choice of lethal suicide missions seemed to emulate the strategies of religiously motivated groups, most of all the fellow-Palestinian Hamas organization. Extremists from other religions were also ready to die for their causes. The young fundamentalist Jew Yigal Amir, who assassinated Prime Minister Yitzhak Rabin in order to stop the peace process between Israelis and Palestinians, claimed to have acted in accordance with the Torah and Jewish law and God. "Everything I did was for the sake of God," he said (Greenberg 1996, A9). While the assassin was not killed during the incident, he certainly considered the possibility and was ready to die for his cause. The same was true for Brooklyn-born Dr. Baruch Goldstein, a follower of the Rabbi Meir Kahane and the organizations that survived the militant Jewish leader, who massacred twenty-nine Palestinians as they worshipped in a Hebron mosque. Goldstein must have expected that he would be killed in his attack—which, indeed, he was.

While North American extremists with hate-based belief systems drawn from the Christian Identity movement and other pseudo-religions have so far shied away from suicide terrorism, some of these factions have pondered and actually attempted catastrophic tactics. Thus, a white supremacy group planned to poison water reservoirs in the American Northwest that supply drinking water to densely populated urban centers. And like-minded extremists tried to release toxic chemicals through ventilation systems into buildings in the Southwest. In both instances, the terrorists failed. Opposition to the vision of a new world order with greater political, economic, and military cooperation among the family of nations revitalized the leaders and followers of the old white supremacy gospel in the Christian Identity movement and related racist, anti-Semitic, and xenophobic conspiracy theories in the United States (Stern 1996; Kaplan 1995). With communists and the Cold War threat out of the way, these groups attacked Washington's alleged compliance in the country's takeover by a world government. The prospect of UN "storm troopers" and other international fighters eradicating the United States as we know it justifies, in the eyes of these groups, violence against the government and its agents. These sorts of ideas, whether spread by neo-Nazi, militia, patriot, white supremacist, or Christian identity groups (and they converge in their conspiracy theories) are, in one way or another, attractive abroad as well—especially in Canada, Europe, and Australia. The Internet provides these apostles of hate and their adherents an easy means of communication, where they can promote each other's sites in the hunt for recruits.

Thirdly, another post–Cold War change playing into the hands of terrorists is that there has been a proliferation of weapons of mass destruction. The United States, Germany, and other Western industrial powers have long been involved in massive arms exports, especially to countries in the developing world. And during the Cold War era, countries east of the Iron Curtain supplied extremists in the West with arms—even with some of the most potent and least detectible ones. The Semtex plastic explosives, for example, that terrorists used to blow up Pan Am Flight 103 over Lockerbie, Scotland, were produced in and supplied by Czechoslovakia. Following the dismantling of the Eastern bloc and the Soviet Union, stockpiles of nuclear weapons became accessible as a few scientists and technicians who had lost their jobs sold some of those weapons to illegal entities, such as the Russian Mafia. Some of these scientists made their way into countries with known ties to terrorist groups. Since then, the idea that terrorists might resort to weapons of mass destruction has been the ultimate nightmare (Allison et al. 1996; Stern, 1999).

Groups like Japan's Aum Shinrikyo and al-Qaeda failed in the past in their efforts to buy highly enriched uranium from sources in Russia and other republics of the former Soviet Union in order to build their own nuclear weapons. However, before his death bin Laden let it be known that he did not exclude the use of nuclear, chemical, and biological weapons in his holy war against Israel and its supporters; his group allegedly "obtained phials of anthrax and the lethal viral agent botulism" (Reeve 1999, 216). And it does not take the financial muscle of a bin Laden to acquire potent weapons. Just as the U.S. Army lost track of large quantities of explosives stored in military facilities, such as Fort Bragg, it is not impossible that groups or individuals could steal nuclear, biological, or chemical material by breaking into some laboratory.

So real is the threat of catastrophic terrorism that the professional response community did not take a chance, not even before the mailing of deadly anthrax letters shortly after 9/11. Thus, in the summer of 2000, when eight businesses in New York City received anonymous letters allegedly containing hazardous biological agents, the Mayor's Office of Emergency Management responded swiftly by dispatching and alerting medical and hazardous material specialists and a host of other response specialists. The "day of eight letters" turned out to be a hoax, but the terrorist response professionals knew that it was not an unlikely scenario for a real act of terrorism. Even without getting their hands on weapons of mass destruction, amateurs, whether working alone or in groups, can build crude, homemade bombs by mixing a few hundred pounds of legally sold materials—as the Oklahoma City and the first World Trade Center bombings showed.

Finally, political change in some parts of the world has opened up channels of communication that were controlled and censored in the past by autocratic governments. As a result, mass-mediated terrorism has become a more attractive weapon. Let's return for a moment to the example of the long-lasting Russian–Chechen conflict that has involved a great deal of violence on both sides. In late March of 2001, three simultaneous car explosions killed twenty-three and injured more than one hundred civilians in southern Russia. If this had happened in the old Soviet Union, the state-controlled mass media probably would not have reported the incident. Although Russian authorities were far from granting press freedom along the lines of Western democracies and, in fact, threatened at this particular time the very existence of NTV television, the only major channel outside of the Russian government's control, the Russian public and the rest of the world learned about these particular bombings and many similar bombings, hostage situations, and hijackings by extremists among Chechen separatists. Indeed, domestic critics of the Putin government suspected that the government-controlled television channels showed the shocking visuals of terrorism's victims in order to justify and enlist support for Russia's military actions against Chechnya. Whatever the motives, based on their earlier terrorist threats there was no doubt that Chechen leaders welcomed the publicity that their actions received in the Russian and international media.

This last point brings the discussion back to the central theme of this book—the inevitable and primary role of communication and propaganda in the terrorist design and the contemporary mass media's appetite to facilitate the need of virtually all terrorists to have their deeds publicized. Former British Prime Minister Margaret Thatcher had it right when she proclaimed that publicity is the oxygen of terrorism. If anything has changed in the last decades, it is the increased availability of the sort of oxygen of which Mrs. Thatcher warned and on which mass-mediated terrorism thrives.

In the years since the Berlin Wall came down and the Soviet Union crumbled, the mass media of communication have changed in dramatic ways—mostly because of the emergence and global reach of the Internet. The latest advances of communication technology added mass self-mediated terrorism to the traditional mass-mediated terrorism. As the following chapters will show, both exist side by side and feed off each other.

And terrorists are very much aware of this! Nothing proves this more than the Islamic State, whose barbaric violence is topped only by its most advanced use of communication technology to spread its brutal propaganda.

Notes

1. The remarks were made during the Landon Lecture at Kansas State University, November 26, 2007. The transcript of the speech, accessed September 1, 2008, is available at http://www.defenselink.mil/speeches/speech.aspx?speechid=1199.

2. These words were part of Yousef's statement before his sentencing by Judge Kevin Thomas Duffy of the Federal District Court in Manhattan. See "Excerpts from the Statements in Court," *New York Times*, January 8, 1998, B4.

3. As it turned out, the same man, Eric Rudolph, was responsible for both attacks.

4. The text of the fatwa, accessed October 15, 2014, is available at http://www.pbs.org/newshour/updates/military-jan-june98-fatwa_1998.

5. According to an Al Jazeera report, accessed October 15, 2014, available at http://www.aljazeera.com/news/middleeast/2010/11/2010118204835107675.html.

6. The text of the interview, accessed October 15, 2014, is available at http://www.aljazeera.com/focus/2010/02/2010271074776870.html.

7. The Anti-Defamation league's report, accessed October 16, 2014, is available at http://www.adl.org/assets/pdf/combating-hate/anwar-al-awlaki-2013-6-4-v1.pdf.

8. "The Facing Grayzone [*sic*]." *Dabiq* 4 (October 2014): 44. Text, accessed October 16, 2014, is available at https://ia601403.us.archive.org/0/items/Dabiq04En/Dabiq_04_en.pdf.

9. The Thanh Phong incident was investigated by Gregory L. Vistica, who also interviewed Bob Kerrey. See Gregory L. Vistica, "What Happened in Thanh Phong," *New York Times Magazine*, April 29, 2001.

10. Peres is quoted here from Clyde Haberman, "In the Mid-East This Year, Even Words Shoot to Kill," *New York Times*, August 5, 2001, section 4, 3.

11. Ariel Sharon is quoted here from Haberman, section 4, 3.

12. "Remarks by the President at the 'Change of Office' Chairman of the Joint Chiefs of Staff Ceremony," White House, September 30, 2011. The text of the speech, accessed October 16, 2014, is available at http://www.whitehouse.gov/the-press-office/2011/09/30/remarks-president-change-office-chairman-joint-chiefs-staff-cere-mony.

13. Ibid.

14. U.S. Government Printing Office (GPO), accessed November 7, 2014, http://www.gpo.gov/fdsys/pkg/PPP-2001-book2/pdf/PPP-2001-book2-doc-pg1111.pdf.

15. GPO, accessed November 8, 2014, http://www.gpo.gov/fdsys/pkg/PPP-2001-book2/pdf/PPP-2001-book2-doc-pg1515.pdf.

16. White House, accessed November 7, 2014, http://www.whitehouse.gov/the-press-office/2011/05/02/remarks-president-osama-bin-laden.

17. Senator Nunn is quoted here from Christopher Drew, "Japanese Sect Tried to Buy U.S. Arms Technology, Senator Says," *New York Times*, October 31, 1995.

18. This remark was made during Rumsfeld's confirmation hearings before the Judiciary Committee of the U.S. Senate in early 2001. See Charles Aldinger, "Bush Pentagon Nominee Says Missile Defense Need," accessed April 1, 2002, http://dailynews.yahoo.com/h/nm/20010111/pl/rumsfeld_missiles_dc_2.html.

19. The Jordanian on death row was quoted in Judith Miller, "On Jordan's Death Row, Convicted Terrorist Says He Has No Regrets," accessed April 1, 2002, http://www.nytimes.com/2001/01/15/world/15TERR.html.

2

The Communication Calculus of Terrorism

Tuesday, August 19, 2014. The media center of the Islamic State of Iraq and Syria (ISIS) uploads its video "#NewMessagefromISIStoUS" to YouTube. The four-minute, forty-second production shows the American journalist James Foley in an orange jumpsuit reminiscent of Arab prisoners held in the U.S. detention facility at Guantanamo Bay. Kneeling next to a black-clad, masked ISIS fighter, Foley delivers an extensive statement in which he calls on his "friends, family and loved ones to rise up against my real killers—the U.S. government— for what will happen to me is only a result of their complacent criminality." He ends with the sentence, "I wish I wasn't an American."

After blaming strikes against the Islamic State for Foley's death the ISIS fighter pulls out a knife and decapitates his hostage.

The camera then moves over to another kneeling captive, the American journalist Steven Joel Sotloff. According to the executioner, he will be the next victim.

Less than two weeks later, an eerily similar two-minute, forty-six-second video captures the beheading of Sotloff and ends with a death threat against British citizen David Haines, who is already wearing an orange prison gown. This time, the video is posted on a file-sharing website.

Ten days later, ISIS releases a two-minute, twenty-seven-second video of Haines's beheading on Twitter. Shortly thereafter, there are more videos with the same images, the same threats.

But nothing is more shocking than the twenty-two-minute film that culminates in the burning of captured Jordanian pilot Moaz al-Kasasbeh alive. While the pilot was presumably executed weeks earlier, the video's release in early

February 2015 indicates that ISIS's production staff needed time to present a "sophisticated" production. Earlier videos, except for the ones showing the killing of two Japanese men, were of Hollywood caliber and proved that ISIS has Western-trained experts in their midst. But the filmed execution of the burning Jordanian is not merely longer but contrasts the uniformed, pale, somewhat removed from full earthly reality ISIS jihadists with the very real, bright colored hostage as the fire slowly embraces and kills him. One assumes that the filmmakers aimed at evoking images of heaven and hell—effectively shot with different camera angles and frightening effects.

∾

Although the social media sites quickly blocked access to the videos and relatively few people knew about the website that ISIS used to post the brutal clips, the world learned almost instantly about the executions via the traditional mass media that in ever more "breaking news" versions aired alarming details of the unspeakably cruel acts. While not playing the complete videos, most news organizations publicized the visuals of helpless hostages kneeling next to the ISIS killer with the threatening image of the black ISIS flag in the picture.

Fox News broke with this pattern, when the news organization posted the complete video of the Jordanian pilot's execution on its website at a time when social media providers had blocked access to the shocker film. Network officials decided that the only way to prove ISIS's barbaric behavior was by providing access to the material. As a Fox News executive put it, "After careful consideration, we decided that giving readers of FoxNews.com the option to see for themselves the barbarity of ISIS outweighed legitimate concerns about the graphic nature of the video. Online users can choose to view or not view this disturbing content."[1]

With all of those video releases, ISIS communication experts achieved the immediate goals of their organization: getting the attention of publics and political elites around the globe, shocking and threatening their foes, and impressing supporters and potential recruits. Moreover, as TV commentator Jeff Greenfield noted, these sorts of images tend "to force, I think, our policymakers into taking decisions they might not take absent the emotional punch of those pictures. They tend to maybe say more than what reality lets them say."[2]

Indeed, a day after the first video release, President Barack Obama appeared in front of cameras and microphones and declared, "The entire world is appalled by the brutal murder of Jim Foley by the terrorist group, ISIL." He promised that "the United States of America will continue to do what we must do to protect our people. We will be vigilant and we will be relentless.

When people harm Americans, anywhere, we do what's necessary to see that justice is done. And we act against ISIL, standing alongside others."[3] Following Steven Sotloff's death Obama said, "Whatever these murderers think they'll achieve by killing innocent Americans like Steven, they have already failed. They have failed because, like people around the world, Americans are repulsed by their barbarism. We will not be intimidated."[4] British Prime Minister David Cameron took to Twitter to condemn the murder of Haines, calling it "an act of pure evil."[5] The same highest-level responses followed subsequent killings. Each of them resulted in President Obama and other leaders commenting on and condemning ISIS's latest videotaped barbarism. ISIS had found a recipe to provoke the U.S. president and other leaders to respond to their inhumanity. They were triumphant as subsequent ISIS video productions included clips of President Obama and other high U.S. officials commenting on their deeds.

Although the media had reported earlier about the beheadings of Muslims in Syria and Iraq by ISIS fighters, it was the sight of Western victims that heightened the awareness and outrage of political leaders and the general public in the U.S, UK, and elsewhere in Western countries. Following the killing of Foley and Sotloff, President Obama said in a nationally televised address, "U.S. airstrikes have been hitting the jihadists in Iraq. Those strikes will be expanded to ISIS targets in Syria." And after the murder of Haines, the British Parliament approved Prime Minister Cameron's request for the UK military to join the growing anti-ISIS coalition in Iraq. Although war-weary after the controversial invasion of Iraq and more than a dozen years of military deployments in Afghanistan, the American public turned hawkish with majorities supporting airstrikes against ISIS both in Iraq and Syria. No doubt, America reacted to the brutal terrorist messages and images.

Ahead of the mid-term election in November 2014, Republican candidates who linked their Democratic opponents to what they characterized as President Obama's failure to deal with the terrorist group before it became a major regional and global problem raised issues surrounding the Obama administration's handling of the ISIS threat in several campaigns. While this may have been campaign politics as usual, it was surprising that even major figures in the Democratic Party criticized Obama for not recognizing and acting on the ISIS threat earlier. Former President Jimmy Carter, for example, said in an interview, "We waited too long. We let the Islamic State build up its money, capability and strength and weapons while it was still in Syria."[6] Leon E. Panetta, who served as CIA Director and Secretary of Defense in the Obama administration before resigning, was just as damning as Carter. In his memoirs, he criticized the president's decision to withdraw all U.S. troops from Iraq and Obama's failure to intervene in the Syrian civil war and in the process stop the growth and expansion of ISIS.[7] As one commentator wrote of Panetta's book, it "is not as scathing as the one by Mr. Panetta's predecessor, Robert M. Gates, but more openly critical than those of former Secretary of State Hillary Clinton or former Treasury Secretary Timothy F. Geithner."[8] One way or the other, the ISIS threat took center stage in American inter- and intra-party politics.

Beheadings or what one ISIS operative labeled "demonstration killings" as the most outlandish parts of the organization's comprehensive online propaganda elevated ISIS into a global player and a headline maker that the world's most influential leaders would not ignore. To be sure, ISIS was a nasty problem at the time. Governments in the region and in the West had looked on as an assembly of fanatic fighters from all over the world exploited the Syrian civil war and the failure of Iraq's Shiite-dominated government to include Sunnis and Kurds in the country's governance to smooth out sectarian hostilities in the wake of the withdrawal of U.S. troops. Before the outside world pondered responses to the ISIS threat, the well-organized jihadists had expanded their reign of terror to one-third of both Syria's and Iraq's territory. ISIS documented its fighters' territorial advances and atrocities as the centerpiece of the group's psychological warfare. Rather than risk being captured and killed by jihadists, even well-trained and well-equipped members of Iraq's army abandoned their military hardware and fled the battlefield. And all of this was captured in swiftly publicized videos and still photographs that ISIS's propaganda arm posted on social media sites.

A few years earlier, Osama bin Laden had written in a letter to Taliban leader Mullah Muhammad Omar, "It is obvious that the media war in this century is one of the strongest methods; in fact, its ratio may reach 90% of the total preparation for the battles."[9] Before and after its leader's demise, al-Qaeda exploited both traditional and new media, but bin Laden's prediction of the dominant role of media in terrorist fights against nation-states was never before showcased as well as by ISIS's propaganda management. ISIS carried out horrendous acts of violence and had its media corps record every detail of its unspeakable brutality. Early anarchists described terrorism as "propaganda by deed." They knew that one way to achieve publicity was via news coverage in the mainstream media. However, even in the nineteenth and early twentieth centuries, leading anarchists tried also to find their own communication means to disseminate propaganda by words—their own words in terrorist alternative media (for more on this, see chapter 3).

If publicity is indeed the oxygen or lifeblood of terrorism, as both terrorism scholars and politicians have argued, ISIS's own propaganda apparatus and the traditional media's frenzied coverage of the group's online postings were akin to providing concentrated oxygen or massive blood transfusions to the group's quest for publicity and propaganda. Indeed, ISIS had seemingly elevated mass-mediated terrorism to an unprecedented level.

How Mass-Mediated Terrorism Works

The preceding chapter introduced a definition of the term *mass-mediated terrorism*. Years ago, when I thought about a fitting terminology to capture the centrality of media in the propaganda scheme of terrorism I came across Sissela Bok's (1998, 6–7) thoughtful book *Mayhem: Violence as Public Entertainment*. The author defines what she calls *media violence* as "the conveyance or portrayal of such exercises of force in the press or on the radio or on the screen" and what she labels *entertainment violence* as including "forms of media violence offered as entertainment." These concepts prove useful in Bok's critical observations about the mass media's preoccupation with the most brutal cases of violence, whether they are presented "over and over again" in local and national news reporting or "reflected, repeated, and echoed in endless variations through the lens of entertainment violence" in motion pictures, TV movies, and novels" (ibid.). Applying Bok's notion of media violence to terrorism, one comes up with a similar and perhaps even more compelling concept: media terrorism. Bok mentions terrorism and the Oklahoma City bombing in particular as she describes television's obsession with images of violence, but her focus is on violence-as-crime—not on violence as political statement or message. This distinction between criminal violence and the term media violence on the one hand and terrorist violence and the concept of media terrorism on the other hand is a significant one. After all, most people who commit violent crimes do not consider their deeds as politically motivated, nor do they seek public awareness in order to further their political agenda. In sharp contrast, groups and individuals who commit or threaten terrorist attacks consider their actions as means to get news coverage and thereby the attention of friends and foes. For violent criminals, more often than not the persons they target matter—for terrorists, as Schmid and de Graaf (1982, 14) have pointed out, "the message matters, not the victim."

While the term *media terrorism* is comparable to Bok's *media violence* and captures the media's eagerness to publicize the violent deeds of terrorists and thereby magnify the terrorist "propaganda by deed," this phraseology seems to overstate a compliant role on the part of the mainstream media. For that reason, I prefer the wording *mass-mediated terrorism*, which conveys the centrality of communication via all kinds of mass media in the calculus of terrorism on the one hand and media gatekeepers' preference for shocking violence on the other hand. The idea here is that most terrorists calculate the consequences of their carefully planned strikes and assume that they are very likely to gain access to what I call the triangle of political communication.

What is this triangle of communication? In mass societies in which direct contacts between governors and the governed are the exception, not the rule, the media provide lines of communication between public officials and the general public (see figure 2.1). Indeed, Thomas Hollihan (2001, chapter 1) explains that in mass societies "politics is communication" and that "political communication is therefore the means by which people express both their unity and their differences. Through communication we petition our government, plead our unique and special interests, rally those who agree with us to our causes, and chastise those who do not share our world views" (ibid., 9).

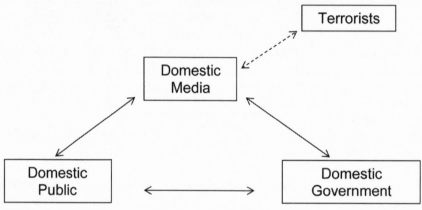

FIGURE 2.1
The Triangle of Political Communication

Groups and individuals with views far removed from the mainstream may not get access to conventional media or, from their perspective, not enough access. The fact is that the news media are not simply neutral and passive information and communication conduits but control the most important space in the triangle of communication. From this perch, media gatekeepers include and exclude, magnify and minimize. A nonviolent fringe group with political grievances may not get the attention of newsrooms but when it resorts to violence, there will be news coverage and often over-coverage. Heavily reported and prominently placed news will result in heightened attention by those situated at the other two corners of the communication triangle: government officials and the general public. Governments, in the American setting in particular the president and high administration officials as well as members of the U.S. Congress, are well positioned in the communication triangle and can use their ready media access to communicate with the general public. This advantage puts governments into an ideal position when communicating with the public during a terrorist crisis or enlisting popular support for their counterterrorism policies (See chapter 10 on counterterrorism and media).

As figure 2.2 shows, apart from the domestic triangle in any given country, there is a larger, international triangle of communication along the lines of the domestic model. When anything as spectacular as a major terrorist attack occurs and generates domestic breaking news, say in the United States, this will move immediately into the international or global communication triangle and from there into other domestic media-government-public entities around the world. Thus, after jihadist gunmen stormed the offices of the French satirical magazine *Charlie Hebdo* in January 2015 and killed and injured two dozen staff members in cold blood, the first news reports came via French mainstream media, alarming the public and officials in France, but in no time dominating the international news networks and domestic media in countries around the world.

Terrorists are well aware of the news value of lethal violence and of the media's, especially television's appetite for horrific images. Take the example of Timothy McVeigh, the man responsible for the Oklahoma City bombing in 1995 that killed 168 men, women, and children and injured several hundred more. While the former U.S. Army sergeant who shared the ideals of the right-extremist militia and patriot milieu did not show any remorse in the years following the bombing and preceding his execution in June 2001, he expressed deep satisfaction that his deed had received not only domestic but indeed global attention. He told an interviewer, "I don't think there is any

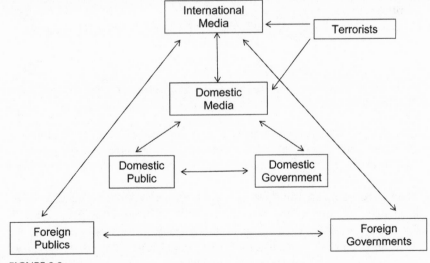

FIGURE 2.2
Terrorism and the Triangles of Political Communication (Mass Communication)

doubt the Oklahoma City blast was heard around the world."[10] McVeigh also revealed that he selected the Alfred P. Murrah Federal Building in Oklahoma City for the attack because it had "plenty of open space around it, to allow for the best possible news photos and television footages." He was determined to "make the loudest statement . . . and create a stark, horrifying image that would make everyone who saw it stop and take notice."[11] Learning about the death of a group of young children who had attended the day-care center in the Murrah Building, McVeigh showed no emotion for the innocent little boys and girls. Instead he expressed regret that the death of those children "would overshadow the political message of the bombing."[12] McVeigh left nothing to chance. To make sure that the world learned about his motives, he left an envelope filled with revealing newspaper clips and documents in his getaway car just in case he was killed in the explosion or during a violent confrontation with law enforcement officers.

Equally revealing was the publicity obsession of a pair of terrorists who in November 2008 directed an unprecedented series of terrorist attacks on a dozen different sites in Mumbai, India, that killed 173 people and injured several hundred more. During the sixty-hour ordeal, the two men communicated with several of their comrades who held hostages in various buildings in Mumbai. The following is the transcript of a phone conversation between the two men in Pakistan and Abdul Rehman and Fahadullah, who held hostages in the Oberoi Hotel.

Caller: Brother Abdul. The media is comparing your action to 9/11. One senior police officer has been killed.

Abdul Rehman: We are on the 10th/11th floor. We have five hostages.

Caller 2 (Kafa): Everything is being recorded by the media. Inflict the maximum damage. Don't be taken alive.

Caller: Kill all hostages, except the two Muslims. Keep your phone switched on so that we can hear the gunfire.

Fahadullah: We have three foreigners, including women. From Singapore and China.

Caller: Kill them.

(Voices of Fahadullah and Abdul Rehman directing hostages to stand in a line, and telling two Muslims to stand aside. Sound of gunfire. Cheering voices in background).[13]

The terrorist masterminds at headquarters were obviously delighted that the media compared their operation to the 9/11 attacks, the gold standard of media coverage for terrorist spectaculars. Their eagerness in ordering the execution of more hostages was indicative of their calculation that more dead victims would result in more media attention.

Osama bin Laden and his al-Qaeda directorate, too, had publicity in mind, when they planned the 9/11 attacks with the destruction of the World Trade Center's twin towers as centerpiece. New York, as the news media capital of the United States and the world's media, would guarantee the desired coverage. Before fleeing their headquarters in Afghanistan, bin Laden and a group of supporters, among them a sheik named "Al Ghamdi," discussed how they waited for and received news of the 9/11 strikes. The following is from the transcript of the videotaped conversation:

> BIN LADEN: We were at . . . [inaudible] . . . when the event took place. We had notification since the previous Thursday that the event would take place that day. We had finished our work that day and had the radio on. It was 5:30 p.m. our time. I was sitting with Dr. Ahmad Abu-al-Khair. Immediately, we heard the news that a plane had hit the World Trade Center. We turned the radio station to the news from Washington. The news continued and no mention of the attack until the end. At the end of the newscast, they reported that a plane just hit the World Trade Center. . . . After a little while, they announced that another plane had hit the World Trade Center. The brothers who heard the news were overjoyed by it.
>
> SHEIK: I listened to the news . . . we were not thinking about anything, and all of a sudden, Allah willing, we were talking about how come we didn't have anything, and all of a sudden the news came and everyone was overjoyed, and everyone until the next day, in the morning, was talking about what was happening, and we stayed until 4 o'clock listening to the news every time a little bit different. Everyone was very joyous and saying, "Allah is great," "Allah is great," "We are thankful to Allah," "Praise Allah."[14]

Before al-Qaeda struck in the United States, its leaders were well aware that the attack on Israeli athletes during the 1972 Olympic Games in Munich, Germany, by the Palestinian Black September group had received more news coverage than any other terrorist incident. After 9/11, Abu Ubeid al-Qurashi, a leading al-Qaeda operative, boasted that "September 11 was an even greater propaganda coup. It may be said that it broke a record in propaganda dissemination" (Rubin and Rubin 2002, 274).

Bin Laden himself was aware of what generations of terrorists before him recognized, namely, that terrorism is propaganda by deed and that this sort of political violence is best understood as communication. After 9/11 the al-Qaeda boss said,

> Those youth who conducted the [9/11] operations . . . those young men [inaudible] said in deeds, in New York and Washington, speeches that overshadowed all other speeches made everywhere else in the world. The speeches are under-

stood by both Arabs and non-Arabs—even by Chinese. . . . It is above all the
media said."[15]

And then there were the brothers Said and Cherif Kouachi who told survivors of their 2015 killing spree in the Paris headquarters of the satirical magazine *Charlie Hebdo*, "You say to the media, it was al-Qaeda in Yemen!"—a
brazen message that was promptly publicized in news reports around the
world.

The discussed links between the various corners of both the domestic and
international triangles and the connections between domestic and international media illustrate the communication models before the digital revolution. As figure 2.3 shows, today the Internet hovers over, circumvents, and
connects with the triangular mass communication model. Instead of depending solely on traditional media or traditional alternative media, individuals
and all kinds of groups and organizations, including terrorists, have now
direct, easy, and fairly inexpensive access to computer-aided communication, most of all social media networks. Terrorists of the past did not trust the
mainstream press or broadcast media because they considered them as agents
of the very powers they fought. For this reason, terrorists always searched
for ways to circumvent the mainstream media's gatekeepers and publicize
their messages in alternative media, preferably those they controlled. While
the Internet serves this function today, it has not replaced the mainstream
media in the overall publicity calculus of terrorism, as we will see in the following chapters. Manuel Castells (2009, 55) recognizes this coexistence of
old and new communication in general, not only in the context of terrorism.
Distinguishing between three forms of communication—interpersonal, mass
communication, and mass self-communication—he points out that these
three "coexist, interact, and complement each other rather than substitut-
ing for one another." For Castells (2009, 302) the massive growth of mass
self-communication and what he calls multimedia communication networks
offers social movements and insurgent politics greater opportunities "to
enter the public space from multiple sources." To be sure, communication
scholars and regular media consumers tend to applaud the clever use of mass
self-communication, when they support the objectives of the communicators,
but the same people may have second thoughts, when terrorists disseminate
their propaganda of hate and violence via the same means of communication.

Yet, as described in chapter 5, for all the buzz about the starring roles of
social media, for the time being, the mainstream news media remain indispensable for terrorist propaganda because conventional news outlets tend to
alert the general public to the most sensational features and developments
in terrorists' mass self-communication via Internet sites and social media
networking.

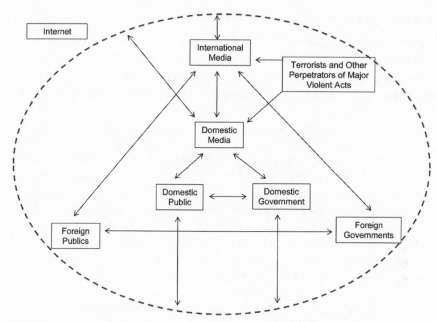

FIGURE 2.3
Terrorism, the Triangles of Political Communication, and the Internet

Terrorists and Their Media-Centered Goals

All terrorists, including those who claim to act in the name of their religion, have ultimate, political, or long-term objectives. For example, al-Qaeda and ISIS want to establish a Caliphate with borders roughly resembling those of the Ottoman Empire. Chechen and Basque terrorists want independence from Russia and Spain respectively; the self-proclaimed Army of God in the United States demands an end to all abortions. Germany's Red Army Faction and the Italian Red Brigades were Marxists who wanted to end capitalism and imperialism. Often, terrorists have short-term goals as well. To secure the financial resources they need, some terrorists rob banks, get involved in drug trafficking, or take hostages to collect ransom. They may kidnap persons to exchange them against imprisoned comrades.

Publicity and propaganda have different values in the terrorist calculus in that they add up to universal goals; publicity and propaganda here are means or instruments to further political ends. For terrorists their media-related goals are universal. To summarize, then, while terrorists' ultimate objectives are by definition political, they have crucial media- or communication-related goals. In particular, terrorists have the following communication-related imperatives:

1. Public Attention and Intimidation

Whether terrorists opt for kidnappings, bombings, or other violent means, their deeds will result in news coverage and all kinds of other communications. To be sure, the more spectacular, the more daring, and the more lethal an attack is the more news it will receive. The awareness of societies under attack is the precondition for terrorists' ability to frighten and intimidate their targets. Once a society is intimidated, the mere threat of more attacks will heighten fear and anxiety.

In terms of getting the attention of friends and foes in literally all parts of the world, the architects and perpetrators of the 9/11 attacks were more successful than those responsible for any previous terrorist attack. With very few exceptions, people all around the globe knew about the attacks soon after they occurred. In 2001, many people received and followed the news of the 9/11 strikes on their television sets or computer screens and communicated their reactions via telephone, e-mail, and in online chat rooms or discussion boards. The unspoken message that bin Laden and al-Qaeda transmitted to America and the world was first of all that they were a formidable foe. By shrewdly planning and staging their brand of media event against the superpower America, the architects of 9/11 were assured news coverage of the horrific attacks not only in the aftermath but in fact during these events. The mass-mediated images of the burning and falling twin towers in New York and the damaged Pentagon outside of Washington worked in favor of al-Qaeda's leaders in that they shocked and intimidated the American public and, albeit to a lesser extent, people in western Europe as well.

In the following weeks, months, and years, bin Laden, al-Qaeda's second in command Ayman al-Zawahiri, and the Californian convert to Islam Adam Gadahn ("Azzam the American" who climbed up the al-Qaeda ranks into a major propaganda role) produced dozens of propaganda videos and released them to the Arab satellite TV network Al-Jazeera or friendly Internet sites. Subsequently finding their way into traditional and new media around the globe, these mass-mediated messages typically threatened more terrorism against Americans and other Western societies, refueling people's anxieties—especially in previously struck countries. Once heavily struck by terrorists, the al-Qaeda leadership recognized, the mere threat of more violence heightened the anxieties of both populations and public officials.

2. Recognition of Grievances and Demands

Once they have the attention of their target audiences, terrorists want to inform them about their motives. They want their targets to learn why they are hated and why they are the targets of attacks. On this count, too, bin Laden and his comrades in arms were utterly successful. Before September 11, 2001, the American news media did not report a great deal about the growing anti-American sentiments among Arabs and Muslims in the Middle East and in other parts of the world; this changed after 9/11 in that they expanded their reporting from these regions. Suddenly, there were many stories that pondered the question that President George W. Bush had posed shortly after the events of 9/11: Why do they hate us? The focus of this sort of reporting was not simply on the motives of the terrorists themselves but also on the vast majority of nonviolent Arabs and Muslims who resented the United States for their foreign policies affecting the Middle East and South Asia. Besides the reporting of the mainstream media there was the distribution of CDs and DVDs among Muslims in the Western diaspora; these were instrumental in spreading al-Qaeda's grievances against their "Crusader-Zionist" enemy and in recruiting new jihadists. This propaganda went into a higher pitch once U.S.-led coalition forces attacked the Taliban and al-Qaeda in Afghanistan and, even more so, in response to the Iraq invasion. Again, al-Qaeda and similar groups exploited all kinds of media to publicize their grievances.

A good example was Hamdi Isaac, one of four participants in a failed London bombing attack on July 21, 2005, designed as a carbon copy of a deadly, quadruple bombing attack of the city's commuter system two weeks earlier. It seems that Isaac had followed news reports from the Middle East and was an alienated young man in the United Kingdom. After he had fled from London and was arrested in Rome, he told the Italian police that he had been recruited by another would-be bomber by the name of Said Ibrahim. As Isaac recalled,

> We met each other at a muscle-building class in Notting Hill and Muktar (Said Ibrahim) showed us some DVDs with images of the war in Iraq, especially women and children killed by American and British soldiers. . . . During our meetings we analyzed the political situation and the fact that everywhere in the West Muslims are humiliated and that we must react.[16]

3. Respect and Sympathy

Osama Bin Laden and al-Qaeda did not win the respect of the American people by committing anti-American terrorism on U.S. soil and abroad, nor did the Madrid and London bombers endear themselves to the Spanish and British people or the self-proclaimed members of al-Qaeda in Yemen to the French populace by striking a controversial satirical magazine. On the contrary, for many Americans, Spaniards, Englishmen, and Frenchmen the architects and actual perpetrators of terrorist spectaculars became the personification of evil with bin Laden and other al-Qaeda leaders seen as the villains-in-chief. This reaction did not come as a surprise to bin Laden and his kind. After all, when international terrorists strike, they do not strive to be loved by their target audiences; they want to be feared, they want to be taken seriously, they want to cause the public and government in a struck country to react. But at the same time, they aim for increased respectability and sympathy among people on whose behalf they claim to act. This is precisely what bin Laden, his closest aides, and the al-Qaeda organization achieved in the post–9/11 years: They won the respect and sympathy of many people in Arab and Muslim countries and of a few in the Western diaspora as well. Important here was the al-Qaeda leadership's ability to produce their own propaganda material, especially audio- and videotapes, and place it with TV networks, such as Al-Jazeera and Al-Arabiya. As time went by, the respect for bin Laden in Muslim countries declined gradually but there remained strong support for al-Qaeda's policy preferences in the Middle East and even among Muslims in the West. Similarly, al-Qaeda in the Arabian Peninsula, Al Shaabab in Somalia, Boko Haram in Nigeria, ISIS in Syria and Iraq and elsewhere, or fanatics of the Army of God and neo-Nazi/white supremacy variety in the United States did not win the hearts and minds of the majority of people they hoped to influence, but all of them won over sympathizers and different numbers of individuals willing to respond to the respective groups' propaganda of hate with violence.

4. A Degree of Legitimacy

A few weeks after the 2004 train bombings in Madrid, bin Laden offered to halt terrorism in European countries if they were to withdraw their military forces from Muslim lands. In an audio message, taped by al-Qaeda's in-house production team and first aired on the Arab television network Al Arabiya, bin Laden said, "The door to a truce is open for three months. The truce will begin when the last soldier leaves our countries" (Bernstein 2004, 3). Within hours, high-ranking officials in several western European countries went public with responses from their respective governments. Although all of these governments rejected the truce offer categorically, their immediate reaction was a testament to bin Laden's quasi-legitimate status. Government officials were prompted to respond immediately by the high degree of attention the European media paid to bin Laden's tape. It was "breaking news" all the time. As German TV commentator Elmar Thevessen noted,

> I think it would be better not to react to the tape in the way many governments did. Of course, one shouldn't keep quiet about it, but by talking about bin Laden's message all the time, we are upgrading him to a global player. (Ibid.)

British Prime Minister Tony Blair learned his lesson: He promised that he would not respond to or comment on any al-Qaeda messages in the future. President George W. Bush did not follow Blair's example. Instead, he often mentioned and spoke at length about America's number one enemy in the "war against terrorism." In July 2007, for example, President Bush spoke at an Air Force base near Charleston, South Carolina. It was another of his "al-Qaeda speeches." By my count, in his 3505-word and less than thirty-minute speech, the president mentioned al-Qaeda ninety-one times, Osama bin Laden twenty-three times, and Ayman al-Zawahiri and other al-Qaeda and alleged al-Qaeda leaders eighteen times.[17] Terrorist leaders love this kind of attention by presidents, prime ministers, and other high officials—especially, if these officials represent governments that are high on their priority list of targets. They perceive this sort of attention as a sign that they are treated like legitimate political leaders—or, actually, better.

If there were any doubts that bin Laden longed for a status generally reserved for recognized political leaders, they were laid to rest when the al-Qaeda boss released a videotape five days before the 2004 presidential elections in the United States. Instead of wearing his familiar military attire, holding a weapon, and using threatening language, bin Laden wore a softly flowing robe and spoke in the measured tone of a statesman. This change in style was not lost on experts, who concluded that this particular speech was "carefully staged and worded to present him as a polished statesman and the voice of a broad movement, instead of a terrorism-obsessed religious fanatic" (Whitlock 2004, A20). While this image of a seemingly new persona hardly attested to a change in bin Laden's attitude toward the United States, the West, and foes elsewhere, the news media nevertheless offered extraordinary airtime and column inches to a "news event" that was staged by the al-Qaeda leader and his media experts. The two major presidential candidates did not play into bin Laden's ploy and refused to comment on his preelection message, but sources in their respective camps gave their takes on al-Qaeda's propaganda rationale in another score for terrorist propaganda.

A Contrary View on Terrorist Publicity

When terrorists struck in the 1970s and 1980s, they typically claimed responsibility for their deeds. But beginning with the downing of Pan Am flight 103 in late 1988 and continuing with terrorist spectaculars in the 1990s and in the beginning of the new millennium (i.e., the World Trade Center bombing in 1993, the Oklahoma City bombing in 1995, the sarin gas release in the Tokyo subway system the same year, the bombings of U.S. embassies in

Kenya and Tanzania in 1998, the suicide attack on the USS *Cole* in 2000), the perpetrators did not claim responsibility by identifying themselves and/ or their affiliations in explicit and timely communications. For this reason, some observers and experts in the field concluded that a new terrorism of expression had emerged. Typically committed by religious or pseudo-religious fanatics, the new kind of political violence has supposedly no media-centered goals, and its perpetrators are said to "lack clearly defined political ends" but give "vent to rage against state power and to feelings of revenge" (Margalit 1995, 19). The point here is that those fighting a holy war of terror against an evil enemy do not need to make public claims since they inflict the greatest possible harm, whereas earlier and typically secular terrorists needed to claim responsibility because they were primarily sending powerful messages to their target audiences in order to further their political agenda.

Even apart from the alleged emergence of "expressive terrorism," some students of terrorism have questioned the inevitable relationship between terrorism and communication. Michel Wieviorka (1993), for example, has argued that some terrorists do not seek media attention and the furtherance of their propaganda. But whether terrorists claim responsibility for their deeds does not matter at all with respect to media coverage. As Wieviorka (1993, 46–47) recognized, even when the perpetrators of political violence seem unconcerned about news coverage, other actors can and do confer media attention upon them—such as the press and government authorities. It is difficult to imagine that terrorists who fail to claim responsibility or do not otherwise release statements are not aware and pleased that their deeds will be highlighted in the news. I fully agree with Paul Wilkinson's unequivocal argument,

> Terrorism has been a remarkably successful means of publicizing a political cause and relaying the terrorist threat to a wider audience, particularly in the open and pluralistic countries of the West. When one says "terrorism" in a democratic society, one also says "media" for terrorism by its very nature is a psychological weapon which depends upon communicating a threat to a wider society. (Wilkinson 2001, 177)

The journalist and columnist Dale Van Atta, who reported on national security issues for decades, warned that the press should not buy the suggestion of the media's diminished role in the terrorist calculus but argued, "The very act of intending to kill hundreds in airplane and building explosions means they [terrorists] seek sensational coverage for their deeds. . . . Like it or not, the media is still an integral part of achieving the terrorist's aim—and therefore must be as judicious and responsible as possible in its reportage" (Van Atta 1998, 68).

Also, when terrorists do not claim responsibility for a particular act of political violence, they are often aware that they will be recognized as the primary or only suspects and that the news media will report on them and their motives. Thus, following the simultaneous bombings of the U.S. embassies in Kenya and Tanzania in August 1998, bin Laden was discovered as the likely architect of these terrorist strikes, although there was no claim of responsibility on his part. But two months earlier, he had told journalists during a press conference in Afghanistan that Americans were "easy targets" and that this would be obvious "in a very short time."[18] And eventually, after the arrest, indictment, trial, and sentencing of several men, the link between the bombings and al-Qaeda was not in doubt.

Pulitzer Prize winner Thomas Friedman suggested that Osama bin Laden "is not a mere terrorist" but a "super-empowered" man with geopolitical aspirations who does not seek headlines but aims to kill as many Americans as possible (Friedman 2002). Yes, bin Laden had big geopolitical plans, and, yes, he wanted to bring America down. But bin Laden knew the importance and power of propaganda. Accordingly, the Manual of the Afghan Jihad, used as a training guide for al-Qaeda's jihadists, attests to the centrality of publicity considerations in the organization's operations and planning. Thus, the manual recommends targeting "sentimental landmarks," such as the Statue of Liberty in New York, Big Ben in London, and the Eiffel Tower in Paris, because their destruction "would generate intense publicity with minimal casualties."[19] In short, if at all possible, terrorists of all ideologies and religions—just like actors in the legitimate political process—want and need publicity.

At the time of this writing, the well-coordinated 9/11 strikes remain the most lethal attacks in the modern history of terrorism. For that reason and because of al-Qaeda's long practice of "propaganda by deed" and, what one might call "propaganda by word," I illustrated the above explanations of the four media-centered objectives of terrorists mostly with examples from 9/11, al-Qaeda, and Osama bin Laden. However, I am fully aware that al-Qaeda affiliates, such as those in Yemen (al-Qaeda in the Arabian Peninsula), Somalia (Al Shabab), Nigeria (Boko Haram), and in Syria (al-Nusra), as well as autonomous organizations, such as ISIS (Syria and Iraq and increasingly North-African affiliates) or Lashkar-e-Taiba (Pakistan) are equally as media savvy and in the case of ISIS have actually surpassed al-Qaeda in terms of propaganda. That is hardly surprising because unlike al-Qaeda, more recently established groups operated from the outset in a new digital communication environment that was in a rudimentary stage or did not exist when the events of 9/11 unfolded and for years thereafter.

Of Symbols, Rituals and Terrorism

What I have described so far testifies to the media savviness of the purveyors of terrorism who are well versed in exploiting all aspects of communication and propaganda to persuade friends and foes. Part of their communication success is based on their skillful use of symbols and rituals. In his book *Symbolism in Terrorism*, Jonathan Matusitz (2014) analyzes a multitude of symbols he associates with terrorism. Of particular interest here is the notion of behavioral symbols. As Matusitz (ibid., 12) explains,

> Behavioral symbols refer to symbols that are enacted through rituals, ceremonies, behaviors, and performances. They help to preserve kinship, affinity, relationships, and brotherhood. They serve to define and delimit the boundaries between ingroups and outgroups. Those who relate to and sanction behavioral symbols are part of the ingroup; those who do not are left out.

When surrounded by special police forces after their bloody attack on the Paris headquarters of the satirical magazine *Charlie Hebdo* in early 2015, the two gunmen told a police negotiator and a reporter in phone conversations that they wanted to become "martyrs." Then they stepped out of their hiding place, faced an overwhelming number of security forces, but nevertheless aimed their AK-47s in a last aggressive gesture at the police before being killed in a hail of bullets. Their associate, who had shot to death several persons as he stormed into a Parisian kosher market, told his hostages that he was ready to be a martyr; he, too, died as he confronted skilled SWAT team members. Thus, all three men, after committing unspeakable murders, performed last acts of what they perceived as heroism and martyrdom in the name of their cause—the most extreme form of jihadism. They invoked the values of their in-group, most of all the will to die for the group's cause. While the mass of people condemned the perpetrators and rejected their claim of being heroes and martyrs, there were others in France and elsewhere around the world who felt a religious and social connection; these people were convinced that the three jihadists would be rewarded in paradise for their heroic actions against infidel enemies of their religion. Olivier Roy, an expert on political Islam, explained in the immediate aftermath of the terrorist strikes in Paris,

> We have a terrible problem in France of disenfranchised young people, with no opportunities. Many of them start off in petty delinquency, but for some of them, radical Islam is a way to find a second life—not in society, but in terms of self-image and self-esteem. We tend to transform them [jihadi terrorists] into negative heroes, but what is a negative hero for the rest of society is a positive one for disenfranchised people.[20]

Simply by reporting spectacular and horrific terrorist incidents like the simultaneous ones in Paris the mass media transmit powerful images that capture gestures of behavioral symbolism. To stay with the terrorist attacks in Paris, by describing and showing in video clips and still photographs the powerful AK-47s or Kalashnikovs in the hands of the three terrorists, the media reflected the empowerment of individuals and groups. For terrorists, according to one expert, weapons "are 'prestige symbols' that indicate or communicate what the group is able to do with them" (Matusitz 2014, 208).

Communication scholars distinguish between communication as transmission (of messages typically to persuade the receiver) and communication as ritual with the latter referring to the "sacred ceremony that draws persons together in fellowship and communality" (Carey 1992, 17–18). However, there are also rituals of excommunication that divide and separate communities rather than draw them together (Carey 1998). While these concepts are typically applied to domestic settings, they are equally useful in the transnational and global contexts, especially in view of the advances in global communication technology.

When it comes to terrorists, they are well versed in ritual communication of both types. Whether Osama bin Laden as head of al-Qaeda Central, Anwar al-Awlaki as influential member of al-Qaeda in the Arabian Peninsula (AQAP), ISIS leader Abu Bakr al-Baghdadi, other prominent terrorists, or their foot soldiers charged with carrying out terrorist acts, their messages, symbols, and rituals are designed to unify active members, supporters, and sympathizers while at the same time emphasizing the existential gap between the community of jihadists and the infidels, their enemies. The following paragraph from AQAP's online magazine *Inspire* is an excellent example of ritual communication in that the first message divides by highlighting the evilness of the West, "the other," that must be fought and destroyed whereas the second one draws Muslims together into a community of jihadists that follows the call of Allah:

> Outrageous slander, blatant smearing of Muḥammad, desecration of the Qurān, and the insulting of over a billion Muslims worldwide are done under the pretext of "freedom of speech." They are never called what they really are: a deeply rooted historic hatred for Islām and Muslims. Yesterday it was in the name of Christianity; today it is in the name of Democracy.
>
> What the West is failing to realize is that these attacks are also serving as a mobilizing factor for the Muslims and are bringing more and more Muslims to the realization that jihād against the West is the only realistic solution for this problem along with a host of other problems that cannot be cured without fighting in the path of Allāh.[21]

Because jihadist terrorism has been predominant in the last decades around the world this chapter's discussions and examples concerning terrorists' media imperatives have dealt in large part with extremist and violent Muslim groups and individuals. It must be noted, however, that other secular and religiously motivated terrorists strove in the past and strive today for the same mass-mediated communication objectives as jihadist groups as will be shown in the next chapter. At this point, though, I want to provide one example from the Army of God, an extremist and fanatical American anti-abortion group that encourages members to kill and maim abortion providers in the name of God and Christ. Just like jihadists who consider themselves as carrying out the will of God, members of the Army of God make the same claim. And just like jihadists, anti-abortion terrorists make great efforts to get attention, have their motives and justifications widely publicized, and when imprisoned or killed consider themselves martyrs.

A good example is Paul Hill, a former minister of the Presbyterian Church in America and the Orthodox Presbyterian Church, who shot and killed Dr. John Bayard Britton and his bodyguard James Herman Barrett as they drove into the parking lot of a Florida abortion clinic. After being arrested, Hill did not express any regrets. Instead, he was proud that he had acted as an instrument of God and he made great efforts to publicize his satisfaction and pride of being a faithful soldier of God. "If I had not acted when I did, it would have been a direct and unconscionable sin of disobedience," he wrote from prison. "One of the first things I told my wife after the shooting was, 'I didn't have any choice!' That cry came from my soul. I was certain, and still am, that God called me to obey his revealed will at that particular time."[22] The day before his execution, Hill asked for and was allowed to hold a press conference for a dozen reporters in a visiting room of Florida State Prison. He told reporters that he was honored to die and that he expected God to welcome him in heaven. "I'm certainly, to be quite honest, I'm expecting a great reward in heaven for my obedience," he said.[23] He also called for other opponents of legalized abortion to follow his example. "I think it was a good thing [killing abortion providers] and instead of people being shocked at what I did, I think more people should act as I acted," he said.[24] Just as jihadist groups celebrate martyrs, the Army of God has for a long time done the same on its website.

In conclusion, then, terrorists rely on the communicative power of their violent acts. Without publicity, a terrorist attack would be like the tree that falls down in the forest without the press there to report. It would be as if the tree did not fall or, with respect to terrorism, as if the strike never occurred.

Notes

1. As reported at Inquirer.net, accessed February 25, 2015, http://newsinfo.in quirer.net/670613/fox-news-posts-jordanian-pilot-burning-video-on-website.

2. CNN, Reliable Sources, "Should Media Air ISIS Propaganda?" September 14, 2014. Text, accessed Oct. 2, 2014, is available at http://reliablesources.blogs.cnn.com/tag/isis.

3. White House, "President Obama Delivers a Statement on the Murder of James Foley." Text of statement, accessed October 1, 2014, is available at http://www.whitehouse.gov/photos-and-video/video/2014/08/20/president-obama-delivers -statement-murder-james-foley.

4. White House, "President Obama Gives a Statement on the Murder of Steven Sotloff." Text of statement, accessed September 30, 2014, is available at http://www .whitehouse.gov/blog/2014/09/03/president-obama-gives-statement-murder-steven -sotloff.

5. David Cameron tweet, accessed October 8, 2014, https://twitter.com/David_ Cameron/status/510924902577479681.

6. Jonathan Topaz, "Jimmy Carter: President Obama Blew It on ISIL," *Politico*, October 8, 2014. Text, accessed Oct. 8, 2014, is available at http://www.politico.com/story/2014/10/jimmy-carter-barack-obama-isil-111692.html?hp=l2.

7. Leon Panetta and Jim Newton, *Worthy Fights: A Memoir of War and Peace.* New York: Penguin, 2014. Following the publication of his book, Panetta gave many interviews repeating his criticism of President Obama's Iraq and Syria policies to which he related the rise of ISIS.

8. Peter Baker, "In Book, Panetta Recounts Frustration with Obama," *New York Times*, October 6, 2014.

9. Combating Terrorism Center, Document No. AFGP-2002-6000321.

10. As I learned in a phone interview with Lou Michael, a reporter for the *Buffalo News*, McVeigh revealed a great deal about his extreme ideology, his motives, and his desire for publicity in a series of interviews with Michael and his colleague Dan Herbeck. See also Lou Michael and Dan Herbeck, *American Terrorist: Timothy McVeigh & the Oklahoma City Bombing* (New York: Regan Books, 2001), especially pages 168, 169, 227, 245, and 382.

11. Ibid.

12. Ibid.

13. The transcript of several phone conversations, made available online by the *New York Times*, accessed October 10, 2014, is available at http://graphics8.nytimes .com/packages/pdf/nyregion/city_room/20090109_mumbaitranscripts.pdf.

14. "Excerpts from the Videotape Transcript." *Washington Post*, December 14, 2001, A37.

15. Ibid.

16. "Italy Arrests Another Brother of London Bomb Suspect." Agence France Presse, July 31, 2005, retrieved from Yahoo! News, July 31, 2005, at http://news.yahoo .com/afp/20050731/wl-uk-afp/britainattacksitaly-050731153552&prin...

17.   The transcript of the speech, accessed January 9, 2015, is available at http:// www.gpo.gov/fdsys/pkg/PPP-2007-book2/pdf/PPP-2007-book2-doc-pg1005.pdf.

18.   Based on what bin Laden said in this particular news conference as well as in other communications, it was not difficult to pinpoint him as the driving force behind the bombings in East Africa. The quotes from his news conference in Khost, Afghanistan, are from Dale Van Atta (1998, 66).

19.   See Hamza Hendawi, "Terror Manual Advises on Targets," accessed February 11, 2002, http://story.news.yahoo.com/news?tmpl=story&u=/ap/20.../afghan_spreading -terror-.

20.   Roy was quoted by Liz Alderman, "After Terrorist Attack, Many French Muslims Wonder: What Now?" *New York Times*, January 10, 2015, accessed January 11, 2015, http://www.nytimes.com/2015/01/11/world/europe/french-muslims-worry -about-backlash-after-charlie-hebdo-attack.html?_r=0.

21.   Paragraph is from page 27 of the first issue of *Inspire* magazine, accessed January 15, 2015, available at https://info.publicintelligence.net/CompleteInspire.pdf.

22.   Excerpts are from Paul Hill, "Defending the Defenseless," http://www.armyof god.com/PHill_ShortShot.html.

23.   Leonora LaPeter, "Facing Execution, He Expects Glory," accessed January 12, 2015, http://www.sptimes.com/2003/09/03/State/Facing_execution__he_.shtml.

24.   "Antiabortion Killer Executed," CBS News, September 3, 2003, accessed January 11, 2015, http://www.cbsnews.com/news/anti-abortion-killer-executed.

3

Terrorists Always Found Alternative Media

Same Objectives, Different Technologies

Here is another way to make bombs: take a piece of iron pipe, as commonly used for water or gas mains, and cut it into short lengths. For home-made "hand-grenades," six inch lengths of pipe of one and a half to two inches in diameter are suitable. . . . We carried out tests with these bombs, also, and the results were always satisfactory. It should be clear to everyone that such devices are easy to make, and not expensive at all (which is very important to us), and that they can achieve spectacular results when used against large assemblies of people (riff-raff of the upper-class variety). . . . These weapons are to the proletariat an effective substitute for artillery, and inflict surprise, confusion and panic on the enemy.

—Johann Most, 1885[1]

Make a bomb in the kitchen of your Mom. Can I make an effective bomb that causes damage to the enemy from ingredients available in any kitchen in the world? The answer is yes. . . . My Muslim brother: we are conveying to you our military training right into your kitchen to relieve you of the difficulty of traveling to us. If you are sincere in your intention to serve the religion of Allah, then all that you have to do is enter your kitchen and make an explosive device that would damage the enemy. . . . Here are the main ingredients. . . . In one or two days the bomb could be ready to kill at least ten people. In a month you may make a bigger and more lethal bomb that could kill tens of people. . . . The open source jihad is America's worst nightmare.

—The AQ Chef, 2010[2]

In 1885, after working in a New Jersey explosives plant and learning the nuts and bolts of handling potent explosive material, the leading anarchist of his time, Johann Most, self-published an instruction manual titled "Revolutionary War Science: A Little Handbook of Instruction in the Use and Preparation of Nitroglycerin, Dynamite, Gun Cotton, Fulminating Mercury, Bombs, Fuses, etc. etc." Originally written in German with the title "Revolutionaere Krieg-swissenschaft" (in translation, "Revolutionary Science of War") the volume was used as a "how-to" text by anarchists of the time. It also served "Alexander Berkman in his aborted attempt to construct a bomb with which to attack the principal opponent of the Homestead strikes, Henry Clay Frick, whom he later unsuccessfully tried to kill using a gun" (Thorup 2008, 338).

One hundred twenty-five years later, al-Qaeda in the Arabian Peninsula (AQAP) devoted ten pages in the first issue of the group's online magazine *Inspire* to describe in text, drawings, and photographs how to "make a bomb in the kitchen of your Mom." The detailed instructions helped among others the Boston Marathon bombers Tamerlan and Dzhokhar Tsarnaev to build two pressure cooker bombs that the manual described as the "most effective method" of homemade explosives. The brothers ignited the bombs at the finish line of the 2013 Boston Marathon, killing three persons and injuring another 264.

In both cases, the advocates of political violence utilized alternative media to publicize their instructions. Early anarchists were then and contemporary jihadists are now very critical of the mainstream media. In 1853, the early anarchist theorist and fierce advocate of political violence Karl Heinzen self-published a pamphlet titled "Murder and Liberty," in which he mocked the mainstream media of his time, daily and weekly newspapers, as mouthpieces of the ruling class and asked fellow radicals to distribute his brochure "in all places, in letters, in clothes, in parcels, in warehouses."[3] One hundred sixty years later, in 2013, when the first issue of the new al-Qaeda magazine *Azan* was posted online, the editors complained about the "vicious propaganda" carried by the "satanic" international media. They claimed that "the biased portrayal of international events coupled with a perspective on life that has nothing to do with the Quran and Sunnah has confused the majority of the Muslim masses with regards to their stances in this war."[4] Explaining the need for an alternative media controlled by those committed to the jihadist movement, the editors wrote, "It is important that the masses of the Muslims be informed of the real nature of the contemporary battle" and assured readers that "*Azan* is a platform for the Muslims of the world to see the truth for what it is and also a way for them to participate in this global effort to destroy the enemies of Allah and His Messenger."[5]

Whereas both the early anarchists succeeded in their times and contemporary jihadists succeed in our time in circumventing what in their view are biased gatekeepers of the mainstream media, there is one distinct difference: The early anarchists could reach only a rather limited number of readers in some locations and over time; ISIS, al-Qaeda, and other contemporary terrorist groups can and do reach supporters and potential recruits around the globe as soon as they post their messages and images on Internet sites and networks.

The previous chapter characterized terrorism as a communicative act, as a means utilized by terrorists to get the attention of friends and foes, to advertise their grievances and demands, to enlist support and sympathy among potential supporters, and to become a political factor in various environments. When it comes to this kind of political violence by non-state actors, one can and should examine terrorism in the context of contentious politics and in some cases in the framework of social movements. More recently, foremost social movement scholars, such as Sidney G. Tarrow, Doug McAdam, and Charles Tilly, have in fact argued "for an integration of social movement studies with the analysis of more violent forms of contention [including terrorism]" (Tarrow 2011, xvii). To be sure, not all terrorist groups amount to or are part of a larger social movement but they all are at minimum involved in acts of contentious politics. Moreover, from the transnational Anarchist movement in the latter part of the nineteenth century and the early years of the twentieth century to the post–WWI Fascist movements, the post–WWII Colonial Liberation movements, the Marxist movements in the second half of the twentieth century, the contemporary jihadist movements, and domestic movements, such as the American white supremacy and the extremist anti-abortion movements, there have been a multitude of larger and smaller groups that seem to qualify.

Tilly and Tarrow (2007, 27) point out that "contentious politics involves many different forms and combinations of collective action." While social movement studies concern in large part peaceful protests, they include increasingly "vigilante violence, military coups, worker rebellion, and social movements [that] involve very different sorts of contention." For terrorist groups and networks to rise to the level of a movement would require first of all that they express political contention in the form of *frequent* public violence and threats of violence. Tilly and Wood (2009, 3–4) list a combination of three characteristics that social movements display, namely,

- sustained, organized public efforts making claims on target authorities;
- combinations of political actions or performances, what they call a repertoire; and
- public representations of WUNC (worthiness, unity, numbers, and commitment).

Political actions, whether peaceful or violent, are here compared to performances that are drawn from repertoires and staged in theaters or arenas for the benefit of those who are watching—in our times via various media of mass communication. Interestingly, terrorism scholars, too, have invoked the theater metaphor. Brian Jenkins (1974, 6) explained that "terrorism is aimed at the people watching, not the actual victims. Terrorism is theater." And Gabriel Weimann and Conrad Winn (1994, 52) wrote perceptively that "modern terrorism can be understood in terms of the production requirements of theatrical engagements." Social movements, whether violent or nonviolent, require publicity and most try to stage mass-mediated events to propagate the worthiness of their motives and strength through unity, numbers, and commitment to their causes.

Although recognizing that case studies of social movement media exploded in the twenty-first century because of the role played by Internet-based social media networks, John Downing (2008, 40–42) criticized nevertheless that on the whole social movement theory and media studies have paid little attention to the importance of media in general and alternative media in particular. Similarly, while contemporary media and terrorism scholars are paying increasing attention to terrorists' utilization of social media, the long history of terrorist alternative media has been mostly or completely ignored by past and present research. This chapter puts the explosion of computer-based terrorist self-communication into a historical context and demonstrates that the use of alternative media, now of the digital variety, is nothing fundamentally new in the long-standing terrorist communication calculus—except for the significant advances in information and communication technology that changed the speed and reach and affordability of self-communication.

Early Anarchists and Propaganda by Deed and Word

Scholars are not clear about the origin of the characterization of terrorism as "propaganda by deed." Some credit the 1881 international anarchist conference with adopting this doctrine, others attribute the term to Johann Most, and still others to the Italian immigrant and anarchist Luigi Galleani. But regardless who first coined this slogan there is no doubt that Most was the most tireless promoter of both violent action and the use of alternative media for the sake of public attention and awareness of anarchist ideology. An admirer of Karl Heinzen, Most reprinted and interpreted his idol's pamphlets in *Freiheit* (Liberty), a weekly newspaper he established in England and revived in the United States in the 1880s. He recognized political violence as acts of communication. In his article "Action as Propaganda," Most wrote, "We preach not only action in and for itself, but also action as propaganda."[6] But he also understood that action alone would not always get the desired results. Thus, he advised his fellow revolutionaries to prepare and put up posters to explain "the reasons for the action in such a way as to draw from them the best possible benefit."[7] Convinced that the mainstream presses were on the side of the enemy, Most urged fellow radicals, "The important thing is that the world learns of it [the act of terrorism] from the revolutionaries, so that everyone knows what the position is."[8] To put it differently, Most recognized and preached the importance of both "propaganda by deed" and "propaganda by word."

The most important propaganda vehicles for him were the anarchist presses; he urged their editors and reporters to "glorify and explicate the deeds at every opportunity."[9] In the late 1800s, the city of Chicago was a hotbed of anarchists who were inspired directly or indirectly by Most. According to James Green (2006, 140), "the call for revolutionary action was gaining new converts in Chicago in early 1886, especially among hundreds of German anarchists who had read Johann Most's extremist views in the provocative newspaper *Freiheit*." In the mid-1880s, "Chicago had five major anarchist newspapers, three in German, one in Czech, and one, *The Alarm*, in English. The combined circulation was about 30,000" (Miller 1995, 49). Whether in Chicago or elsewhere, anarchist newspapers subscribed to Most's radical ideas and used their own pages to urge radicals to build bombs and stand up to the oppressive authorities in government and industry. As one article in the *Alarm* stated, "One man with a dynamite bomb is equal to one regiment" (ibid.). That was the essence of Johann Most's revolutionary philosophy.

While on a speech-making tour, Most fell ill and died in early 1906, but that did not mean the end of his doctrine of propaganda. On the contrary, Luigi Galleani, an Italian immigrant, was already several years in the United States when Most passed away and ready to work for the anarchist cause with the same passion that characterized Johann Most's activities. Before long, Galleani had a committed group of followers (called Galleanists at the time) who carried out what he preached. As editor of *Cronaca Sovversiva* (Subversive Chronicle), an Italian language newsletter, Galleani became "the leading Italian anarchist in America" in the first two decades of the twentieth century. Paul Avrich (1991, 48, 50) recognized Galleani's and his newsletter's influence beyond the United States as well, noting that "though its [*Cronaca Sovversiva's*] circulation never exceeded four or five thousand, its influence, reaching far beyond the confines of the United States, could be felt wherever Italian radicals congregated, from Europe and North Africa to South America and Australia." Galleani preached the most militant type of anarchism without any room for compromise; he called for violence in the battle against capitalism and capitalist governments. As Susan Tejada summarized,

> In the pages of *Cronaca* and in *his other writings* [emphasis added], Galleani promoted social revolution, endorsed the use of violence to win the "good war" against capitalism, and published practical tips for aspiring bomb makers— where to buy explosives, how to avoid arousing suspicion, how to build devices to injure the maximum number of people.[10]

A good example of Galleani's "other writings" was a brochure titled "Health is in You" that was advertised in the pages of *Cronaca Sovversiva* as must reading for proletarian families; the pamphlet was in fact a manual for building homemade bombs. In this respect, too, Galleani followed Most's example of providing teaching material for building homemade bombs. Galleani was also a gifted orator who was welcomed by Italian anarchist groups around the country. Both his written and spoken words fell on fertile ground among like-minded Italian immigrants, most of them factory workers. Many of them spread anarchist ideology in meetings and in their own leaflets, newsletters, and even newspapers after work in their spare time. According to one account, "After ten or twelve hours in the factory or mine, the anarchists would come home, eat supper, then go to their clubs and begin to churn out their journals and leaflets on makeshift presses" (Avrich 1991, 54).

In the second decade of the twentieth century, Galleanists were the most active group among anarchists in America. They practiced both "propaganda by word" and "propaganda by deed." In April 1919, for example, Galleanists mailed thirty letter bombs to a cross-section of prominent public officials (including the Attorney General of the United States, a Supreme Court Justice, and the Postmaster General) and prominent businessmen, including John D. Rockefeller.[11] In June, more powerful bombs were delivered by messengers to carefully selected targets in seven cities with the explosions occurring simultaneously. As with the earlier letter bombs, the new wave of explosives contained messages printed on pink paper in which "The Anarchist Fighters" claimed responsibility and issued the following threat:

> You have jailed, deported, and murdered us. We accept the challenge. The workers have a right to defend themselves; and since their presses have been silenced and their voices muzzled, we mean to speak for them with dynamite. There will have to be bloodshed; we will not dodge; there will have to be murder: we will kill, because it is necessary; there will have to be destruction; we will destroy to rid the world of your tyrannical institutions.[12]

By the time Galleanists delivered those letter and package bombs to targets across the country the Department of Justice had outlawed *Cronaca Sovversiva* for good. Earlier, the Justice Department had called Galleani's publication "the most rabid, seditious and anarchistic sheet ever published in this country."[13] After Galleani published an article asking his followers to avoid being drafted to serve, *Cronaca Sovversiva* was banned from being delivered by the postal service by order of the postmaster of Lynn, Massachusetts, and the newspaper's offices were raided. Galleani and printer Giovanni Eramo were arrested on charges of conspiracy to obstruct the draft. They were taken to Boston and later released on a $10,000 bond. Both men pleaded guilty to conspiracy charges in a federal court in Boston. They were fined $300 and $100 respectively.

Although Galleani was deported back to Italy in mid-1919 and many of his followers were jailed, hardcore anarchists continued to follow Most's and Galleani's "propaganda by deed" and "propaganda by word" strategies, which required not only spectacular acts of violence but immediate explanations of the attackers' motives or demands and often threats of further violence. Thus, after an explosives-packed horse-drawn wagon exploded in the Wall Street area on September 16, 1920, killing thirty-three and injuring more than 200 people, "a crudely printed leaflet" was found a short distance away in which "American Anarchist Fighters" warned, "Free the Political Prisoners or it Will Be Sure Death for All of You" (Davis 2007, 1).

This precursor of the later car or truck bombs achieved exactly the publicity-centered objectives that anarchists wanted with their propaganda by deed and word. In the assessment of one scholar of the 1920 Wall Street bombing, "the number of victims, large though it was, cannot convey the extent of the inferno produced by the explosion, the worst of its kind in American history" (Avrich 1991, 204). Like the attacks on the World Trade Center on September 11, 2001, the Wall Street bombing eighty-one years earlier was also "immediately construed as a national emergency" (Davis 2007, 2).

Anarchists in the second half of the nineteenth and early twentieth centuries recognized the communicative qualities of violent deeds but also utilized from the outset brochures, newspapers, posters, and flyers as alternative media to explain their motives and to issue threats. To put it differently, anarchist public displays of violence (that were amply covered by leading newspapers) and their own messages delivered via anarchist presses and printed claims of responsibility left at the sites of attacks added up to public displays of the unity, strength, and devotion to their cause. These kinds of representations dovetail with several of social movement theory's characteristics mentioned above (Tilly and Wood 2009, 3–4).

Post–World War I Fascist Movements in Germany and Italy

It may well be, as social movement scholars suggest, that most social movements want to have their policy goals enacted and strive for "acceptance of the movement as representative of legitimate interests" (Cowell-Meyers 2014, 65). This is particularly the case for nonviolent movements in democratic settings. But there are also movements that resort to violence in order to move into the legitimate political process. Benito Mussolini's and Adolf Hitler's post–World War I fascist movements in Italy and Germany carried out violence against political opponents before they rose to prevail in the electoral arena. Joseph Goebbels, Hitler's propagandist-in-chief, expressed in his speech "Knowledge and Propaganda" how he viewed a movement's rights once in power:

> If a movement has the strength to take over government positions of power, then it has the right to form the government as it wishes. Anyone who disagrees is a foolish theoretician. Politics is governed not by moral principles, but by power. If a movement conquers the state, it has the right to form the state. You can see how these three elements combine ideals and personalities. The idea leads to a worldview, the worldview to the state, the individual becomes a party, the party becomes the nation.[14]

From the outset, Hitler's and Mussolini's populist movements relied heavily on "propaganda by deed" carried out by Mussolini's combat squads or Black Shirts and Hitler's storm troopers (Sturm Abteilung or abbreviated S.A.) or Brown Shirts. On their way to power, I argue, both movements resembled modern-day terrorist organizations in that they had political and paramilitary or terrorist wings with the latter intimidating and physically attacking political opponents all the while claiming that these squads were merely protecting fellow partisans. Fascist Black Shirts proved as brutal as Hitler's Brown Shirts in their clashes with socialist and communist demonstrators. Both leaders and their movements utilized alternative media as disseminators of propaganda. Mussolini established early on the newspaper *Il Popolo d'Italia* (The People's Daily) as his propaganda outlet. For Hitler and the Nazis *Voelkischer Beobachter* (People's Observer) was the "fighting newspaper" of the movement. Both Mussolini and Hitler spoke at mass rallies to persuade the masses to join their movements.

However, when it came to propaganda, the Nazis were in a league by themselves. Adolf Hitler was a natural propagandist. In his two-volume autobiographical manifesto *Mein Kampf*, which he wrote while imprisoned for his role in a failed coup attempt, he devoted three chapters to propaganda focusing on the effects of various forms of self-communication. Considering textual and oral propaganda, he stated,

> The one-page circular was also adopted by us to help in this propaganda. While still a soldier I had written a circular in which I contrasted the Treaty of Brest-Litowsk [*sic*] with that of Versailles. That circular was printed and distributed in large numbers. Later on I used it for the party, and also with good success. Our first meetings were distinguished by the fact that there were tables covered with leaflets, papers, and pamphlets of every kind. But we relied principally on the spoken word. And, in fact, this is the only means capable of producing really great revolutions, which can be explained on general psychological grounds.[15]

Comparing textual and visual propaganda, Hitler felt that still photographs and motion pictures were more effective than the written word. As he noted,

> Only a leaflet or a placard, on account of its brevity, can hope to arouse a momentary interest in those whose opinions differ from it. The picture, in all its forms, including the film, has better prospects. Here there is less need of elaborating the appeal to the intelligence. It is sufficient if one be careful to have quite short texts, because many people are more ready to accept a pictorial presentation than to read a long written description. In a much shorter time, at one stroke I might say, people will understand a pictorial presentation of something which it would take them a long and laborious effort of reading to understand. (Ibid.)

While Hitler was well versed in propaganda, the Nazi party's propagandist-in-chief Joseph Goebbels understood the power of persuasion in theory and practice. Goebbels had studied American public relations literature and was a fan of Edward L. Bernays, the so-called father of public relations. According to Bernays,

Karl von Wiegand [foreign correspondent for the Hearst newspapers stationed in Berlin] was telling us about Goebbels and his propaganda plans to consolidate Nazi power. Goebbels had shown Wiegand his propaganda library, the best Wiegand had ever seen. Goebbels, said Wiegand, was using my book *Crystallizing Public Opinion* as the basis for his destructive campaign against the Jews in Germany. This shocked me, but I knew any human activity can be used for antisocial ones.[16]

So, Goebbels was a master in the use of propaganda for sinister purposes. In 1931, Goebbels wrote in the first issue of the Nazi magazine *Wille und Weg* (Will and Path),

No other political movement has understood the art of propaganda as well as the National Socialists. From its beginnings, it has put heart and soul into propaganda. What distinguishes it from all other political parties is the ability to see into the soul of the people and to speak the language of the man in the street. It uses all the means of modern technology. Leaflets, handbills, posters, mass demonstrations, the press, stage, film and radio—these are all tools of our propaganda. . . .

In the long run, propaganda will reach the broad masses of the people only if at every stage it is uniform. Nothing confuses the people more than lack of clarity or aimlessness. The goal is not to present the common man with as many varied and contradictory theories as possible. The essence of propaganda is not in variety, but rather the forcefulness and persistence with which one selects ideas from the larger pool and hammers them into the masses using the most varied methods.[17]

Goebbels studied the history of communication and like Hitler recognized the superior power of the spoken word. During a speech that celebrated the radio as a new means of communication he said,

Napoleon spoke of the "press as the seventh great power." Its significance became politically visible with the beginning of the French Revolution, and maintained its position for the entirety of the nineteenth century. The century's politics were largely determined by the press. One can hardly imagine or explain the major historical events between 1800 and 1900 without considering the powerful influence of journalism.

The radio will be for the twentieth century what the press was for the nineteenth century. With the appropriate change, one can apply Napoleon's phrase to our age, speaking of the radio as the eighth great power. Its discovery and application are of truly revolutionary significance for contemporary community life. Future generations may conclude that the radio had as great an intellectual and spiritual impact on the masses as the printing press had before the beginning of the Reformation.[18]

Goebbels was right; no other movement and no other leaders understood the communicative power of public displays better than Nazi propagandists. In their propaganda manuals for local and regional party functionaries, they not only detailed the use of the written and spoken word but also listed public rallies or marches as effective propaganda means. In one propaganda manual, there is even a reference to choral propaganda but only if the singers had rehearsed and, ideally, were "supported by a trumpet."[19] The mass marches of uniformed Nazis, men and women as well as children, were most carefully orchestrated displays designed to publicly demonstrate the movement's growing strength, unity, worthiness, and the absolute commitment of its members.

Once in control of the government and all aspects of life, the Nazis continued and indeed perfected their propaganda machine. Their official squads of hooligans openly carried out violence against "un-German" targets, most of all Jews, whereas the unspeakable state terror in concentration camps that systematically killed ten million persons was not publicized as typical for those committing genocide.

Post–World War II National Liberation and Leftist Movements

After World War II, the European colonial powers, such as the British, French, and Dutch, came under pressure in Africa and Asia as the quest for national independence and self-determination became intensive and often violent. In Latin America, part of the growing opposition of revolutionary demands for a new social order was directed against American interference on behalf of the ruling class and oppressive government. Powerful voices used propaganda by word to justify propaganda by deed. One of them was Frantz Fanon, who focused on the case of Algeria to indict the inhumanity of colonialism and the Western capitalist model. In justifying all-out violence against the colonial oppressors Fanon endorsed violence not merely as a means to a noble end— national liberation—but also as an end in itself. His point was that violence against the colonial power and victory would free liberated individuals from marks of oppression and empower them. As he wrote, "At the level of individuals, violence is a cleansing force. It frees the native from his inferiority complex and from his despair and inaction; it makes him fearless and restores his self-respect" (Fanon 1963, 94). But Fanon's theoretical underpinnings of liberation terrorism transcended the Algerian case in that he thought it to be applicable to the struggle for independence in other Third World settings. Fanon rejected both the European and American models and called on the Third World to create their own, a new and better solution.

Regis Debray, another leading voice among post–WWII revolutionary theorists, preached to Latin Americans in favor of rising against imperialism and capitalism for the sake of social change. But unlike Fanon, Debray did not favor propaganda by deed—terrorism—but called for larger scale guerrilla warfare. Fanon (born in Martinique in the Caribbean) and Debray (a native of France) were outsiders in the region they wrote so passionately about. They were wide-ly read but did not speak as directly to terrorist and guerrilla movements as did Carlos Marighella. The latter was a Brazilian Marxist revolutionary and thus a homegrown Latin American who was not only a highly skilled practi-tioner of propaganda by deed but also a resourceful propagandist by word who recognized the value of mass self-communication along with the utilization of the mainstream media. Indeed, Marighella wrote the script for urban guer-rilla warfare and his "Minimanual of the Urban Guerrilla" became the bible for a generation of activists in guerrilla and terrorist movements. To begin with, like Karl Heinzen more than a hundred years earlier Marighella asked the readers of his self-published manual to circulate it by making copies or producing small brochures and making the material accessible to many more people. He differentiated between armed propaganda and self-communicated propaganda. Marighella wrote that all kinds of violent actions "become propa-ganda material for the mass communication system. Bank robberies, ambushes, desertions and the diverting of weapons, the rescue of prisoners, executions, kidnappings, sabotage, terrorism and the war of nerves are all cases in point."[20] He knew that the mainstream media had no choice but to report about violent actions.

Like his predecessors at the right and left of the political spectrum, he preached the value and absolute necessity of self-communication, of media controlled by those fighting against the existing power holders and structures. Thus, he advised,

> The urban guerrilla must never fail to install a clandestine press, and must be able to turn out mimeographed copies using alcohol or electric plates and other duplicating apparatus, expropriating what he cannot buy in order to produce small clandestine newspapers, pamphlets, flyers and stamps for propaganda and agitation against the dictatorship.[21]

His recommendations were as detailed as those of anarchist and fascist propagandists. "Tape recordings, the occupation of radio stations, the use of loudspeakers, graffiti on walls and other inaccessible places are other forms of propaganda," Marighella wrote. "A consistent propaganda by letters sent to specific addresses, explaining the meaning of the urban guerrilla's armed ac-tions, produces considerable results and is one method of influencing certain segments of the population."[22]

In the second half of the 1960s when opposition against the war in Viet-nam grew rapidly in the United States and western Europe, radical breakaway groups from the New Left's student organizations began to go underground to wage their fight against capitalism and imperialism, as they put it. These groups, whether the Weather Underground in the United States, the Red Bri-gades in Italy, or the Baader-Meinhof group or Red Army Faction (RAF) in Germany, embraced Marighella's urban guerrilla concept. The RAF was a case in point. Although often referring to the writings of Mao Tse-tung, the group borrowed most of their terrorist know-how from Marighella. According to one of the group's communications, "The urban guerilla requires the organization of an illegal structure, including safe houses, weapons, cars, and documents. What one needs to know about this, Marighella describes in his Minimanual of the Urban Guerilla."[23] Describing themselves as guerrillas was an exaggeration because the RAF was never a paramilitary entity that could openly fight security forces. Instead, they utilized propaganda both by deed and by word.

Like earlier terrorists, the RAF attacked the mainstream media—newspapers, news magazines, TV, and wire services relentlessly. But this did not mean that leaders and rank and file members ignored the news in television, radio, and newspapers. Quite the contrary, the RAF followed the news reporting of print and broadcast media very closely and often responded to particular articles and corrected "false reporting" and "fascist material." Moreover, they wrote letters to the editors of major news organizations or to Deutsche Presse Agentur, the major German wire service, complaining about what they called biases. They also understood the importance of self-communication, which they practiced via newsletters, such as *Fizz* and *Agit*, pamphlets, declarations, and audiotapes.

The Red Army Faction focused on publicizing programmatic material during its formative period but after both Andreas Baader and Ulrike Meinhof were arrested in the early 1970s, the remaining RAF leaders and followers were forced to operate even more clandestinely than before, focusing primarily on "propaganda by deed." In the final phase, the remaining cells' public messages were mostly claims of responsibility for terrorist strikes (Elter 2008, 115).

Altogether, the RAF's actions and even more so its alternative media left the false impression that the original Baader-Meinhof gang and its successor groups had far more members and supporters than they actually had. Moreover, contrary to the internal conflicts among the Baader-Meinhof gang and its successors, their propaganda reflected the earlier described WUNC displays associated with social movements and resulted in the false belief among government officials and the general public that the terrorists were far more of a threat than they were in reality.

PIRA and Breakaway Extremists: A New Propaganda War

In September 2014, the online version of Sinn Fein's weekly *An Phoblacht* carried the following announcement,

Every week over the next two years, An Phoblacht is making all the editions of The Irish Volunteer—the newspaper of the Irish Volunteer movement—available online exactly 100 years after they were first published. The Irish Volunteer—tOglách na hÉireann—was first published on 7 February 1914 and every week until 22 April 1916, just days before the Easter Rising.[24]

The announcement was a reminder of the long history of Irish resistance against British rule, the longevity of Sinn Fein (established in 1905) and the Irish Republican Army (IRA, founded in 1917 as successor of the Irish Volunteers organization that was formed in 1913), and the equally long tradition of militant Irish propaganda in the perennial conflict. In spite of subsequent splits, the modern-day IRA and later the Provisional Irish Republican Army (PIRA) as well as their political wing Sinn Fein considered themselves all along the heirs of the early Irish dissidents. Like the Irish Volunteers and Sinn Fein in the early 1900s, subsequent IRA generations understood propaganda by word and demonstrated considerable skill in written, spoken, and visual persuasion that was directed at recruits, potential supporters among the Irish at home and abroad, and, of course, the enemy.

The IRA's "Green Book," first published in 1957 with a second edition coming out in 1977, contained detailed instructions for members and especially new and potential recruits. The booklet characterized IRA soldiers as "the legal representatives of the Irish people" and told volunteers that they were "expected to wage a military war of liberation against an numerically superior force" and that this "involves the use of arms and explosives." The Green Book instructed IRA volunteers to distinguish between different categories of enemies and single out "the enemy through ignorance" who was thought to have the potential for education. In an instructive propaganda section, the Green Book authors explained,

> Our means are marches, demonstrations, wall slogans, press statements, Republican press and publications and of course person-to-person communication. But as has already been stated, we must first educate ourselves, we must organise the protests and demonstrations efficiently, we must be prepared to paint the wall slogans and to sell and contribute to Republican press, publications and press statements.[25]

While most propaganda targeted friends and foes in Ireland but also the rest of the United Kingdom, Sinn Fein and the PIRA "even catered to overseas sympathizers by publishing the quarterly *Iris: The Republican Magazine* and *The Irish People*, the newsletter published in New York by NORAID, the Irish Northern Aid Committee" (Kingston 1995, 206). Both publications were primarily vehicles to raise funds for the PIRA.

As a result of the 1998 Good Friday Agreement, the PIRA announced in 2005 that it would end its armed campaign. With Sinn Fein sharing governmental power in Northern Ireland, the group's newspaper *An Phoblacht* began to promote peace and compromise while criticizing the factions that had split from the Provisional Irish Republican Army to continue violent resistance campaigns. Thus, in 2010 a Sinn Fein editorial stated,

> Some of the individuals who are involved in these small militaristic factions may genuinely but mistakenly believe they are furthering a republican

cause. . . . Others are—without a shadow of a doubt—working to sabotage the republican movement. (Whiting 2012, 484)

Like the PIRA, the two breakaway paramilitary groups have political wings with the Real Irish Republican Army (RIRA) linked to the 32 County Sovereignty Movement (32CSM) and the Continuity Irish Republican Army (CIRA) allied with the Republican Sinn Fein (RSF). Before the peace agreement in the late twentieth century, the propaganda war of words was fought between the Sinn Fein and the mainstream British media. Since then, a fierce rhetorical battle has been fought on the pages of Sinn Fein's *An Phoblacht*, 32CSM's *Sovereign Nation*, and RSF's *Saoirse Irish Freedom*. As Sophie A. Whiting points out, "*An Phoblacht* is used to strongly denounce the existence and actions of dissident groups, acting as part of the 'normal' media's 'responsibility' to promote peace and highlight the isolation of dissidents."[26]

In the Provisional Irish Republican Army's long history, both its propaganda by deed and propaganda by word added up to public displays of WUNC as described by social movement scholars. The mentioned breakaway groups made efforts to follow the example of the PIRA before it laid down its arms.

From Self-Communication to Mass Self-Communication

During the 1990s, when Western television and radio networks, wire services, and leading print outlets still dominated the global media market and the Internet was not yet the major communication means, Osama bin Laden invited Western reporters to interview him in order to get his message across to friends and foes. At the time, bin Laden had a follower in the United Kingdom establish an office as "media wing of al-Qaeda" with the understanding that a physical presence in important media markets was essential for effective publicity campaigns. According to British and American intelligence, bin Laden's media man in London was Khalid al-Fawwaz, a citizen of Saudi Arabia. He followed the content of Western media and issued communiques and statements in the name of bin Laden and the al-Qaeda organization. Arrested in the United Kingdom for his alleged role in planning the deadly bombings of the U.S. embassies in Nairobi, Kenya, and Dar Es Salaam, Tanzania, in 1998, al-Fawwaz fought the American extradition request for many years before in 2012 he was finally extradited from Britain to the United States. In early 2015, when al-Fawwaz's trial finally began in New York City, his past as al-Qaeda's media liaison in London was a stark reminder of the revolutionary communication changes of the two previous decades. There was no longer a need to have media representatives in key locations. Instead, declarations, condemnations, threat messages, claims of responsibility, demands, and the like were easily released on Internet sites and/or posted on social media networks.

That was not yet the case twenty years earlier. In 1996 and 1998, bin Laden's declarations of war against the United States, Western crusaders, and Zionists were first published by the London-based Arab language newspaper *Al Quds Al Arabia*. While he figured correctly that the Western media would not publish the full text of his declarations, bin Laden could be sure that the Western mainstream media would pick up those threatening messages in which he called for the first time for attacks not only against Western military but civilians as well. He relied for publicity in the West on Western mainstream media. However, after Al-Jazeera emerged as the first non-Western global television network during the earliest phase of the war in Afghanistan against the Taliban and al-Qaeda, bin Laden and his associates no longer needed direct contacts with the Western press but made printed statements and videos available to the Arab TV network. They knew, of course, that their propaganda would make its way—via Al-Jazeera and later occasionally via Al Arabiya, another new Arab satellite network—to the global news media.

In the early 2000s, while al-Qaeda utilized the Internet to search for information and communicated via satellite telephones, the group relied predominantly on the mainstream mass media for the global and regional dissemination of its propaganda. While al-Qaeda Central established eventually its own media production company, produced its own DVDs and videos, and utilized Internet sites and social media for its propaganda, the group was a latecomer to mass self-communication compared to other terrorist organizations.

Before and after bin Laden and his followers moved from Sudan to Afghanistan in the mid-1990s, other jihadist and secular terrorist movements had established their own radio and television stations, some of which expanded into global satellite networks. From the Colombian FARC's "Voice of Resistance" to the Sri Lankan Tamil Tigers' "Voice of Tigers," secular groups utilized for many years their own on- and off-shore radio transmitters for the dissemination of propaganda news and entertainment programs. While the reach of these radio transmitters was limited, FARC beamed its programs across the borders into Ecuador. In some instances, mobile transmitters were used since they could be quickly moved in the event of counterstrikes by armies or police squads. Before the advent of Internet radio, the precondition for the establishment of terrorist onshore broadcast media was control of a particular region and/or backing by a tightly knit net of supporters.

I mentioned above the term mass self-communication several times. Manuel Castells distinguishes between mass media or mass communication that are controlled by gatekeepers in the interest of elites on the one hand and mass self-communication based on digital social media and communication networks that are also available to actors and movements pushing insurgent politics on the other hand.[27] Without discounting Castells's analysis of recent communication advances, I suggest that even before the spread of Internet sites and the establishment of social media networks some terrorist organizations operated in favorable environments and had enough resources to establish their own media arms that transcended limited self-communication means and added up to mass self-communication with regional and global channels for the distribution of their propaganda.

The best example is the Lebanese Hezbollah with its sophisticated media platforms. Established in 1982 with the assistance of Iran, Hezbollah followed soon the example of earlier terrorist groups and established propaganda. In 1984, the weekly newspaper *Al-Ahed* (The Pledge) was founded followed by several other weekly and monthly periodicals. In 1988, Al Nour 9 (The Light) radio began to operate; in 1991 Hezbollah's television station al-Manar (The Beacon) beamed its first programs into parts of Beirut and thereafter steadily expanded its domestic and regional reach. By 2000, when al-Manar became a satellite TV powerhouse in the Arab world, the station was the leading pro-Palestinian and anti-Israeli propaganda voice. This was reflected in its reporting during the Second Intifada. The following is an excerpt from a CNN report from late October 2000 that described Hezbollah's propaganda via al-Manar:

Frank Sesno, CNN Anchor: As efforts continue to salvage the Mideast peace process, there was new violence between Israelis and Palestinians today. A 24-year-old Palestinian on a bicycle blew himself up outside an Israeli army post in Gaza, the first suicide attack in four weeks of clashes.

An Israeli soldier was slightly wounded. The Palestinian militant group Islamic Jihad claimed responsibility.

In the West Bank, Israeli troops fired rubber-coated and metal bullets and tear gas to disperse Palestinians throwing stones.

Over these past weeks, one organization has gone to great lengths to convey its own version of events, and of the violence to the Arab world.

CNN's Beirut bureau chief Brent Sadler has their story.

(Begin Videotape)

Brent Sadler, CNN Beirut Bureau Chief (voice-over): The Beirut studios of Al-Manar, or The Lighthouse TV, nerve center for a relentless media assault on Israel, created and operated by Hezbollah, one of the world's most highly motivated guerrilla organizations. Images of Palestinian-Israeli conflict are turned into weapons of war, a drum beat of carefully selected, dramatically composed, one-sided visual accounts of West Bank and Gaza violence beamed across Lebanon and, via satellite, to a vast regional audience, transmissions which incite the Arab world to mobilize popular support for the Palestinian cause.

This montage says Arab states number 300 million people. In occupied Palestine, it states, there are five million Jews. "What are you waiting for?" screams this headline.

Transmissions urging Palestinians to follow Hezbollah's lead by standing up to Israel, as the guerrillas did in formerly occupied South Lebanon.

Unidentified Male (through translator): We are trying to plant this idea in the minds of the Palestinian people inside the territories that it's possible to repeat the same experience and liberate their land in the West Bank and Gaza.

Sadler: Claiming to be the first Arabs to use modern psychological warfare in an effective way against the Israelis, Hezbollah's TV station now broadcasts some 18 hours of programming every day.

(voice-over): A barrage of anti-Israeli propaganda pours out of Hezbollah's TV station, as well as its Internet sites, now the focus of a high-tech clash of self-interests, Hezbollah and Israel waging a cyberspace war, trying to overload each other's Web pages.

Hezbollah's journalists stand shoulder-to-shoulder with the Palestinian intifada, or uprising.

Farah Noureddine, News Editor, Al-Manar TV: Of course, we are part of a [*sic*] intifada because we are resisting. Our enemy is one.

Sadler: And resistance, says Hezbollah, will continue in many different ways.[28]

While Hezbollah had a website at the time, al-Manar was the most effective propaganda weapon. Since then, Hezbollah's TV station went global, airing its programs in several languages around the clock. With the help of Hezbollah, Hamas established its own radio (The Voice of Al Aqsa) and television (Al Aqsa Television) stations. Both glorify jihad, suicide terrorism, and martyrs. Both target especially children for their propaganda programs to socialize young boys and girls into a culture of total war against Israel and Jews. Not surprisingly, during the 2006 conflict between Israel and Hezbollah, the Israeli Defense Forces (IDF) hit the compounds of al-Manar television and al-Nour radio, forcing them off the air temporarily. Similarly, during the 2014 conflict between Hamas and Israel, the IDF struck the headquarters of Al Aqsa TV with the same result.

It was Anwar al-Awlaki, imam and influential member of al-Qaeda in the Arabian Peninsula, who embraced social media as preferred platforms for his propaganda and recruitment mission like no other jihadist leader before. His Facebook page, YouTube videos, blog posts, and online magazine *Inspire* were designed to convince Muslims around the world to join the jihadist war against Western infidels. After al-Awlaki, the "bin Laden of the Internet," was killed in 2011 in an American drone attack, *Inspire* magazine was discontinued but soon replaced by the new online magazine *Azan*. Following al-Awlaki's comprehensive computer-aided propaganda model, ISIS managed to improve the quality of its productions thanks to the seemingly unlimited financial resources and the professional expertise of people in its media center.

As described in this chapter, publicity was central in the terrorist calculus in the past and remains central to terrorism in our time. Nothing has changed in that respect. However, unlike their predecessors, contemporary terrorists operate in a global information and communication environment with opportunities for mass self-communication that earlier terrorists could not have imagined. This new e-terrorism or computer-assisted terrorism is explored in the following chapter.

Notes

1. From the English translation of Johann Most, *Science of Revolutionary War-fare* (El Dorado, AZ: Desert Publications, 1978 [1885]).
2. "Open Source Jihad: Make a bomb in the Kitchen of Your Mom," *Inspire* 1 (2010). The AQ stands for al-Qaeda.
3. Karl Heinzen, "Murder and Liberty." New York: Self-published by Author, 1853. Newly translated text in Daniel Bessner and Michael Stauch, "Karl Heinzen and the Intellectual Origins of Modern Terror," *Terrorism and Political Violence* 22, no. 2 (2010): 143–76.
4. In the same context the *Azan* editors described "this war" as "conflict between the forces of Allah and the forces of satan [*sic*]," *Azan*, March 2013, 3, accessed Jan. 2, 2014, http://jihadology.net/2013/05/06/new-english-language-magazine-azan-issue-1.
5. Ibid.
6. Johann Most, "Action as Propaganda," *Freiheit*, July 25, 1885, accessed July 3, 2014, http://libcom.org/library/action-propaganda.
7. Ibid.
8. Ibid.
9. Ibid.
10. Susan Tejada, "Boston's Other Terrorists," SusanTejada.com, June 18, 2013, accessed September 7, 2014, http://susantejada.com/bostons-other-terrorists.
11. See *Chicago Tribune* of May 1, 1919, accessed September 11, 2014, http://www.fold3.com/image/153511600.
12. Avrich 1991, 149. There are different accounts on the number of people killed in the incident ranging from thirty to forty.
13. According to the "Emma Goldman Papers," accessed September 10, 2014, http://editorsnotes.org/projects/emma/topics/174.
14. Joseph Goebbels, "Knowledge and Propaganda," speech, 1928, accessed October 31, 2014, http://research.calvin.edu/german-propaganda-archive/goeb54.htm.
15. Adolf Hitler, *Mein Kampf*, vol. 2, chap. VI, English translation, accessed September 17, 2014, http://www.hitler.org/writings/Mein_Kampf/mkv2ch06.html. The first volume of *Mein Kampf* was first published in 1925, the second volume in 1926.
16. Cited by Stuart Ewen, *PR! A Social History of Spin* (New York: Basic, 1996), 446.
17. Joseph Goebbels, *Wille und Weg* 1 (1931), 2–5, English translation, accessed July 1, 2014, http://research.calvin.edu/german-propaganda-archive/wille.htm.
18. Joseph Goebbels, "The Radio as the Eighth Great Power," speech, accessed September 15, 2014, http://research.calvin.edu/german-propaganda-archive/goeb56.htm.
19. From a pamphlet on "modern political propaganda," accessed June 12, 2014, http://research.calvin.edu/german-propaganda-archive/stark.htm.
20. Carlos Marighella, "Minimanual of the Urban Guerrilla," 1969, accessed June 12, 2014, http://www.ballistichelmet.org/school/urban_warfare.pdf.
21. Ibid.
22. Ibid.

23. From the RAF's "Urban Guerrilla Concept," 98, accessed September 17, 2014, http://www.socialhistoryportal.org/sites/default/files/raf/en/0019710501%2520EN_2.pdf.

24. *An Phoblacht*, accessed November 30, 2014, http://www.anphoblacht.com.

25. The IRA Green Book, accessed September 20, 2014, http://cain.ulst.ac.uk/othelem/organ/ira/ira_green_book.htm.

26. Ibid.

27. Castells 2009.

28. CNN Newsday, "Crisis in the Middle East: Al Manar Airs Hezbollah's High Tech Propaganda Campaign," October 26, 2000, accessed September 21, 2014, http://transcripts.cnn.com/TRANSCRIPTS/0010/26/nd.02.html.

4

Computer-Assisted Political Violence or E-Terrorism

January 2001: "I can't say goodbye to you—I already miss you," Ofir Rahum, a sixteen-year-old Israeli from Ashkelon told twenty-five-year-old Sali, whom he met in an Internet chatroom and corresponded with via email. Sali, who had introduced herself as an Israeli woman of Moroccan background answered passionately. "You know how much I am waiting for Wednesday." Wednesday, January 18, 2001, was the Internet lovebirds' first personal rendezvous in Jerusalem.

Without telling his parents, Ofir took a bus to Jerusalem, where Sali met him with her car. As they drove north, the teenager did not notice that they entered Palestinian territory and headed towards Ramalla. Suddenly, Sali stopped the car. A man appeared and pointed a Kalashnikov at Ofir's head. When the boy's bullet-ridden and stabbed body was found later and transferred by Palestinian authorities to their Israeli counterparts, Ofir's grief-stricken parents warned fellow Israelis, "Keep your children off the Internet. The Internet kills."

As Israeli investigators soon found out, Sali was in reality Amneh Muna, a Palestinian journalist from Ramallah who was active in Yasir Arafat's al-Fatah organization. After covering the funerals of Palestinians killed in the conflict with Israel, she told investigators after her arrest, she wanted to inflict pain on an Israeli family. To that end, she struck up chat room relationships with several Israeli men but none was as vulnerable as Ofir.[1]

~

October 2014: Three girls from a Denver suburb, two sisters seventeen and fifteen years old and their sixteen-year-old friend, are reported missing by their worried parents after skipping school. The local police alert the FBI. A day later, the girls are stopped by FBI agents at Frankfurt Airport, Germany, before they are able to board a plane to Turkey and make their planned journey to join ISIS in Syria. Sent back to Denver by the authorities, the girls are reunited with their parents. The following is from a report published in the local newspaper.

Authorities believe that three Colorado teenagers likely were recruited online to travel to Germany, apparently on their way to join the Islamic State, school officials said Wednesday. "Our understanding, our belief is that they were recruited online," said Cherry Creek School District spokeswoman Tustin Amole. "That's our belief based on information we have from various sources, including investigators. . . . That's my understanding of what likely happened." The teens also tweeted with fellow students about their trip, Amole said. "Students came in on Monday morning and reported the tweets to us," Amole said. "They said they were going to Germany and try to go to Turkey. Some of the students (on Twitter) told them it was a bad idea; others said good luck."[2]

$\sim$

In the first case, an early Internet chat room was the setting for luring an unsuspecting victim into what seemed a romantic relationship and subsequently into a real-life death trap under the disguise of a first rendezvous between two young people seemingly in love. Nothing like that had happened before. At the time, there were Internet service providers and media organizations providing chat rooms and discussion boards. There were no social media networking sites yet. More than a decade later, social media networks and particularly Facebook facilitated similar efforts by individual terrorists or groups to get enough information about individuals to either kidnap and kill them or recruit them as informers. But by then many intelligence agencies were aware of such schemes and issued warnings. According to one report,

> The Shin Bet security agency (part of the Israeli Ministry of Defense) has recognized terrorist use of social networking sites for remote reconnaissance, warning Israeli soldiers about posting sensitive information: "terror organizations are using these [social networking] sites to tempt Israelis to meet up in person in order to either abduct them, kill them or recruit them as spies." The English-language Lebanese media outlet, Ya Libnan, has also reported that an Israeli soldier was sentenced to 19 days in a military brig after posting a photograph of the base where he was assigned.[3]

In the thirteen years between the cases in Israel and Colorado, the virtual communication landscape changed massively and in favor of terrorists. There were thousands of terrorist websites and opportunities for terrorists and their sympathizers to open accounts and post on Facebook, Twitter, YouTube, Instagram, Flickr, Tumblr, and many more online networks. Also, it was widely reported that terrorists made great efforts to recruit visitors to their social media networking sites that did not exist when the young Israeli Ofir Rahum was killed. Ofir's parents had no idea about the dangers that vulnerable people could encounter on the Internet. One parent of the three Colorado teenagers became alarmed when he learned that his daughter had disappeared with her passport; he immediately alerted the police. When FBI agents examined the computers of the teenagers, two of them of Somali descent and their friend of Sudanese background, they found that these girls had posted very frequently on jihadist social media sites.

When listening to news reports about the Denver teenagers' interrupted trip, I was not at all surprised. I thought of social media sites designed to target young Muslim women and girls in the Western diaspora. One of those female-directed sites was that of a woman of Somali descent who called herself Um Umbaydah and hinted that she came from somewhere in northern Europe. She answered the "notes" posted by "sisters" who expressed interest, often eagerness in following her lead. Here are a few examples of posted question-and-answer exchanges in their original versions:

Anonymous: hello sister! I am 17 years old and I want to come to Syria very much. I have done my research but the only obstacle i am facing is my family. They have no Idea i want to join isis. I want to come very badly but how? do i leave without telling them? what did you do?

[Answer] I tried giving them daw'ah. They were completely at the end spectrum of the correct aqeeda, then I knew they would be an obstacle, so I came without telling them.

Anonymous: Asalamu aaleykum ukhti fillah am a last born of a huge family and am planing on soon making Hijra but I happen to be one the last person who stays with my mom it's only me and her now all the other siblings are busy with this or that, here or there can I still make Hijra with the other ukhtis, I keep asking this question to myself but I keep on saying I'd prolly get married and leave her anyway.

[Answer] Wa alaykum Salām. I suggest you give daw'ah to your mum and try to bring here with you, if this cannot be done then I suggest you leave and once you leave in sha Allāh your siblings would have to look after her.

Anonymous: If a teen muslimah wants to. Make hijrah even tho her parents would be against it do u think she should.

[Answer]: If a human being wants to obey Allāh but his creations don't want him to, should they still obey Allāh?

As the following exchanges show, questions and answers concerned also the living conditions in ISIS-held territory, the availability of beauty-care products, reading material, and electronic equipment:

Anonymous: Ukhti, I plan to buy a smart phone like sumsung s4 or s5 since I am leaving behind my laptop, what apps do you recommend i download before i come and also what islamic books. I'm guessing english books are not that available. What medicince should i bring too. Sorry for the weird questions.

[Answer] Subhāna Allāh these are not weird questions at all and download PDFs, you can go to kallamullah.com if it's still up, but download all of anwars series (Audio : and there are many) try to get sheikh Ahmed musa jibrils lectures, and books I would say from Abdullah Azzam, Abu muhammed al maqdisī (despite his opinion on dawla I highly recommend his books on aqeeda, they're really good) download books from Ibn qayyim, sheikh Yusuf al uyari, you can find these books in english. And if you have any condition please bring medicine for it because the ones here are not good, get medicine on diarrhea and constipation because you'll most likely get it here, and get a first aid kit. Asalāmu alaykum.

Anonymous: Can one find good hair dryer and straighter there and hows the weather like, I have no winter cloth with me.

[Answer] A sister I know just got one yesterday. So in sha Allāh if you look you can find but bring with you. And SubhānaAllāh bring as maaannnnyyy winter clothes with you, brothers and sister were begging for shahadah even more during the winter, It is that cold and the clothes here are crap. Right now the weather is hot but if i was in your shoes 80% of what I would bring would be winter clothes such as thermal sweaters, big coats, good shoes etc.

Anonymous: Ukhtee, weird question but, are tea and coffee available where you are?

[Answer] Lool everywhere.[4]

The two cases described above, one facilitating computer-assisted terrorism in the early phase of the publicly used Internet and the other attesting to the allure of social media networking put faces and emotions on online terrorists, online would-be recruits, and a victim of computer-assisted terrorism. Although indicative of terrorists' ability to exploit communication means in cyberspace, these cases merely scratch the surface of online terrorist activities.

Why Terrorists Drop "Media Bombs" on Internet Sites and Social Media

As ISIS conquered and ruled more cities and towns in Syria and Iraq Nassar Bolochi posted a picture of several bombs labeled Twitter, Facebook, and YouTube on his Twitter site. The caption explained, "Media Bombs: This is a war of ideologies as much as it is a physical war, and just as the physical war must be fought on the battlefield, so too must the ideological war be fought in the media."[5] Bolochi, one of the most prolific disseminators of hard-hitting jihadist propaganda, made a valid point. By the second decade of the twenty-first century, Bolochi personified the growing army of online jihadists who came to be as respected in the jihadist milieu as were fighters on the battlefield. The propaganda arms of al-Qaeda in the Arabian Peninsula (AQAP) and ISIS made perfectly clear that not every one of their followers had to fight on the battlefield but that their relentless online warfare elevated them to the same status. This was also spelled out in an article about "electronic jihad" posted in a leading jihadist online forum (al-Fida and Shumukh al-Islam):

Any Muslim who intends to do jihad against the enemy electronically is considered in one way or another a mujaheed as long as he meets the conditions of jihad such as the sincere intention and the goal of serving Islam and defending it, even if he is far away from the battlefield. He is thus participating in jihad indirectly as long as the current context requires such jihadi participation that has effective impact on the enemy.[6]

The elevation of online jihadists to the level of their brothers on the battlefield was not lost on terrorism experts. As Rita Katz pointed out, it was the ISIS (also IS) propaganda arm that revolutionized the way jihadists exploit the Internet:

In the past, jihadi activities used to take place almost exclusively within password-protected forums. IS's revolutionary approach to social media, however, brought the jihadi community into the mainstream of the internet and exponentially increased jihadis' audience. IS uses social media to create what I like to call, for all practical purposes, a wireless caliphate—fighting enemies on the ground as well as on the web.[7]

The division of labor between those fighting in the war of words and others carrying out terrorist deeds or fighting against the military of states was nothing new. As the previous chapter described, starting with the early anarchists there were always those who theorized and wrote about the need for and the justification of political violence on the one side and others who heeded and carried out those calls on the other side. But the communication and information and propaganda specialists of the most threatening terrorist organizations in the twenty-first century, such as ISIS and AQAP, belonged to the first generation growing up with the Internet and social media networks. Their propaganda machinery explored every aspect of new and old communication technology. According to one account,

ISIS is online jihad 3.0. Dozens of Twitter accounts spread its message, and it has posted some major speeches in seven languages. Its videos borrow from Madison Avenue and Hollywood, from combat video games and cable television dramas, and its sensational dispatches are echoed and amplified on social media. When its accounts are blocked, new ones appear immediately. It also uses services like JustPaste to publish battle summaries, SoundClod to release audio reports, Instagram to share images and WhatsApp to spread graphics and videos.[8]

Younger members of left-extremist and right-extremist groups as well as single-issue radicals had the same backgrounds but unlike the leading jihadist groups did not control territory or operated from not easily accessible hiding places; they also lacked the financial resources for producing sophisticated propaganda products for online consumption that the big jihadist organizations had available.

So, why is the Internet an ideal vehicle for terrorist information and communication needs? To begin with, the Internet has many qualities that serve
terrorists well. It is:

- global;
- accessible;
- inexpensive;
- mostly unregulated;
- anonymous;
- inclusive in that it reaches huge audiences; and
- exclusive in that it can grant and deny access.

Given these ideal conditions, terrorists exploit the World Wide Web for
literally all their goals associated with information and communication. In
particular, they utilize their own and sympathetic websites and social media
networks for the following purposes:

- mining the Internet for valuable information;
- planning and coordinating terrorist operations;
- reporting and glorifying terrorist attacks and attackers
- radicalizing and recruiting;
- waging psychological warfare;
- taking group rivalries public; and
- raising funds to finance their operations.

Mining the Internet for Valuable Information

Before the overabundance of information available on the Internet, it took far
more time, money, and effort for terrorists to find what they perceived as ideal
targets. Timothy McVeigh's selection of the Alfred P. Murrah Federal Building
in Oklahoma City for the April 1995 catastrophic bombing of the building was
a case in point. According to Lou Michel and Dan Herbeck (2001, 166–69), he
checked telephone books for the pages listing federal government agencies to
find their locations in various states. He looked for a building that housed at
least two of the three federal agencies that were involved in the 1993 lethal conflict between the Branch Davidian sect and federal law enforcement. He and
his accomplices Terry Nichols and Michael Fortier visited federal buildings
in several states, among them Texas, Arizona, Arkansas, and Missouri, before
McVeigh settled on Oklahoma City. McVeigh had been a computer whiz kid
in high school but when he planned his horrific attack information that was
easily accessible on the Internet a decade or so later was not yet available.

When bin Laden and his al-Qaeda group fled their camps in Afghanistan in late 2001 for Pakistan, they left behind their computers. An examination of their hard drives revealed that al-Qaeda had used the equipment to data mine open sources for all kinds of information—site maps, anti-surveillance methods, the location of possible targets, components of weapons of mass destruction, and so on. The personal computer of one al-Qaeda operative contained information about "all the structural features of a dam, and it was used to simulate catastrophic damages caused by the dam's failure" (Weimann 2006, 112). In 2003, speaking about an al-Qaeda manual found in the deserted camps in Afghanistan, U.S. Defense Secretary Donald Rumsfeld noted, "Using public sources openly and without resorting to illegal means, it is possible to gather at least 80 percent of all information required about the enemy."[9] And an American expert on computer-based information revealed,

> Many Web sites constitute a gold mine for potential attackers. Audits have found descriptions of physical locations of backup facilities, the number of people working at specific facilities, detailed information about wired and wireless networks, and specifications on ventilation, air conditioning and elevator systems. Other sites give graphical representations of floor plans, cabling connections and ventilation ductwork.[10]

The architects of a dozen bombing and shooting attacks that killed 164 persons in Mumbai, India, in 2008, used Google Earth to gather information about soft targets in the city and the distances between likely targets. This information was crucial for the planners of the Pakistani terrorist organization Lashkar-e-Taiba to select various targets with the most victims they intended to kill and maim. Once they had made their first cut, they sent a scout to Mumbai to personally survey the selected sites. David Coleman Headley, a U.S. citizen and the son of a former Pakistani diplomat and an American socialite, traveled to Mumbai and, as he admitted after his arrest, made surveillance videos and conducted other intelligence in the pinpointed areas.

The Mumbai model is widely used by terrorists. While terrorists themselves or their associates continue to scout the selected sites personally and make dry runs on commuter trains, buses, or airlines depending on the chosen methods of attack, the Internet tends to provide the initial information about buildings, security measures, opening hours, timetables, and the like.

Just as most people use the Internet for job-related information, terrorists, too, mine the World Wide Web for data not immediately related to planning terrorist strikes. The media and propaganda specialists of terrorist organizations, for example, follow the mainstream media for news about politics and policies, political and business leaders, public opinion, election results, and anything else they can use to strengthen their propaganda scheme and demagoguery. While Amedy Coulibaly, a self-described admirer of Osama bin Laden and follower of ISIS, held hostages at gunpoint in a Parisian Jewish market in January 2015, he engaged his captives in a heated debate. His shouted arguments revealed that he was well informed about public affairs, for example, concerning the size of the French military budget and the more recent counterterrorist deployments of the French military in African countries. To be sure, Coulibaly lived in France where this sort of information was available in print, radio, and television. But especially young people like Coulibaly get most of their information from Internet sites. More importantly, regardless where terrorists reside or hide, they typically use computers and have access to the Internet to gather information.

Planning and Coordinating Terrorist Operations

The masterminds of 9/11 and the foot soldiers who carried out the attacks used the Internet to put their plan together and coordinate with each other. According to one account, evidence was found on the computers left behind by al-Qaeda in Afghanistan that the group "was collecting intelligence on targets and sending encrypted messages via the Internet. [Moreover], as recently as 16 September 2002, al-Qaeda cells operating in America reportedly were using Internet-based phone services to communicate with cells overseas."[11] Before 9/11 when the members assigned to carry out the attack lived on and off in different parts of the United States and made occasional overseas trips, they visited local libraries in order to use computers available to patrons to communicate with each other via encrypted messages.

While the 9/11 case indicates that terrorists used the Internet for planning, preparing, and coordinating operations effectively at the beginning of the new millennium, the rapid technology advances of the following years offered terrorist organizations far more sophisticated communication options that escaped discovery by even the best spy agencies. The most spectacular computer-assisted coup in the planning and execution of a major terrorist mission concerned the above-mentioned multiple bombing and shooting attack in Mumbai. Although the British, Indian, and American intelligence agencies had Zarrar Shah, the technology chief of Lashkar-e-Taiba, on their radar and tracked many of his communications, they were unable to pinpoint the date and other details about an expected major terrorist strike in Mumbai. It turned out that he set up an Internet phone system that was routed through a New Jersey–based company through that U.S. state. This particular voice-over-Internet service (VoIP) was selected by Shah, because it disguised the origins of calls between Lashkar's headquarters in Pakistan and the terrorists in Mumbai making believe they were exchanged between parties in New Jersey and Austria. During the four-day-long incident, these Internet phone links were used. At that time, the intelligence communities were able to listen to the conversations between Lashka's leaders in Pakistan and operatives in Mumbai. But it was too late. Here are excerpts from those conversations:

Excerpts from Conversations between Terrorists and Operation Leaders in Pakistan during Multiple Attacks in Mumbai, India, November 2008

Hotel Taj Mahal: 27.11, 2008; 0310 hrs.

Receiver: Greetings!

Caller: Greetings! There are three Ministers and one Secretary of the Cabinet in your hotel. We don't know in which room.

Receiver: Oh! That's good news! It is the icing on the cake.

Caller: Find those 3–4 persons and then get whatever you want from India.

Receiver: Pray that we find them.

Caller: Do one thing. Throw one or two grenades on the Navy and police teams, which are outside.

Narriman House: 27.11, 2008; 1945 hrs.

Caller: Greetings! What did the Major General say?

Receiver: Greetings. The Major General directed us to do what we like. We should not worry. The operation has to be concluded tomorrow morning. Pray to God. Keep two magazines and three grenades aside, and expend the rest of your ammunition.

Hotel Taj Mahal: 27.11, 2008: 0126 hrs.

Caller: Are you setting the fire or not?

Receiver: Not yet. I am getting a mattress ready for burning.

Caller: What did you do with the dead body?

Receiver: Left it behind.

Caller: Did you not open the locks for the water below? [this referred to the terrorists leaving their boat upon arrival at Mumbai]

Receiver: No, they did not open the locks. We left it like that because of being in a hurry. We made a big mistake.

Caller: What big mistake?

Receiver: When we were getting into the boat, the waves were quite high. Another boat came. Everyone raised an alarm that the Navy had come. Everyone jumped quickly. In this confusion, the satellite phone of Ismail got left behind.

Oberoi Hotel: 27.11, 2008: 0353 hrs.

Caller: Kill all hostages, except the two Muslims. Keep your phone switched on so that we can hear the gunfire.

Fahadullah: We have three foreigners, including women. From Singapore and China.

Caller: Kill them.

Hotel Taj Mahal: 27.11, 2008: 0137 hrs.

Caller: The ATS Chief has been killed. Your work is very important. Allah is helping you. The Vazir (Minister) should not escape. Try to set the place on fire.

Receiver: We have set fire in four rooms.

Caller: People shall run helter skelter when they see the flames. Keep throwing a grenade every 15 minutes or so. It will terrorize.

Ajmal Kasab, the only surviving Mumbai terrorist, testified in court about training sessions in Lashkar's big media center during which Khan and his fellow planners used Google Earth, videos, and reconnaissance reports to familiarize him and the other nine members of the mission with the selected targets. At these occasions, according to Mumbai police officials, "the terrorists were trained to use Google Earth and global positioning equipment themselves."[12] They were trained to locate everything they wanted to find in Mumbai before they left Pakistan. During the four-day ordeal, the New Jersey–based VoIP service was used for frequent conversations between operation chiefs in Lashkar's Pakistani headquarters and terrorists at various sites in Mumbai.

The expertise of Khan and others in Lashkar-e-Taiba's technology strata was no exception among contemporary terrorist organizations. Instead, the Mumbai example demonstrated how difficult it is for intelligence services of different countries to share valuable pieces of their respective intelligence efforts and thereby solve the whole puzzle before it is too late. As the investigative report noted,

> The story of the Mumbai killings has urgent implications for the West's duel with the Islamic State and other groups. Like Lashkar, the Islamic State's stealthy communications and slick propaganda make it one of the world's most technologically sophisticated terror organizations. Al-Qaeda, which recently announced the creation of an affiliate in India, uses similar tools.[13]

Reporting Attacks and Glorifying Attackers

In the past, terrorists were notorious for issuing threats that they often followed up with actual attacks. But they did not provide graphic descriptions of their brutality and the suffering of their victims. Contemporary terrorists can and do utilize the Internet to go public even in the midst of staging horrific terrorist strikes. Particularly shocking were the communication tactics of the Somalian terrorist organization al-Shabaab during its attacks inside the upscale Westgate Mall in Nairobia, Kenya, when sixty-seven persons were killed and many more injured. Christopher Anzalone's research revealed that the group's media department used its Twitter account to tweet "a continuous stream of 'updates' and commentary throughout the assault."[14] The terrorists inside the mall, too, tweeted "updates" of their own horrible killing spree. Intelligence experts suspected that the terrorists themselves had set up a mobile command center before they launched their attack and used it to communicate with al-Shabaab headquarters and via tweets with friendly and hostile publics. Most of all, al-Shabaab's press office HSM (Harakat al-Shaabab al-Mujahidin) used Twitter to attract the greatest possible attention. According to one account,

> The HSM Press account purportedly posted "updates" on the ongoing siege at a time when conflicting reports abounded. These included tweets announcing

the attack on the "Kenyan Kuffar [unbelievers] inside their own turf," denying the cessation of fighting between "the mujahidin" and the Kenyan military and police, alleging that the Kenyan government was "pleading" with the attackers inside the mall to negotiate, and reports of the calmness of the attackers despite being under siege by Kenyan security forces. Al-Shabab also claimed via Twitter that it had "singled out" only "unbelievers" in the attack and had "escorted out" Muslims before the attack began, announcing that the defense of Muslim lands "is one of the foremost obligations after faith & defending against the aggressive enemy is our right as Muslims."[15]

Even more conspicuous examples of self-reporting are part and parcel of ISIS's propaganda scheme with its meticulous documentation of literally all terrorist activities that the organization's jihadists commit in the name of holding up the strict edicts of their religious beliefs. According to Natascha Bhuiyan (2014, 12), ISIS "is more than comfortable to admit to their violent deeds online. Just by following their brutal propaganda on social media it seems as if one is watching a horror show. ISIS presents not only scenes of crucified, stoned, or beheaded victims, but also the dead bodies of innocent, bleeding Iraqi children, the victim's intestines packed up in boxes or heads hanging on spikes." Indeed, no other terrorist group has publicized its unspeakably brutal violence as meticulously and widely as ISIS.

Followers and sympathizers of terrorist groups also use social media to celebrate high-profile terrorist attacks and glorify the attackers. Thus, following the attacks on *Charlie Hebdo* magazine and a Jewish market in Paris, there was an outpouring of jubilant messages in social media networks. ISIS released an audio clip online that celebrated the attack by "heroic jihadists" on a publication that had ridiculed Mohammad. As one news report summarized, "Islamic extremists and their supporters were praising the killings and lauding the attackers on social media under hashtags like #we_avenged the_prophet and #lone_wolves."[16] This was especially remarkable because ISIS was a competitor of al-Qaeda and the *Charlie Hebdo* attackers announced that they acted in the name of AQAP, the most potent of all remaining al-Qaeda affiliates.

In addition to these online communication streams during and after spectacular terrorist strikes, there are permanent posts on many websites of terrorist organizations or of their sympathizers that celebrate those who carried out terrorist violence as heroes and martyrs. As mentioned in another context, this glorification is not peculiar to jihadist groups but also occurs in those claiming to act in the name of other religions. In the American setting the "Army of God" is a good example. Its various websites celebrate those who killed or injured abortion providers as heroes and martyrs who followed God's will.

Hate groups that do not openly recommend violence but have been known to incite frequent posters and commenters on their online discussion boards also glorify the founding fathers of their movements. Thus, when most of the world mourned the murder of twelve members of the *Charlie Hebdo* staff and honored their stand for press freedom with the slogan "Je suis Charlie," a post on Vanguard News Network Forum, a most vicious neo-Nazi site, showed Adolf Hitler's picture and proclaimed, "Je suis Hitler!" The attached video starred the uniformed Nazi leader in one of his many ugly anti-Semitic speeches that blamed Jews for all evils he could think of. For these kinds of hate sites, white Caucasians are the superior race whose purity and dominance are threatened by Jews, Blacks, Hispanics, Asians, and Muslims. It was not surprising that immediately after the attack on the French magazine *Charlie Hebdo* conspiracy theories were forwarded in one discussion threat.

One poster wrote, "Something to keep in mind: These murderers claim to be 'al-Qaeda in Yemen.' Hmmmm! Yemen is predominately Shia, as is Syria and Iran. Now who really hates, and I mean really hates Shia (Syria and Iran?). Who is always screaming that the US should attack Syria and Iran? I'm guessing that if these murderers are not caught, or are killed before they can be interrogated, then plain-and-simple . . . this was an Israeli operation."

Another conspiracy theorist calling himself AntiZOG (in neo-Nazi circles, ZOG stands for Zionist Occupied Government) was sure that "Mossad had a hand in this, the motivation could be to take some of the pressure off jews [*sic*] in France, and further vilify, and point the spotlight on, Islamists—not that they aren't dangerous scum—but . . . net result: this works out for jews, in that outrage is directed away from jews, and quite likely, no jews were killed—only a dozen sacrificial goyim, most of whom were left-wing pets, who would not dare write such cartoons against the self-chosen or criticize the Holohoax."

Yet another contributor wrote, "Folks, this [*Charlie Hebdo*] is precisely and exactly the sort of publication that National Socialist would have thrown on a pyre, along with all the other dirty Jew books that they burned, porn etc. In 2014, we have white people rushing to the defence [*sic*] of the sort of filth that Hitler would have ordered to be destroyed. Ironically, while we do that, the only people that appear to have retained the spirit of Hitler are . . . Muslims."[17]

At the same time, the oldest neo-Nazi/white supremacy website "Stormfront," which the one-time Ku Klux Klan leader Don Black established in 1995, carried a fake magazine cover depicting Horst Mahler and the title "Je suis Mahler." Mahler was once a prominent German lawyer and sympathizer of the left-extreme Baader-Meinhof terrorist group and at first sight an unlikely hero for anti-Semitic Stormfront adherents. However, since Mahler became a vocal right-extremist and was imprisoned for publically denying the Holocaust, he became an idol in neo-Nazi circles. "Freedom for Horst Mahler," the Stormfront post demanded. There was also a link to a contact address for visitors planning to write to Mahler.[18]

A survey of these U.S.-based right-extremist online discussions revealed that the participants were mostly but not solely Americans. There were many foreign, especially European, commenters equally as supportive of white supremacy ideology and actions as their American counterparts.

Radicalizing and Recruiting

Terrorist propaganda tends to be directed at followers, potential recruits, and the enemy. In many instances, sophisticated communiques and videos are designed to trigger strong reactions from all three target audiences. When terrorist groups publicize proofs that they hold hostages or killed captives, they do so in order to demonstrate their power and the impotence of states with military forces. This can increase adhesion and conviction within a particular organization and impress others to become sympathizers or even join a ruthless but winning group. However, the same propaganda may terrify the declared targets of terrorist violence. Thus, videos showing in horrific detail the beheadings of foes are likely to impress fanatic followers, radicalize already sympathetic persons, convince still others to join, and shock the declared enemy.

In early 2015, when ISIS released a video of two Japanese men in orange jumpsuits standing next to the jihadist organization's executioner responsible for the beheading of several Western journalists, some observers believed this was a move to get once again global attention. While the group demanded a $200 million ransom payment for the release of the hostages, the Japanese government was unable to make contact with the ISIS leaders. They were obviously not interested in ransom money but rather in demonstrating that they remained powerful actors at a time when U.S. officials claimed that thousands of ISIS fighters and half of the group's leadership had been killed. On an ISIS website, a clock was posted ticking down to the announced execution of the Japanese hostages. Eventually, videos depicting the execution of the men were posted on social media sites. This incident, again, horrified many people around the world and pleased ISIS supporters, precisely the effects that the terrorists wanted to accomplish.

Before the advent of Internet and social media, the recruitment of terrorists was strictly the result of person-to-person contacts. Radical extremists convinced members of their families, their friends, acquaintances, and colleagues to join. As Marc Sageman's (2004) research shows, the recruitment of members of the original al-Qaeda group or al-Qaeda Central was based on kinship and friendship. But this changed, when terrorists discovered the power of larger, global appeals—even before the advent of social media networks. During the second Iraq War, for example, al-Qaeda did not merely post videos of alleged Western atrocities against Muslims on Internet sites but distributed large numbers of DVDs with the same material. The graphic images proved to be powerful recruiting tools. Hamdi Isaac, one of the participants in a failed London bombing plot in 2005, told Italian interrogators after he was arrested in Rome about watching these kinds of DVDs with other would-be bombers. According to Isaac, the men met at a muscle-building class in Notting Hill and watched "some DVDs with images of the war in Iraq, especially women and children killed by American and British soldiers. During our meetings we analyzed the political situation and the fact that everywhere in the West Muslims are humiliated and that we must react."[19]

Ten years later, social media carried this sort of material and made it accessible throughout the world. And no other organization used online media more skillfully and more successfully than ISIS. After carefully analyzing ISIS's beheading videos, David Carr (2014) wrote about the group's effectiveness in sending medieval messages by modern communication technology. According to Carr,

> While the videos convey barbarism on an elemental level, dismissing them as crude or one-dimensional would be wrong. The Islamic State in Iraq and Syria, known as ISIS, clearly has a sophisticated production unit, with good cameras, technically proficient operators and editors who have access to all the best tools. What they made are modern media artifacts being used to medieval ends. The videos serve as both propaganda and time machine, attempting to wipe away centuries of civilization and suggest that the dreamed-of-caliphate flourishes and blood is cheap currency.

To be sure, contemporary terrorist organizations engage in mass self-communication. But as Bhuiyan (2014, 15–16) concluded, ISIS propaganda has shown consistently that the group knows also the value of market segmentation "that involves the division of a broad market into subdivisions of consumers, who share common interests and needs, and then develop and execute strategies to target these people." To that end, the online magazine *Dabiq* targeted from the outset Muslims around the world and made great efforts to convince them to join ISIS's jihad either in the growing "Caliphate" in Syria and Iraq or as autonomous cells or lone wolves in the Western diaspora. The narrative in issue after issue was consistent: After enumerating the evils done by the enemy in many details on the one hand and the great achievements of ISIS in terms of conquering large parts of two nation-states, there are direct, urgent, and sometimes threatening appeals to Muslims to partake in the fight. A call for professionals and students in the diaspora to come to the Middle East and join ISIS in the third issue of *Dabiq* begins with citing the Prophet, who condemned a decision of not joining jihad as "a trait of hypocrisy." This is followed by this recruiting hard sell:

> Therefore, every Muslim professional who delayed his jihād in the past under the pretense of studying Sharī'ah, medicine, or engineering, etc., claiming he would contribute to Islam later with his expertise, should now make his number one priority to repent and answer the call to hijrah, especially after the establishment of the Khilāfah. This Khilāfah is more in need than ever before for experts, professionals, and specialists, who can help contribute in strengthening its structure and tending to the needs of their Muslim brothers. Otherwise, his claims will become a greater proof against him on Judgment Day.
>
> As for the Muslim students who use this same pretense now to continue abandoning the obligation of the era, then they should know that their hijrah from dārul-kufr to dārul-Islām and jihād are more obligatory and urgent then

spending an unknown number of years studying while exposed to doubts and desires that will destroy their religion and thus end for themselves any possible future of jihāh.

There were also efforts to show sympathizers and potential recruits the human face of ISIS in its social work assisting people in the areas under their control. You see jihadists providing medical services, distributing food, repairing houses, and organizing games for children. On Twitter, the "Islamic State of Cat" posted pictures of jihadists holding or feeding their cat as "the mujahideen's best friend." The same site also featured other images of loving jihadists, for example, sharing "Ramadan with the poor and families." But none of these efforts to portray ISIS fighters as benevolent human beings came close to overshadowing the endless stream of terrifying visuals released by the group's official media center Al-Hayat.

Official ISIS news and propaganda productions were never the only online activities supporting the organization's war of words and images. Sympathizers with no formal ties to the group also utilized social media, most of all Facebook, YouTube, and Twitter to constantly support the group and attack its enemies. During the 2014 World Cup events in Brazil, for example, ISIS fans "posted videos including the beheading of a man identified as a Sunni police officer. 'This is our ball,' said a tweet accompanying a photo of the decapitated head. 'It's made of skin #WorldCup.' The World Cup hashtag ensured it would pop up on news feeds of the tournament's followers until Twitter Inc. could take down the posting."[20] A study of messages posted by online jihadists on Facebook sites revealed that social media networking in general and Facebook in particular were highly praised as effective means to disseminate propaganda as the following posts attest.

- This [Facebook] is a great idea, and better than the forums. Instead of waiting for people to [come to you so you can] inform them, you go to them and teach them! God willing, the mujahedeen, their supporters, and proud jihadi journalists will [use the site, too]. [First,] it has become clear that the market of social networking websites is developing in an astonishing manner and that it fulfills important needs for Internet users, particularly younger ones.
- Facebook has become very successful in this field; therefore, it is our duty to use it, as adherents of jihad and [members] of the blessed jihadi media. [I] mean, if you have a group of 5,000 people, with the press of a button you [can] send them a standardized message. [That] means if you send one message with a link to [forum names], a clear [path] to jihadi media is open.
- I entreat you, by God, to begin registering for Facebook as soon as you [finish] reading this post. Familiarize yourselves with it. This post is a seed and a beginning, to be followed by serious efforts to optimize our Facebook usage. Let's start distributing Islamic jihadi publications, posts, articles, and

pictures. Let's anticipate a reward from the Lord of the Heavens, dedicate our purpose to God, and help our colleagues.[21]

Besides targeting and segmenting men and women, some terrorist groups also aim their propaganda material to attract children. ISIS was not the first and only terrorist group to indoctrinate and train children to hate and kill. From the children corps of the Tamil Tigers to child suicide bombers on behalf of the Taliban in Pakistan or youngsters recruited by Hamas, child terrorists and child soldiers have been used by many groups in many parts of the world. Religious schools—madrassas, especially in South and South-East Asia—have been identified as places where children are indoctrinated and prepared to become jihadists. Schools in Pakistan have been singled out in this respect and by some observers identified as providing cannon fodder for terrorist organizations. Children are taught that Muslims everywhere are under attack by infidels, by evil forces, and that they must join the fight against those enemies to the death.

But ISIS is the first terrorist enterprise that documents and publicizes how it runs its training camps for young boys, many not older than nine and ten years and some significantly younger. Nor does ISIS make a secret of its objective to use its "Sharia camps" to produce a whole new generation of jihadists. Indeed, in one of these readily available online propaganda videos, one jihadist in an ISIS training camp for young boys declares proudly, "This generation of children is the generation of the Caliphate." Some fathers are complicit in transforming young children into eager killers. In one video, a man called Abdullah, the Belgian, is shown with his little son, perhaps five or six years old. The father prods the little boy again and again to say "The Islamic State." He asks questions like, "What have the infidels done?" The son finally answers, "They kill Muslims."[22]

One result of these indoctrination methods was shown in the most shocking online video in ISIS's long list of horror shows that depicted a young boy as executioner of two men who were allegedly Russian spies. In the video, the boy, holding a pistol, stands next to a grown-up jihadist who recites religious verses. The two condemned men are kneeling when the boy steps toward them, firing several shots before and after the men collapse. The video ends with footage from an earlier production in which the same boy identified himself as Abdallah and said that he wanted to grow up to kill infidels.[23] There could not be a more troubling case of ruthless indoctrination, recruitment, and training with the sole purpose of producing killers and publicizing all of this online.

Noting that U.S. officials' wondered about ISIS's success in attracting so many foreign fighters "outstripping recruitment in the war against the Soviets in Afghanistan and the war against Saddam Hussein in Iraq," Sarah Birke (2015, 27) pointed first to the organization's "unprecedented use of social media to attract people." Indeed, exposure to online radical extremism tends to be crucial in the radicalization of vulnerable individuals who may or may not actually try to meet with like-minded people.

At the beginning of this section I mentioned three teenagers from Colorado trying to travel to Syria to join ISIS. A case study by the SITE Intelligence Group that examined the social media accounts of the girls revealed their stunning change from typical American teenagers with many friends who liked playing tennis, swimming, and traveling to religious fanatics who came to hate their friends and non-religious activities. Besides taking on the screen names Grape, Ikram, and Umm Yassir, the study found,

> [The girls] spent a substantial proportion of their time on social media. The three girls' respective Twitter accounts show approximately 7,000, 9,000, and nearly 13,000 tweets. Tweeted content across the three accounts shows a strong focus on Islam, particularly on marriage and the role of women. For example, "Umm Yassir" tweeted 11 Qur'anic verses on October 13 and 14, 2014. Furthermore, tweets from the accounts show posts rejecting Western culture and values, embracing Islamic ideology and IS propaganda, and, perhaps most importantly, communications with IS activists and online recruiters.[24]

As Rita Katz concluded, ISIS's "shift from near-exclusive use of password-protected forums to the utilization of social media platforms like Twitter exported the war from the distant battlegrounds of Syria and Iraq into the homes of tens of thousands in the West, rendering any social media user a prospective recruit."

While much of this section on radicalization and recruitment addressed the online efforts of jihadist organizations that do not have to hide their aggressive recruitment pitches and their calls to arms, the explicit hate messages and interactions on online discussion boards of secular extremist groups attract large numbers of people as well. An investigation of possible connection between the above-mentioned Stormfront web forum and deadly terrorist attacks inside and outside the United States found, "In the last five years alone—since the election of the nation's first black president—registered members of Stormfront (an incredible 286,000 people, though many inactive) have been responsible for the murders of close to 100 people."[25] According to the report, the killers "typically posted for years before beginning to kill, drawing sustenance and support from their fellow racists and anti-Semites."[26] Posters and commenters on similar neo-Nazi/white supremacy web forums, too, ended up committing violence against members of the groups they hate. Frazier Glenn Cross, for example, who in 2014 shot three people to death as he stormed onto the grounds of Jewish institutions in Kansas, was a regular participant in the above-mentioned Vanguard News Network Forum, posting more than 12,000 messages over several years.

Waging Psychological Warfare

When the self-proclaimed Army of God utilizes its website to post the names of abortion providers and their families and of judges and politicians who support legalized abortion, they aim for more than attention: They wage psychological warfare in efforts to intimidate their declared enemies in the hope of forcing abortion providers to stop these legal procedures.[27] Often, the sites do not simply list names of "abortionists" or "baby butchers" but also the phone numbers and addresses of their places of work plus what days and hours they are on duty. Who would not be intimidated by these tactics of people who openly celebrate the assassination of abortion providers, calling it "justifiable homicide" and laud imprisoned and executed "soldiers of God" as "heroes who stood up for the unborn."[28] The graphic visuals of aborted fetuses and simulated blood dripping onto the pages have as much shock value as the target lists. Even old and rudimentary sites such as those of the Army of God and the related Christian Gallery website embrace new communication technologies. Thus, the latter offers a daily web-TV program and calls on supporters to use their web cameras to film "people going in and out of Baby Butcher Shops in your city or town." The idea is to post those videos on the site and show people "who kills God's little babies."[29]

Organizations with top communication experts and plenty of financial resources raise their psychological warfare to another level. Thus, in early January 2015, hackers claiming to work for ISIS hacked the social media sites of the U.S. Military's Central Command, occupying both the Twitter and Facebook sites with their pro-ISIS propaganda. Calling themselves the Cyber Caliphate, the online jihadists placed their names on top of the pages with the sub-header "I love you isis." A reference to the U.S. military's involvement in fighting ISIS in Iraq and Syria from the air was followed by the threat message,

> We broke into your networks and personal devices and know everything about you. You'll see no mercy infidels. ISIS is already here, we are in your PCs, in each military base. US soldiers! We're watching you!

One of the posts left on the sites was a fifty-two-page spreadsheet titled "Retired Army General Officer Roster" that included the addresses, e-mails, and retirement dates of many former generals. The Pentagon was alarmed enough to call the named officers and inform them of the list that some observers deemed a "hit list."[30]

This reaction in the Pentagon was not far-fetched since AQAP had repeatedly pinpointed people in the West as their targets, among them Stéphane Charbonnier, the editor of *Charlie Hebdo* and one of the satirical magazine's staffers killed during the terrorist attack on the publication's headquarters. For years, the publication of most wanted individuals or hit lists was the domain of AQAP. It is well known that competition between groups results in outbidding and ISIS's posting of a list of retired generals on the Central Command's virtual bases was likely an outbidding coup in the eyes of ISIS supporters.

In March 2015, an ISIS cyber unit that called itself "Islamic State Hacking Division" posted a list of 100 wanted members of the American military with names, photographs, and addresses—on its website. "*With the huge amount of data we have from various different servers and databases, we have decided to leak 100 addresses so that our brothers in America can deal with you," the post warned. This was followed by the following appeal to ISIS followers in the United States: "Now we have made it easy for you by giving you addresses, all you need to do is take the final step, so what are you waiting for?" In other words, this was a hit list. It did not matter whether the data were the result of another hacking incident on the part of ISIS or whether it was gathered from open sources as Defense Department officials claimed. The threat was once again a blow landed by the jihadists in their psychological warfare serious enough for the Pentagon to warn every one of the listed persons.*[31]

Death threats against named individuals are the most disturbing weapons in terrorists' psychological warfare arsenal but more general threats against a whole nation or several nations also can result in public anxiety. This tends to be particularly the case in the wake of major terrorist attacks. After the 9/11 attacks, the U.S. public was significantly more worried that more terrorist strikes inside their country would follow. And when Osama bin Laden threatened more violence against their country, Americans' concerns of becoming themselves victims of terrorism increased measurably (Nacos, Bloch-Elkon, and Shapiro 2011).

Taking Group Rivalries Public

In early 2014, al-Qaeda Central released a statement in which it for the first time declared publicly that ISIS was not an affiliate of the organization that bin Laden founded and led. Although bin Laden's successor Ayman al-Zawahiri had expressed in a private but eventually leaked letter his displeasure with ISIS, the public divorce became the topic of lively online debates on jihadist websites and social media. According to one account,

> Some, but not all, [online] pundits adopted a diplomatic approach. Some called on both sides to unite, but their language betrayed the group with which they sided; others attributed the schism to years of scheming by "the RAND Corporation" and similar think-tanks to create a "good" al-Qa`ida and a "bad" al-Qa`ida, a plot which time has now come to divide jihadists. At times, the forum contributions reached a certain level of vulgarity that saw al-Julani getting cursed, and numerous references gently criticizing Zawahiri and calling on him to renege on his decision.[32]

Rivalries among and within extremist groups occur regardless of their particular ideologies. A good example from the American domestic setting is the National Alliance, founded and led by William Pierce, which was for many years the leading neo-Nazi/white supremacy hate group in the United States. The group's online discussion boards and Pierce's racist writings attracted record numbers of visitors from inside and outside the United States.

The organization's own record label, "Resistance Records," was its money maker, selling White Power Rock to skinheads via the label's own website. After Pierce's death in 2002, neo-Nazi websites were the battlefield for a bitter struggle for his succession. Although William W. Williams, a longtime neo-Nazi, finally took charge of the National Alliance in late 2014, he remained the target of fierce rhetorical attacks by former comrades who split off into the National Alliance Reform and Restoration Group (NARRG) and established its own website and venue of the ongoing rivalry.

Raising Funds to Finance Their Operations

Both domestic and transnational groups have used their websites to raise funds to finance their operations. Typically, donations can be made by charge cards. The NARRG, for example, has a PayPal button on its site so that visitors can donate with their various charge cards. Donators are assured that "NARRG team members work completely on a volunteer basis. Every dollar collected goes to saving our National Alliance." The "Army of God" has a permanent post on its website that begs with great urgency for donations. "By now, you've probably heard about the massive effort launched by the baby butchers and their evil lackeys to destroy the Christian gallery web sites," site visitors read. "Every month that passes our expenses grow in direct proportion to the number of people we impact with this web site. . . . That's why we need your donations every month."

Nobody, however, is as sophisticated as jihadists and their supporters who are known to have discussed in various social media the advantages of Bitcoin as ideal currency for raising donations and purchasing weaponry. As one researcher found,

> Although some websites affiliated with terrorist organizations have begun collecting Bitcoin donations, this practice appears to be relatively limited. One example would be http://kavkazcenter.com. It is possible that as the technical capacity of these organizations increases, their use of digital currencies will also increase. This increase is likely to be small however, in relation to overall terror financing through other channels such as hawala, kidnapping, front companies, narcotics sales, oil sales, and many more.[33]

The Consequences of E-Terrorism

To sum up, the Internet and especially social media networking altered the communication schemes of literally all terrorist and hate groups that incite followers to commit violence and in the process threaten and frighten their declared enemies. Most of all, twenty-first-century online mass self-communication changed the ways in which these organizations disperse their propaganda. Before the emergence of the Internet as vehicle for mass self-communication, the number of people that terrorists could reach with their propaganda was limited—even for those groups that had their radio and TV stations and networks. Contemporary terrorists reach huge audiences via social media and websites. A key question here, of course, is whether a connection between the content of social media and websites do have real-life ramifications and, in fact, are tools to recruit people to join violent extremist groups or motivate lone wolves or small groups to carry out violent attacks without organizational affiliations. This chapter contains examples of people who were radicalized and recruited via social media communications. It is entirely logical to conclude that the proliferation of hate sites and the large number of people online has infected— and will continue to infect—far more people with the virus of hate than did traditional means of communication before the advent of social media.

In the past, besides person-to-person contacts, extremist books were effective in radicalizing certain people and motivating them to commit violence. But whereas these volumes were rarely available in neighborhood bookstores, they were eventually sold online by companies such as Amazon and Barnes & Noble and advertised on extremist websites. This was precisely the point of "Hate.com: Extremists on the Internet," a Home Box Office documentary produced in association with the Southern Poverty Law Center, a nonprofit group that tracks hate groups in the United States. The program contained, for example, an interview with Joseph Paul Franklin, a convicted killer and follower of neo-Nazi William Pierce and his National Alliance. Pierce was the author of several best-selling books, among them *Hunter*, about a white supremacist who fights for the purity of his race. As it turned out, Franklin was the real-life "Hunter," telling "Hate.com" interviewers about two female hitchhikers that he picked up and killed, after one told him about dating a black man and the other one remarked that she would do the same.

Using the pseudonym Andrew Macdonald, Pierce also authored *The Turner Diaries*, about white American supremacists' war against nonwhite minorities and the Jewish-Controlled (Federal) Government. The best-seller was a favorite of Oklahoma City bomber Timothy McVeigh, who modeled his bombing of the Alfred P. Murrah Federal Building on an attack against the Washington FBI Headquarters described in Pierce's book. And one of the three white Texans who beat and decapitated James Byrd Jr., an African American man, as he was dragged on a chain by a pickup truck, said, according to one of his accomplices, "We're starting the Turner diaries early."[34] The notoriety of Pierce's second book, *Hunter*, grew in the wake of news reports revealing that the FBI found a copy of the book in the home of McVeigh's accomplice, Terry Nichols. While both *Hunter* and *The Turner Diaries* were written as fiction in the form of a novel, they contain, in fact, much of the divisive and hateful ideas and violent scenes that Pierce's heirs and other right-wing extremists continued to spread via the Internet and make accessible to increasingly larger audiences.

In more recent times, the openness of Internet propaganda is even more effectively exploited by the well-trained and well-funded media experts of jihadist groups. After conducting a case study on radicalization via social media, one student of violent extremism on the Internet concluded, particularly with respect to ISIS,

The most advanced IS's shift from near-exclusive use of password-protected forums to the utilization of social media platforms like Twitter exported the war from the distant battlegrounds of Syria and Iraq into the homes of tens of thousands in the West, rendering any social media user a prospective recruit. Jihadi propaganda is nearly impossible to avoid on Twitter and, in effect, invaded the homes of numerous thousands in the US, UK, Canada, Germany, Australia, and France, to name only a few. As jihadi material is widely spread on the internet and then shared and retweeted, the once-distant conflict in the Middle East has crossed boundaries and resulted in several hundreds of Americans fighting with IS and dying in Syria and Iraq, only to be replaced by new recruits.[35]

After reading this chapter, readers may wonder whether social media and websites have replaced the mainstream media in the communication calculus of terrorism and whether the gatekeepers of the traditional media have become irrelevant for the preachers of hate and violence. The following chapter will provide answers to those questions.

Notes

1. My account of this case is based on Dan Ephron and Joanna Chen, "Ofir's Fatal Attraction," *Newsweek*, April 2, 2001, and Deborah Sontag, "Israelis Grieve as Youth Who Was Lured to His Death on the Internet is Buried," *New York Times*, January 20, 2001.

2. Carlos Illescas, Tom McGhee, and Jesse Paul, "Officials: Teen Girls Likely Recruited Online to Join Islamic State," *Denver Post*, October 22, 2014, accessed October 22, 2014, http://www.denverpost.com/news/ci_26776829/fbi-investigation -continues-into-denver-teens-stopped-germany.

3. Department of Homeland Security, "Terrorist Use of Social Networking Sites," 2010 report, accessed January 18, 2015, https://publicintelligence.net/ufouoles -dhs-terrorist-use-of-social-networking-facebook-case-study.

4. Like most of these sites, Um Umbaydah's was on and off available on various social media networks; the excerpts were taken from http://al-khanssa.tumblr.com, where the last notes with questions and answers were posted in the second half of October 2014.

5. Steven Stalinsky and R. Sosnow, "Social Media in Syria and Iraq Conflict," Middle East Media Research Institute, December 5, 2014, accessed January 12, 2015, http://www.memri.org/report/en/print8309.htm.

6. Cited by Gabriel Weimann, *New Terrorism and New Media*, vol. 2 (Washington, DC: Wilson Center, Research Series, 2014), 3–4, accessed January 16, 2015, http://www.wilsoncenter.org/sites/default/files/STIP_140501_new_terrorism_F.pdf.

7. Rita Katz, "From Teenage Colorado Girls to Islamic State Recruits: A Case Study in Radicalization via Social Media," accessed January 23, 2015, http://news.sit eintelgroup.com/blog/index.php/categories/jihad/entry/309-from-teenage-colorado -girls-to-islamic-state-recruits-a-case-study-in-radicalization-via-social-media.

8. Scott Shane and Ben Hubbert, "ISIS Displaying a Deft Command of Varied Media," *New York Times*, August 30, 2014, accessed March 14, 2015, http://www.ny times.com/2014/08/31/world/middleeast/isis-displaying-a-deft-command-of-varied -media.html.

9. Rumsfield was cited in Timothy L. Thomas, "Al Qaeda and the Internet," *Parameters* (Spring 2003): 112–23, accessed January 18, 2015, http://www.iwar.org.uk/ cyberterror/resources/cyberplanning/al-qaeda.htm.

10. Dan Verton, "Web Sites Seen as Terrorist Aids," accessed January 15, 2015, http://www.computerworld.com/article/2586194/security0/web-sites-seen-as-terror ist-aids.html.

11. Ibid.

12. James Glanz, Sebastian Rotella, and David E. Sanger, "In Mumbai Attacks, Piles of Spy Data, But an Uncompleted Puzzle," *New York Times*, December 21, 2014, accessed January 20, 2015, http://www.nytimes.com/2014/12/22/world/asia/ in-2008-mumbai-attacks-piles-of-spy-data-but-an-uncompleted-puzzle.html?_r=0.

13. Ibid.

14. Christopher Anzalone, "The Nairobi Attack and Al-Shabab's Media Strategy," *CTC Sentinel* 6, no. 10 (2013): 3, accessed January 12, 2015, https://www.ctc.usma .edu/posts/the-nairobi-attack-and-al-shababs-media-strategy.

15. Ibid, 3–4.

16. Ben Hubbard, "Jihadists and Supporters Take to Social Media to Praise Attack on Charlie Hebdo," *New York Times*, January 10, 2015, accessed January 18, 2015, http://www.nytimes.com/2015/01/11/world/europe/islamic-extremists-take -to-social-media-to-praise-charlie-hebdo-attack.html.

17. VNN Forum, accessed January 15, 2015, http://vnnforum.com/showthread .php?t=232708.

18. Stormfront.org, accessed January 15, 2015, https://www.stormfront.org/ forum. The post shown on the opening page was no longer accessible two weeks later.

19. "Italy Arrests Another Brother of London Bomb Suspect." Agence France Presse, July 31, 2005, retrieved from Yahoo! News, July 31, 2005, at http://news.yahoo .com/afp/20050731/wl-uk-afp/britainattacksitaly-050731153552&prin.

20. David Lerman, "Beheading's World Cup Hashtag Shows Islamic State's Online Savvy," Bloomberg, July 7, 2014, accessed January 22, 2014, http://www.bloom berg.com/news/2014-07-07/beheading-worldcup-shows-islamic-state-s-online-savvy .html.

21. Department of Homeland Security, "Terrorists Use of Social Networking Sites," accessed January 23, 2015, https://publicintelligence.net/ufouoles-dhs-terror ist-use-of-social-networking-facebook-case-study.

22. Vice News, accessed December 20, 2014, https://news.vice.com/video/the
-islamic-state-part-2?utm_source=vicenewstwitter.

23. The video was released on January 13, 2015 but soon was removed from ISIS
sites.

24. Katz, "From Teenage Colorado Girls to Islamic State Recruits," n7.

25. Mark Potok, "Editorial: Frazier Glenn Cross, Murder and the Internet."
Southern Poverty Law Center Intelligence Report, May 24, 2014.

26. Ibid.

27. The list, accessed January 16, 2015, was posted at http://www.christianga
llery.com/atrocity/aborts.html#walsh. Since the courts outlawed the original list, the
so-called Nuremberg Files, new and updated lists are almost always available on one
of the group's websites, www.ArmyofGod.com and www.ChristianGallery.com. Site
visitors are encouraged to send more names of abortion providers.

28. Army of God, accessed January 16, 2015, http://www.armyofgod.com/PHill_
ShortShot.html.

29. Christian Gallery, accessed January 16, 2015, http://www.christiangallery.
com/atrocity/aborts.html.

30. This account is from various stories publicized in the news media.

31. Michael S. Schmidt and Helene Cooper, "ISIS Urges Sympathizers to Kill U.S.
Service Members It Identifies on Website," *New York Times*, March 21, 2015, accessed
March 23, 2015, http://www.nytimes.com/2015/03/22/world/middleeast/isis-urges
-sympathizers-to-kill-us-service-members-it-identifies-on-website.html. See also Security Affairs, accessed March 23, 2015, http://securityaffairs.co/wordpress/35203/
hacking/isis-cell-calls-on-supporters-to-kill-100-us-military-personnel.html.

32. Nelly Lahoud and Muhammad al-`Ubaydi, "The War of Jihadists against
Jihadists in Syria," *CTC Sentinel* 7, no. 3 (2014): 3, accessed January 24, 2015, https://
www.ctc.usma.edu/v2/wp-content/uploads/2014/03/CTCSentinel-Vol7Iss3.pdf.

33. Aaron Brantly, "Funding Terrorism Bit by Bit," *CTC Sentinel* 7, no. 10
(2014): 4, accessed January 23, 2015, https://www.ctc.usma.edu/v2/wp-content/up
loads/2014/10/CTCSentinel-Vol7Iss101.pdf.

34 See Court TV, accessed 1 April 2002, http://www.courttv.com/trials/
berry/102599_ctv.html. The brutal killing occurred in June of 1998 in Jasper, Texas.

35. Katz, "From Teenage Colorado Girls to Islamic State Recruits," n7.

5

Traditional Media, Terrorism News, and the Virus of Contagion

New York City police are calling a brazen, broad-daylight attack by a hatchet-wielding man on a group of police officers an act of terrorism.

The suspect—Zale Thompson, 32—attacked a group of four officers who had stopped to take a photo Thursday when a freelance photographer approached them. The suspect charged at the group for no apparent reason, police said. Thompson was shot dead by one of the officers.

"This was a terrorist attack," Police Commissioner William Bratton said Friday. A clear motive has yet to be established in the case.

It appears Thompson—who converted to Islam two years ago—became "self-radicalized" and was inspired by terrorist groups such as the Islamic State and al-Qaeda, the New York Times *reported.*

"We at this time believe that he acted alone," Bratton said at a news conference, which was also attended by New York City Mayor Bill de Blasio, according to the Times. *"We would describe him as self-radicalized. It would appear at this time that he was self-directed in his activities."*

John Miller, who oversees intelligence and counterterrorism for the New York Police Department, said recent online history showed Thompson had visited websites related to those terrorist groups, the Times *reported.*

"It appears, just from the electronic forensic piece of this, that this is something he has been thinking about for some time and thinking about with more intensity in recent days," Miller said.[1]

~

Leaving behind a rant against the government, big business and particularly the tax system, a computer engineer smashed a small aircraft into an office building

where nearly 200 employees of the Internal Revenue Service were starting their
workday Thursday morning, the authorities said.

The pilot, identified as Andrew Joseph Stack III, 53, of north Austin, apparent-
ly died in the crash, and one other person was unaccounted for. Late Thursday,
two bodies were pulled from the site, though the authorities would not discuss
the identities of those found, The Associated Press reported. Two serious injuries
were also reported in the crash and subsequent fire, which initially inspired fears
of a terrorist attack and drew nationwide attention.

Within hours of the crash, before the death or even the identity of the pilot had
been confirmed, officials ruled out any connection to terrorist groups or causes.

"The main thing I want to put out there is that this is an isolated incident here;
there is no cause for alarm," said the Austin police chief, Art Acevedo, in a tele-
vised news conference at midday. Asked how he could be sure, Mr. Acevedo said,
"You have to take my word at it, don't you?"

As the Department of Homeland Security opened an investigation and Presi-
dent Obama received a briefing from his counterterrorism adviser, John O. Bren-
nan, federal officials emphasized the same message, describing the case as a
criminal inquiry.[2]

~

Following the lethal attack on the I.R.S. office in Austin, Texas, in February
2010, one observer noted that the term terrorism "is simultaneously the single most meaningless and most manipulated word in the American political
lexicon. The term now has virtually nothing to do with the act itself and everything to do with the identity of the actor, especially his or her religious
identity."[3] Indeed, even before the authorities had dug into the background
of the white, Christian perpetrator, they ruled out that this was an act of terrorism. In response, NBC correspondent Pete Williams said that there are "a
couple of reasons to say that, one is he's an American citizen."[4] A sharp contrast
was the case of the hatchet attack on New York police officers when the perpetrator, a Muslim convert, was categorically labeled as a terrorist by the New
York Police Department.

In chapter 1, I discussed the difficulty of defining the term *terrorism*, suggesting a definitional solution that focuses on the link between this particular
kind of political violence and the desire for publicity. In the same way that
students of terrorism have wrestled with defining various types of political
violence, the news media have as well. Indeed, it seems that the press's choice
of terms is most inconsistent in its reporting about political violence perpetrated by groups or individuals. Research has revealed, for example, that the
U.S. media is more prone to label violent acts as "terrorism" when U.S. citizens
are the victims of politically motivated terrorism abroad. A content analysis of
three leading American news magazines from March of 1980 to March of 1988
showed that the t-word was used in 79 percent of the cases when American

citizens were victims, but in only 51 percent when no U.S. citizens were involved (Alali and Eke 1991, 30).

In this respect, the American media are not different from news organizations abroad. Thus, the German press readily called political violence at home or in Europe "Terrorismus" and its practitioners "Terroristen," whether committed by successors of the Baader-Meinhof group that remained active during most of the 1990s or the Basque separatist ETA that unleashed a new round of terror at the beginning of the millennium. But at the same time, the Abu Sayyaf in the faraway Philippines were typically characterized as "militante Moslemrebellen" (radical Muslim rebels) or "Rebellengruppe" (rebel group)— even during the time when they held three German hostages. The British news media were more likely to call acts of violence by the IRA or splinter groups thereof "terrorism" while reporting on politically motivated "bombings" or "hostage-takings" or "hijackings" abroad without using the t-word.

Following the terrorist attacks on the World Trade Center and the Pentagon, Reuters was reported to have banned the use of the term *terrorism* in the context of the 9/11 incidents, and CNN was said to have discouraged its correspondents from using the t-word although the network used *terrorist* all the time in its on-screen banner slogans. The wire services who serve many different members and clients had practiced this kind of strange political correctness long before 9/11. The most plausible reason for banning or discouraging the t-word was probably that all these news organizations, and perhaps others, were concerned that their correspondents would be attacked by or lose access to terrorists and their supporters, who rejected the terrorist label.

When terrorists strike inside the United States, the America-centric bias of the media does not explain why the news tends to characterize some acts of political violence as "terrorism" and similar deeds as "crimes." In the fall of 1998, the media watchdog FAIR criticized the news media for rarely describing the cold-blooded murder of Dr. Barnett Slepian by anti-abortion extremists as an act of terrorism, while readily attaching this label to the burning down of a ski lodge in Vail, Colorado, by extreme environmentalists. A content analysis of more than five hundred print and broadcast stories conducted by the FAIR organization found that "reporters labeled Dr. Slepian's killing as 'terrorist' or 'terrorism' only six times (exclusive of quotes from sources). In contrast, reporters themselves labeled the arson attack at the Vail ski resort 'terrorist' or 'terrorism' 55 times in 300 articles and newscasts."[5]

The conventional wisdom that the news media take their cues from government officials was once again affirmed in the aftermath of the deadly attack on Dr. Slepian when President Bill Clinton declared. "I am outraged by the murder of Dr. Barnett Slepian in his home last night in Amherst, N.Y. . . . No matter where we stand on the issue of abortion, all Americans must stand together in condemning this tragic and brutal act."[6] In fact, almost all news reports that followed called Dr. Slepian's demise "murder" and not "terrorism." The *CBS Evening News* was typical for this pattern, when it opened its broadcast with anchor Russ Mitchell stating, "President Clinton says he is outraged by the murder of a Buffalo, New York, area doctor who performs abortions."[7] One wonders about the news media's choice of terminology, if the president, in his statement only hours after the attack, had spoken about a brutal act of terrorism instead of murder. One of the few exceptions in this particular case was an editorial in the *New York Times* published after James Kopp was arrested abroad for the killing, many months later. Obviously thinking of Kopp's accomplices in the United States, the *Times* wrote that the "case could shed light on whether there is a widespread network of anti-abortion terrorists intent on depriving citizens of their constitutionally protected right to have access to reproductive health services, including abortion."[8]

Besides presidents' and other opinion leaders' influence on many aspects of the news—including the linguistic choices—there may be other reasons that explain why the fourth estate was and is far more inclined to call the violent actions by the Earth Liberation Front or the Animal Liberation Front "terrorism" or "eco-terrorism" and the far more lethal acts of anti-abortion militants "murders" or "bombings." Here, the vastly different resources and the lobbying muscles of interest groups come into play. The fur industry, for example, has made a point of exposing and attacking "terrorist" actions by animal rights and other environmental extremists in their lobbying campaigns, as have other business sectors on the target lists of the Earth Liberation Front and Animal Liberation Front. While pro-choice advocates, too, characterize the attacks on abortion providers and clinics as terrorist acts, their organizations and lobbying efforts have not been successful in changing the terminology used by public officials and by the news media. It is ironic that members of FBI counterterrorism task forces frequently investigate the deeds of violent environmentalists and violent pro-life activists. Thus, FBI agents and police officers assigned to a joint counterterrorism task force in Washington were involved in the hunt for fugitive James Kopp after the assassination of Dr. Slepian, just as special agents trained in counterterrorism investigated cases of eco-terrorism in various parts of the United States. Strangely, though, law enforcement officials spoke frequently of "eco-terrorism," but rarely, if ever, of "anti-abortion terrorism."

In the Cold War era, the mainstream news media in the United States and elsewhere in the West did not hesitate to choose the t-word for the self-proclaimed Marxists of the Red Army Faction/Red Brigade variety in Europe, Latin America, and Asia with suspected (and by now proved) backing east of the Iron Curtain. Also, the terrorist label was readily attached by the American media to militant secular organizations in the Middle East (such as the Palestine Liberation Front or the Popular Front for the Liberation of Palestine), and religious groups (such as Hezbollah in Lebanon or the Egyptian Islamic Jihad). All of these groups were fiercely anti-American (besides being declared enemies of Israel and of the capitalist West in general).

While "Arab" or "Islamic" or "Muslim" groups—or individuals, as the news often identified them—remained most prone to be characterized by the t-word, the old left/right divide no longer guided the choice of words as clearly in the post–Cold War era as it did when the old world order was still in place.

To be sure, some Marxist groups that survived the fall of the Soviet Union and the Communist bloc, for example the Greek 17 November Organization, which committed political violence for more than twenty-five years, was still labeled "terrorist." But the mainstream media were just as reluctant to describe as "terrorists" the violent anarchists who turned anti-globalization protests into riots and street fights with police as they were to attach the t-word to the violent anti-abortion faction. Thus, the suggestion that the media describe violence by left-extremists as terrorist but withhold the word from violence by right-extremists is not justified today. Rather than the result of conscientious bias on the part of the media, the linguistic choices seem to be based on two causes, (1) a tradition of stereotypical reporting patterns, and (2) a follow-the-leader syndrome in the news production that persists in other areas of reporting as well.

Thus, the media in the United States and in other Western countries report on "Islamic" or "Muslim" terrorists and terrorism, but not on "Christian" terrorists and terrorism, for instance in the context of Northern Ireland or anti-abortion violence in the United States committed under the banner of the Christian "Army of God." The same is true for "Jewish" terrorism expressed in violent acts by individual Israelis affiliated with or affected by extremist Jewish groups. A good example was the reporting on the Brooklyn-born Jewish fundamentalist Dr. Baruch Goldstein, who killed twenty-nine Palestinians in early 1994 as they prayed in a Hebron mosque and who was eventually killed by survivors of his attack. In reporting the incident, members of the American media characterized Goldstein's deed as massacre, shooting rampage, murder, and mass murder but not as an act of terrorism. In the following excerpt from the *CBS Evening News*, the anchor called Goldstein "gunman," and the correspondent characterized Goldstein as "mass murderer," but the correspondent referred to a Palestinian who had killed two Israelis several months earlier as "Palestinian terrorist":

> *Richard Threlkeld*: He [Dr. Baruch Goldstein] went to college and medical school here at Yeshiva University in New York. Eleven years ago, he emigrated to Israel. We may never know what turned Baruch Goldstein, a doctor, a healer, into a mass murderer, but there are some clues. . . .
> *Mrs. Barbara Ginsberg [Goldstein's friend]*: He was always there for anybody who was sick. OK, he refused to treat Arabs. He didn't hurt them, but he didn't want to treat them because he said, "I didn't come to Israel to treat my enemies."
> *Threlkeld*: Most likely it was this incident: A Palestinian terrorist machine gunned a bus hear Hebron last December, killing a settler and his son. They were close friends of Goldstein's. And after that, a friend said he became convinced the only answer to terror is more terror.[9]

The remark of Goldstein's friend revealed that Goldstein seemed to consider his deed an act of terrorism, if only in response to terrorist acts by Palestinians. Except for a few citations of non-media sources, reporters, editors, and anchors did not use the t-word and did not refer to an "Israeli terrorist" or to "Jewish terrorism." However, the latter term was thrown into the public debate by some Israelis and Jewish Americans who were quoted in some news reports. Thus, Dean Reynolds reported from Jerusalem that "Israeli commanders [who were blamed by critics for not stopping Goldstein from entering the Moslem house of worship] said they had never even discussed the possibility of Jewish terrorism at the mosque."[10] And in a report by Aaron Brown, a man in a Jewish neighborhood of New York said, "Nine of 10 will condemn it [the attack on worshipers in the Hebron mosque] and say that it is a terrible act of violence, it's an act of terrorism. And Jewish people are not terrorists."[11]

The follow-the-leader syndrome or, more specifically, the tendency of the news media to adopt the language of leading government officials, may have affected the linguistic characterization of the Hebron incident as well. President Clinton, in a special appearance in the White House briefing room, called Goldstein's act in the Mosque of Ibrahim "this crime" and "a gross act of murder." He equated this sort of violence by Palestinians and Israelis, when he said, "Extremists on both sides are determined to drag Arabs and Israelis back into the darkness of unending conflict and bloodshed."[12] He never mentioned the t-word.

After a young white supremacist killed nine African American members of the Charleston Emanuel African Methodist Episcopal Church in June 2015 following his participation in a bible study gathering, a mass-mediated public debate arose over the proper definition of the deed. Officials in Charleston and the U.S. Department of Justice spoke initially about a "hate crime." But this did not sit well with many observers. Even before the mainstream media reported the existence of an online pro-segregation manifesto written by the perpetrator, critics pointed to the most obvious double standard in the definition of these sorts of attacks. Thus, a reader from Illinois wrote in his letter to the editor in the *New York Times,*

> When a white gunman shoots nine people dead in a black church in South Carolina, this is a "hate crime." When two Muslim gunmen open fire at an exhibition of cartoons depicting the Prophet Muhammad in Texas, this is "terrorism." Why isn't the attack on the A.M.E. Church in Charleston not labeled "terrorism" and the assault on the cartoon exhibition a "hate crime?"[13]

Given the inconsistency of labeling these sorts of attacks, one thing was for sure: Had a young Muslim shot those nine church members, officials and the media would have immediately labeled the attack an act of "terrorism."

Over-Covering Terrorism at the Expense of Other Important Problems

One does not need to ignore or minimize the consequences of terrorism and the ever-present threat of this sort of violence to recognize that other problems deserve the same and even greater media attention. This point was not lost on Shanto Iyengar and Donald Kinder, who found that during a six-year period in the 1980s, the evening news of the three major TV networks (ABC News, CBS News, and NBC News) broadcast more stories about terrorism than about poverty, unemployment, racial equality, and crime (Iyengar and Kinder 1991, 27). The overemphasis on terrorism coverage at the expense of other important societal problems has not changed at all.

Table 5.1
News Coverage January 1, 2014–December 31, 2014:
Articles about or Mentioning . . .

	New York Times	*Washington Post*
Terrorism	3,040	2,292
ISIS or Islamic State	1,676	3,516
Health Insurance	1,293	3,567
Medicare	617	1,362
Poverty	1,905	2,808

Source: Compiled by author from the Lexis/Nexis and *Washington Post* archives[14]

As table 5.1 shows, in 2014 the *New York Times* and the *Washington Post*, the two most influential newspapers in the United States, published an extraordinary number of stories about or mentioning terrorism and ISIS or the Islamic State. Indeed, the *New York Times* published more such "terrorism" stories than articles on health insurance, Medicare, and poverty. ISIS or the Islamic State received more coverage in the *Times* than health insurance and Medicare. In the *Washington Post*, ISIS or the Islamic State received more coverage than Medicare and poverty and about the same as health insurance issues. As argued in earlier chapters, the media's over-emphasis and over-coverage of terrorism and the most notorious terrorist organization(s) at a given time provide terrorists with the publicity they crave. Strangely, massive media attention turns certain terrorists and even terrorist organizations into celebrities.

Celebrity Culture, Terrorists, and Media Hype

Just in time for his execution, MSNBC presented a special program about Oklahoma City bomber Timothy McVeigh as part of the series "Headliners and Legends" that is typically devoted to Hollywood and Broadway stars. For Caryn James (2001, A26), a TV critic for the *New York Times*, the program "said everything about the transformation of Mr. McVeigh into a celebrity, however vilified." This was hardly surprising at the time given that "life itself is an entertainment medium" (Gabler 1998, 6). As Gabler noted,

Audiences need some point of identification if the show is really to engross them. For the movies the solution was stars. For the life movie it is celebrity.

Though stardom in any form automatically confers celebrity, it is just as likely now to be granted to diet gurus, fashion designers and their so-called super-models, lawyers, political pundits, hairdressers, intellectuals, businessmen, journalists, criminals—anyone who happens to appear, however fleetingly, on the radar of the traditional media. (Ibid., 7)

While not listing "terrorists," Gabler was well aware that the saturation coverage of terrorist spectaculars makes the perpetrators of mass-mediated political violence excellent candidates for celebrity status, just like O. J. Simpson or Princess Diana. Using one example, Gabler critiqued the glamour treatment that McVeigh received from *Newsweek* magazine this way:

The cover photo of McVeigh staring off dreamily into space, his lips resolute but also soft, was pure Hurrell, the romantic photographer of Hollywood's golden age. (McVeigh had joked with the photographer Eddie Adams not to let any of the trashy magazines get the photos.) Meanwhile, the interview inside was pure *Photoplay*: gushy, reverent, excited. McVeigh looked, wrote *Newsweek*, "a lot more like a typical Gen-Xer than a deranged loner, much less a terrorist. (Ibid., 181)

Certainly, the ever stronger shift from hard news to infotainment—even in serious news organs such as *Newsweek*—figures prominently into this obsession with celebrities on the part of the news media and their audiences. McVeigh's celebrity status was never more obvious than in the days and hours before and after his execution, when news anchors and reporters of all television networks gave "blow-by-blow" accounts of his last hours and minutes—without having access to the actual execution, he was a celebrity for his fans at home and abroad for years—because of his media exposure. According to Michel and Herbeck (2001, 299),

Some women sent nude pictures of themselves. A young woman from Germany sent perfumed letters with lipstick kiss marks and erotic, extremely detailed stories of her sexual fantasies about McVeigh. From a woman in Ann Arbor, Michigan, came the first of several marriage proposals. . . . And a woman in Baltimore sent a one-hundred-dollar check, telling McVeigh, "Don't give up, fight back."

Some of the families that lost loved ones in the Oklahoma City bombing were not happy about the massive news coverage of McVeigh's execution. The daughter of one victim complained bitterly to NBC's Katie Couric that McVeigh "made himself a name" through this kind of television exposure. But she and other family members of victims as well as survivors of the terror had been enlisted shrewdly to take part in this last media circus surrounding McVeigh's final hours. Especially repugnant was the way the TV networks exploited those who survived the Oklahoma blast or lost loved ones in that nightmare by pressing them to articulate their innermost feelings about McVeigh's demise and relive the horror and grief of the past. Jane Clayson, co-host of *The Early Show* on CBS, interviewed Kay Fulton, whose brother was killed in the Oklahoma City bombing, and Tony Brown, whose father-in-law had died in the blast, shortly after they had witnessed McVeigh's execution. The following excerpt from that interview is a good example of the line of questioning:

> *Clayson*: You were hoping to make eye contact with Timothy McVeigh today. Did you?
>
> *Fulton*: I—I was hoping that he would some—somehow acknowledge our presence, and—and he did. However briefly, he did turn and—and look at each of the witness rooms.
>
> *Clayson*: And what was that like when he turned his head to your witness room to acknowledge you?
>
> *Brown*: I took a deep breath, a very deep breath, but knowing that just within a few minutes it would be over.
>
> *Clayson*: Mm-hmm. When you saw that needle inserted, with McVeigh laying there on the gurney, what was going through your mind? Were you thinking of your father-in-law? Were you thinking of the victims? Were you just happy that he was dying?
>
> *Brown*: All the above. All the above . . .
>
> *Clayson*: And when he did die, when he was gone, what was it?

In her discussion of the mass media's role in presenting violence as public entertainment, Sissela Bok quotes a TV reporter who was guided by the belief that "one has to show very strongly emotional images of victims of violence in order to arouse an indifferent public. A wall of indifference has to be overcome" (Bok 1998, 115). The television networks certainly labored hard to exploit and magnify every possible emotional image as they reported the McVeigh execution—whether those images highlighted the grief for the victims, flashbacks to the horrors of the bombing, or pleas of McVeigh's lawyers to explain him as a veteran, a son, and a brother. While many people were relieved that efforts to televise the implementation of the death penalty were rebuffed by the Justice Department and were thus spared of the unthinkable spectacle of a public execution via modern communication technology, Frank Rich (2001, A13) took a different stance when he wrote:

> True, the actual images of our government taking McVeigh's life weren't on the air, but their absence made the show more grotesque. Left to the audience's imagination, a death by lethal injection may be more disturbing than its depiction—especially when the four minute act itself is padded out with flashbacks to the greatest (i.e., goriest) video hits from the murderer's crime and promoted with logos like "Date with Death." Anchors across the TV spectrum talked incessantly about how "somber" the day was, but not so somber that their bosses

forsook selling commercials. Wal-Mart, which banned the sales of a journalistic book about McVeigh in its stores, did not refrain from hawking household wares to those tuning in for his execution. When Home Depot's ads for Father's Day presents and snappy trailers for Eddie Murphy's summer yukfest blurred with interviews with Oklahomans whose loved ones had been slaughtered in the Murrah Building, death not only lost its sting, but became merely another sales tool.

While most flagrant in its self-serving and excessive coverage, television was not the only medium that helped McVeigh to achieve fame. In the last five and a half months of his life, the frequency of news about McVeigh was very generous in television, radio, and print. In all major outlets except the *New York Times*, McVeigh received almost a third as many mentions as the president-elect and then President George W. Bush, and stories about him far exceeded the volume of coverage devoted to Vice President Richard Cheney, who was widely seen as equally influential and important as the new president. McVeigh's death did not end the media's fascination with the Oklahoma City bomber: Three days after his execution it was revealed that CBS purchased the rights to *American Terrorist: Timothy McVeigh & the Oklahoma City Bombing* by two reporters of the *Buffalo News*, Lou Michel and Dan Herbeck, as the basis for a miniseries about McVeigh and the most deadly act of terrorism on American soil.

Just as the mass media was essential in assigning McVeigh's celebrity status, they were instrumental in making Osama bin Laden a household name even before the attacks on New York and Washington on September 11, 2001. Bin Laden was indicted in New York for masterminding the bombings of U.S. embassies in Kenya and Tanzania in 1998, he regularly issued terrorist threats against the United States and the West, and he was listed on the FBI's "Most Wanted List"—certainly enough reasons for the news media to report on him, his organization, and their deeds and causes. But one wonders whether bin Laden deserved nearly as much, equally as much, or more attention than the legitimate leaders of important allies or adversaries of the United States. In 2000, for example, CBS News and NBC News broadcast significantly more stories mentioning bin Laden than segments referring to Great Britain's Prime Minister Tony Blair and Germany's Chancellor Gerhard Schroeder. ABC News presented the same number of stories mentioning bin Laden and Blair, far less referring to Schroeder. Both National Public Radio and the *New York Times* devoted more stories to Blair than to bin Laden, but the *New York Times* devoted far more to the terrorist than to Germany's head of government, Schroeder. As Simon Reeve observed, in Osama bin Laden the "world's media had found a new hate-figure to occupy their attention" (Reeve 1999, 2).

While casting McVeigh and bin Laden (even before 9/11) as celebrities, the mass media in the United States and other Western countries had long provided other terrorist figures opportunities to make their case in the public sphere. Thus, when Unabomber Ted Kaczynski, whose sixteen letter bombs killed three persons and injured twenty-three others, was willing to talk, he was interviewed by Stephen J. Dubner of *TIME* magazine. Dubner's long story explained Kaczynski's background, focused especially on his relationship with his brother, who had turned on him, and gave the Unabomber the opportunity to vent his anti-technology attitude. There was even a plug for the Unabomber's political goal and dream. What Kaczynski wants is a true movement, Dubner wrote, "people who are reasonably rational and self-controlled and are seriously dedicated to getting rid of the technological system. And if I could be a catalyst for the formation of such a movement, I would like to do that."[15]

In fact, had Kaczynski chosen to, he could have had far more publicity for his grievances and objectives than the sole interview with *TIME*. From *20/20*, *60 Minutes II*, *Good Morning America*, and the *Today Show* to *Larry King Live* and the *Roseanne* show, from the *New Yorker* to the *Denver Post*, many well-known media organizations and figures asked the Unabomber to use their platform to explain himself to fellow Americans. Letters that Kaczynski donated to the University of Michigan's Special Collection Library reveal how members of the fourth estate tried very hard to convince the terrorist to talk to them. Here are excerpts from some of the interview requests sent to this inmate in the Florence Correctional Institute in Colorado who had lived as a hermit in a primitive cabin when he assembled and sent his deadly bombs:

I've been a journalist most of my life, but also a wildlife film maker and writer. I'm as intrigued by your comments on the morality of your actions as I am by your strong feelings about the environmental ravages of technology.

—Don Dahler, ABC's *Good Morning America*

I wanted to let you know personally that I would obviously be very interested in also sitting down with you for an interview. It would give you a chance to explain your experiences to our huge audience and also the opportunity to share your views and concerns, which I know you've long wanted to.

—Katie Couric, NBC's *Today Show*

Your case is particularly fascinating since you reject the findings, and no one can dispute that you are an extremely smart man.

—Greta Van Susteren, CNN

Several doctors and some of your lawyers have claimed you suffer from schizophrenia. I want to give you the opportunity to respond point-by-point to their allegations and to show the American people that you are, in fact, rational, clearheaded, and sane.

—Shawn Efron, CBS's *60 Minutes II*[16]

Media figures bent over backward to curry favors with a man who killed and injured people for his political agenda—all for the sake of getting an interview that probably would not tell us anything new about the Unabomber but would offer him opportunities to publicize his agenda. Or take another case: When Sheik Hassan Nasrallah, the leader of the Lebanon-based Hezbollah or "Party of God," one of the most notorious anti-Israeli and anti-American terrorist groups, felt the urge to address the American public, Ted Koppel of ABC's *Nightline* granted him the television stage. While the Unabomber was behind bars and unable to wage his campaign of terror, when showcased by *TIME* magazine and courted by its scooped rivals, Sheik Nasrallah was still leading the organization that continued to engage in mass-mediated political violence.[17]

Table 5.2
Mainstream Media Reporting on ISIS before and after Foley Beheading
(Number of Articles mentioning Islamic State, ISIS, or ISIL)

	The month prior to James Foley beheading video (July 18–August 18, 2014)	The month following James Foley beheading video (August 19–September 19, 2014)
New York Times Articles Mentioning ISIS	124	375
Newsweek Articles Mentioning ISIS	3	15
CNN.com Articles Mentioning ISIS	45	296

Source: Marissa Young (2015)

Fast forward to the second decade of the twenty-first century and the rise of the Islamic State or ISIS, when not Abu Bakr al-Baghdadi, the self-appointed Caliph of the Islamic State Caliphate, but the organization he headed played a starring role in the mass media and one can argue became something like a celebrity. Whatever the ISIS media center produced and posted on social media sites became breaking news in the mainstream media. Every cruel act, every threat of more violence, every recruitment success was covered with the most savage killings raking in the greatest attention. A case in point was the beheading of James Foley in the summer of 2014. As table 5.2 shows, in leading print and TV media the number of articles about or mentioning ISIS, ISIL, or the Islamic State tripled in the month following the release of the decapitation video compared to the month before ISIS made the video available. Similarly, as seen in table 5.3, articles with ISIS, ISIL, or Islamic State in the headlines increased dramatically after the beheading video was released from merely three in the month before the publicized beheading images to ninety-nine in the *New York Times*, from one to five in Newsweek, and from thirty-one to ninety-five on CNN.com. The coverage patterns were no different in the rest of the news media.

The Islamic State's masked executioner, who grew up in England, became well known around the world as "Jihadi John." In mid-2015, a Google search of the term "Jihadi John" produced 6,280,000 results; a search in the archive of the *New York Times* brought up 266 stories; there were seventy-eight such articles in the Washington Post and 229 at CNN.com.

Table 5.3
Mainstream Media: Reporting on ISIS before and after Foley Beheading
(Number of Articles with Islamic State, ISIS, or ISIL in Headline)

	The month prior to James Foley beheading video (July 18–August 18, 2014)	The month following James Foley beheading video (August 19–September 19, 2014)
New York Times Headlines Mentioning ISIS	3	99
Newsweek Headlines Mentioning ISIS	1	5
CNN.com Headlines Mentioning ISIS	31	95

Source: Marissa Young (2015)

The atrocities that are meticulously videotaped and uploaded on social media sites are part and parcel of ISIS's propaganda strategy. According to one source with rare insider information,

> Crucifixions, beheadings, the hearts of rape victims cut out and placed upon their chests, mass executions, homosexuals being pushed from high buildings, severed heads impaled on railings or brandished by grinning "jihadist" children—who have latterly taken to shooting prisoners in the head themselves— these gruesome images of brutal violence are carefully packaged and distributed via Islamic State's media department. *As each new atrocity outdoes the last, front-page headlines across the world's media are guaranteed* [emphasis added].[18]

Those leading the Islamic State's propaganda campaigns are public relations and propaganda specialists. Abu Muhammad al-Adnani al-Shami who is in charge of ISIS's public information operations, has been called "the Goebbels of the Islamic State" and seen as the second most important figure in the organization besides Caliph Baghdadi. Obviously, he understood all along that the traditional media remain major factors in the dissemination of shocking news.

Revisiting the Contagion Theory in the Context of Terrorism

On April 19, 1995, Timothy McVeigh ignited a homemade truck bomb that destroyed the Alfred P. Murrah Federal Building in downtown Oklahoma City, killed 168 persons, injured close to 700 more, and triggered massive news coverage at home and abroad. Five days later the director of the California Forest Association, Gilbert Murray, was killed instantly when he opened a small package that had been mailed to his office. The enclosed message revealed that the sender was the mysterious person, dubbed "Unabomber" by the FBI, who had already killed two other people and injured twenty-three via mail bombs since 1978. That same day, the *New York Times* received a letter from the Unabomber threatening another deadly mailing unless the newspaper published a 35,000-word manifesto he had written to explain his motives.

It is difficult to imagine that there wasn't any link between the nonstop coverage of the terrorist spectacular in Oklahoma City on the one hand and the timing of the simultaneous mailings to Murray's office and the *Times* on the other. My guess was then and is now that the Unabomber Theodore Kaczynski was miffed because of the relatively modest news his mail bombs had received over the years compared to the tremendous attention the mass media paid to the Oklahoma City bombing. More importantly, whereas McVeigh's grievances and motives were prominently covered since he had intentionally posited clues in his car (i.e., Waco, Ruby Ridge), there had been no definitive news about the Unabomber's causes in the wake of his long mail-bombing trail.

Thus, he wasted no time to finally get his share of media attention and recognition of his causes by sending off another mail bomb and a threatening letter to the country's leading newspaper. By September 1995, when the *Washington Post* published his full-length manifesto "Industrial Society and Its Future"—sharing the printing costs with the *New York Times*—the Unabomber had already overtaken McVeigh as terrorist newsmaker-in-chief and saw suddenly his causes widely publicized and discussed in the mass media. If the deadly mail bomb, the letter to the *Times*, a follow-up threat to bomb the Los Angeles airport contained in a letter to the *San Francisco Chronicle*, and a host of demands and threats communicated to several newspapers and magazines were indeed inspired by the high volume and nature of news about Oklahoma City in order to get comparable coverage—and I believe that they were—it is impossible to prove media-related contagion here unless the imprisoned Kaczynski were to confirm such an effect with respect to the timing of a terrorist bombing and a threat sometime in the future.

While this case speaks to the difficulty of finding conclusive evidence for *direct* media-induced contagion with respect to terrorism, it encourages the exploration of media content about terrorist incidents, methods, and, most importantly, ideologies as an agent of terrorist infection. In the following, I revisit the media contagion hypothesis as it relates to terrorism and, to a lesser extent for comparative purposes, to violence-as-crime.

Contagion theories have been forwarded and rejected with respect to terrorism for several decades—often in the context of media effects. While some scholars deny such relationships (Picard 1986, 1991; Schlesinger, Murdock, and Elliott 1984), the notion of mass-mediated contagion seems commonsensical and is supported by anecdotal accounts and systematic research (Schmid and de Graaf 1982; Weimann and Winn 1994).

More than thirty years ago Robert G. Picard (1986, 1) attacked the news-as-contagion theory as "backed by dubious science" and argued, "The literature implicating the media as responsible for the contagion of terrorist violence has grown rapidly, but, under scrutiny, it appears to contain no credible supporting evidence and fails to establish a cause-effect relationship." Several years later, Picard (1991, 55–56) cited the minimal press effect findings of social scientists in the 1940s and 1950s in support of his rejection of the media contagion theory. What he failed to mention was that ample and far from "dubious" research, starting in the 1960s, found far stronger media effects on audiences (most notably with respect to agenda setting, framing, and priming) than the minimal effect school. Writing with Northern Ireland and domestic terrorism in mind, Schlesinger, Murdock and Elliott (1984), too, rejected the idea that the media are spreading the virus of political violence by ignoring the intelligence and good judgment of news consumers and especially television audiences.

However, a decade later, based on their quantitative analysis of media reporting (or non-reporting) of terrorist incidents and subsequent terrorist strikes of the same type (i.e., hijackings, kidnappings) Gabriel Weimann and Conrad Winn (1994, 277) concluded that their data "yielded considerable evidence of a contagion effect wrought by coverage." More specifically, these scholars found that "television coverage was associated with a shortened lag time to emulation in the case of kidnapping, attacks on installations, hijackings, bombings, and assassinations." In the early 1980s, Alex P. Schmid and Janny de Graaf (1982, 142) concluded that "The media can provide the potential terrorist with all the ingredients that are necessary to engage in this type of violence. They can reduce inhibitions against the use of violence, they can offer models and know-how to potential terrorists and they can motivate them in various ways." About the same time, Brian Michael Jenkins (1981, 6) wrote, "Initial research tentatively suggests that heavy media coverage of hijackings, kidnappings and other hostile seizures carried out by terrorists increases the likelihood that similar incidents will occur in the period immediately following. A recent Rand analysis of embassy seizures during the last decade shows them occurring in clusters, clearly suggesting a contagion effect."

Assumptions or inferences about contagion in the area of violent crimes are often based on observations and statistical data in the context of particularly horrific incidents.

For example, Berkowitz and Macaulay (1971, 238) studied crime statistics in the aftermath of the assassination of President John F. Kennedy in 1963 and two mass killings in 1966, when Richard Speck killed eight nurses in Chicago and Charles Whitman shot forty-five persons from a tower at the University of Texas. The researchers found that "statistical and graphic data from 40 U.S. cities indicate" that those incidents "were followed by unusual increases in the number of violent crimes." While the scholars characterized these cases as "widely published crimes" and implied a relationship between heavy news coverage of the three incidents and subsequent jumps in the number of violent crimes, they did not argue that most such crimes are instigated by media reports.

More recently, Loren Coleman explored the links between the Columbine school shooting in 1999, when high school students Eric Harris and Dylan Klebold killed twelve and injured twenty-three fellow students, some 400 similar incidents in the following years, and the Virginia Tech campus shooting in 2007, when student Seung-Hui Cho killed thirty-two people and wounded many others. In many of these cases the killers revealed the copycat nature of their violence by referring directly or indirectly to the Columbine massacre. In Coleman's words, "The copycat effect is what happens when the media makes an event into a 'hot death story' and then via behavior contagion, more deaths, suicides, and murders occur in a regularly predictive cycle."[19]

But just as the media-terrorism connection is embraced and contested by communication, media, and terrorism scholars, there is also disagreement about the impact of media reporting on violent crimes. In a comprehensive recent review of the relevant literature, Barrie Gunter (2008, 1063) cautioned, "Despite the vast volume of published literature that has concluded that the causal link between media violence and antisocial behavior is established, there have been more cautious and even dissenting voices that have challenged the strong effects position. Some writers have accepted that media violence can influence viewers, but not all the time and not always to the same degree in respect of different members of the audience."

As for mass-mediated diffusion of terrorism, the strongest arguments against connections between media content and terrorist incidents are made by those who fear that the notion of the media as agent of terrorist contagion will strengthen the hands of governments in efforts to curb or alter terrorism-related content and thereby interfere with freedom of the press and expression. I share those concerns and oppose censorship categorically. But these concerns must not prevent us from considering possible connections between media content and terrorism contagion and find mitigating factors without media restrictions from government or other outside forces.

The probably most cited example for media-related contagion of violence or the threat thereof is that of D. B. Cooper, who in November 1971 hijacked a commercial airliner on a flight from Portland to Seattle under the threat of detonating a bomb in his briefcase. After receiving a $200,000 ransom and two parachutes at the Seattle-Tacoma airport and ordering the crew to fly at the lowest possible altitude to Las Vegas, he jumped out of the plane and was never seen again. In the wake of heavy media coverage and the release of songs and a motion picture devoted to his daredevil heist, Cooper became a cult hero. More importantly, he inspired a series of copycat hijackings by other criminals during which the hijackers asked for ransom money and parachutes along the lines of Cooper's deed.

As for terrorism, the perhaps best evidence of contagious media content comes from captured terrorists or ex-terrorists. Horst Mahler, one of the founders of the German Red Army Faction recalled years later how television newscasts had triggered the "shock . . . [which led to] self-liberation . . . [and] the basis for RAF ideology" (Weimann and Winn 1994, 217, 218). Several biographical studies of terrorists show that many were motivated by a desire to emulate the publicity achievements of precursors (ibid.). Schmid and de Graaf (1980) cite the case of South Moluccan nationalists who hijacked trains in the Netherlands on two occasions in the 1970s to dramatize their plight and admitted reportedly after their arrest that their deeds were inspired by a similar attack plotted by Arab terrorists. Concerning the South Moluccan train hijackers, media reports affected simply what method of attack the group selected as most likely to succeed from what one would assume were several options the extremists considered.

This copying of terrorist methods seems to be a quite common media-related effect that explains why particular *modes* of terrorist attacks tend to come in clusters or waves. Thus, beginning with the hijacking of commercial airliners by Palestinian terrorists in the late 1960s, other Palestinian and non-Palestinian groups followed suit so that there was a cluster of hijackings with passengers held hostage. This method remained attractive in the 1980s and beyond. But as airlines and governments improved their security systems, the takeover of planes became more risky. While terrorists continued to hijack planes and in the case of the *Achille Lauro*, a cruise ship, it was no longer the preferred method of attack. Instead, terrorist groups embraced other means of attacking different targets and victims, for example, by taking over foreign embassies. Based on incident data collected by the RAND Corporation, Brian Jenkins (1981, 7) found that the forty-three successful embassy takeovers and five unsuccessful attempts between 1971 and 1980 occurred in twenty-seven countries and targeted the embassies of many countries—albeit most of all those of the United States and Egypt. "Like many other tactics of terrorism, hostage-taking [in embassies] appears to be contagious," Jenkins (ibid.) concluded. "The incidents do not fall randomly throughout the decade, but occur in clusters."

The idea here is that one particular mode of attack inspires similar strikes. As for the embassies, presumably, terrorists knew of these takeovers, most of them successful, from media reports since these incidents took place in a host of different countries and on different continents. By late 1979, when the Iran hostage crisis began, the "students" who took over the U.S. embassy in Tehran and the Iranian leaders who backed them must have known (via news accounts) about the prominent news coverage such incidents received. After all, of the embassy takeovers during the 1970s, more than half occurred in the last two years of that decade and thus shortly before the takeover in Tehran.

Or take as the cluster of gruesome beheadings of American, British, Japanese, and South Korean hostages by ruthless terrorists in Iraq and Saudi Arabia starting in the spring of 2004 with the killing of Nicolas Berg, a Philadelphia businessman. Emotionally wrenching videotapes that depicted the hostages begging for their lives were posted on the Internet by the killers and were subsequently reported on by traditional news organizations in shocking detail.

Consider the following, equally shocking description of an American civilian's decapitation by his terrorist kidnappers as published in a lead in the *New York Times* (MacFarquhar 2004):

> As the insurgent speaks, the gray-bearded man identified as Mr. Armstrong appears to be sobbing, a white blindfold wrapped around his eyes. He is wearing an orange jumpsuit. The masked man then pulls a knife, grabs his head and begins slicing through the neck. The killer places the head atop the body before the video cuts to a shot of him holding up the head and a third, more grainy shot showed the body from a different angle.

It is likely that the global wave of shock and outrage ignited by Berg's beheading resulted in copycat actions—first in the Middle East. And then there were a number of cases in which perpetrators beheaded their victims or threatened to do so outside the Middle East. In Haiti, for example, the bodies of three headless policemen were found; they were victims of terrorists who explained their action as "Operation Baghdad"—a label that had no meaning in Haiti's civil strife, except for the cruel method of murder in Iraq. There was also the beheading of a Buddhist official in a village in Thailand, which was described as an act of revenge for violence against Muslim rioters. After the shooting of Dutch filmmaker Theo van Gogh (his killer tried to cut his throat as well), self-proclaimed jihadis in the Netherlands threatened to decapitate other critics of Muslim extremists. These perpetrators must have recognized the shock value and media attractiveness of this particularly gruesome terrorist tactic from afar.

However, all the media attention devoted to the several al-Qaeda beheadings paled in comparison to the media hype in the wake of the beheadings of American and other Western hostages by the Islamic State starting in August 2014. The breaking-news-all-the-time coverage on television and in print was not lost on disgruntled ISIS devotees. A few weeks after the gruesome decapitation of James Foley, thirty-year-old Alton Nolen attacked former colleagues at a food plant in Moore, Oklahoma, beheading Colleen Hufford and seriously wounding a second woman. Nolen was a convert to Islam who had tried to convert his colleagues—without success. A month later, when Zale Thompson, thirty-two, and another convert to Islam attacked a group of New York police officers with a hatchet, the conclusion was that he had planned to behead his targets.

As one terrorism expert, Mark Sedgwick (2007, 102), concluded, "there is no doubt that besides direct contacts between terrorist groups and/or individual terrorists, indirect observations of successful terrorist methods and strategies rely on *traditional news* reports and, more recently, *new media* outlets—especially Internet sites." Examining the diffusion of suicide terrorism, Mia Bloom (2005, 122) explained,

We can discern the direct (patron-client) and indirect (through observation) influences of suicide terror. In some instances, insurgent factions have been physically trained by other organizations and taught how to best use horrifying tactics to devastating effect, who subsequently import the tactic far and wide. . . .

On other occasions, factions observe the successful operations of groups from afar—because of the publicity and media attention engendered by spectacular bombings, and then tailored the techniques to suit local circumstances.

While suicide terrorism spread inside and outside the Middle East well before 9/11, it became an even more popular terrorist weapon after the strikes in New York and Washington, D.C. Examining possible reasons for the post–9/11 wave of suicide terrorism, Paul Marsden and Sharon Attia (2005, 153) argued that the media cannot cause "suicide bombings any more than sex (as opposed to HIV) can cause AIDS," but they also suggested that media might be "a vector of transmission that can precipitate its spread."

Considering the publicity success of the 9/11 attacks from the perspective of al-Qaeda and the organization's supporters and sympathizers, I pointed early on to the likelihood of spectacular homicide-suicide attacks becoming a most attractive model for future acts of terrorism (Nacos 2003) in one form or the other. So far, nobody has repeated the flying-airplanes-into-buildings scenario but there have been many spectacular homicide-suicide attacks since in different countries and continents. The idea of imitating the 9/11 attacks has been discussed among terrorists. Thus, the Colombian FARC wanted to fly a plane into the presidential palace during President Alvaro Uribe's inauguration but the plotters were unable to find a pilot willing to die for the cause—even though the organization offered to give the suicide pilot's family a $2 million reward.

To summarize, besides personal contacts and cooperation between various groups, mass media reports are the most likely sources of information about the efficacy of terror methods and thus important factors in the diffusion of terrorist tactics. Interestingly, based on their analysis of terrorist incidents in the 1960s and 1970s around the globe, Midlarsky, Crenshaw, and Yoshida (1980) concluded that some terrorist methods of attack (hijackings, kidnappings, and bombings) were more contagious than others (assassinations, raids). These scholars recognized also that publicity provided by the news media was a factor in terrorists' decision to imitate terrorist methods deemed effective. As they put it, "Visible and unusual violence is in essence newsworthy and attracts international publicity necessary for cross-regional and cross-cultural spread" (ibid., 279).

The adoption of effective terrorist tactics, however, does not cause terrorism per se because those tactics are imitated or adapted by organizations that already exist and have embraced terrorism. As Mark Sedgwick (2007, 102) explained,

A particular terrorist technique is only of interest to a group that has already made the decision to adopt a terrorist strategy; a technique cannot on its own cause a resort to terrorism. Similarly, a radical group will normally enter into direct contact with an established terrorist group only once the decision to adopt a terrorist strategy has already been made.

Inspirational contagion is more alarming for the targets of terrorism because it is the stuff that makes terrorists tick and leads to the formation of new organizations and cells. The above-mentioned recollection of one of the Red Army Faction's founders, Horst Mahler, about the crucial role of televised terrorism news in formulating his group's ideology and the RAF's raison d'être might not have been a surprise for Midlarsky, Crenshaw and Yoshida (1980, 282), whose data analysis revealed the spread of terrorist thought from the Third World, and particularly from Latin-American and Palestinian terrorist leaders and groups, to western Europe in the early 1970s. Noting that radicals in Germany and elsewhere in western Europe received this sort of inspirational information from the mass media, the three scholars figured that "physical contacts [for example, between RAF and Palestinian groups] followed rather than preceded the decision to adopt terrorism."

Writing more than a quarter century later and considering David Rapoport's categorization of four global waves of terrorism, Sedgwick (2007) suggested,

> Contagion is possible at two levels, and can happen in two ways. On one level, a group might copy a particular terrorist technique, and on another level a group might copy a general terrorist strategy. Either of these might happen directly or indirectly. All these forms of contagion take place. The primary form, however, is the adoption of a general terrorist strategy without direct contact. All other forms of contagion are secondary to this.

One recent case of diffused inspirational contagion originated with the Afghan mujahideen who fought Soviet occupiers in the 1980s and with the establishment of al-Qaeda and its rapidly expanding terrorism network. It is hardly surprising that contagion effects tend to be strongest among groups and individuals that share the cultural and religious background of organizations and leaders with inspirational ideologies. No doubt ISIS has by far outdone al-Qaeda in spreading the virus of inspirational contagion. While the organization's media center's mass self-communication efforts explain a great deal of ISIS's success in the recruitment of followers and copycat terrorists around the world, the traditional media's over-coverage of ISIS is a factor as well.

In conclusion, then, when it comes to international and domestic terrorism various kinds of media figure prominently into both tactical and inspirational contagion. And although the Internet allows terrorists to mass self-communicate, the traditional mass media continue to be a major, perhaps still *the* major sources of information in this respect.

Notes

1. Katharine Lackey, "NYC Police: Hatchet Attack Was Terrorist Attack," USA TODAY, October 25, 2014, accessed June 20, 2015, http://www.usatoday.com/story/news/nation/2014/10/25/new-york-city-hatchet-attack/17899003.

2. Michael Brick, "Man Crashes into Texas I.R.S. Office," *New York Times*, February 18, 2010, accessed June 20, 2015, http://www.nytimes.com/2010/02/19/us/19crash.html.

3. Glenn Greenwald, "The Reluctance to Apply the Term 'Terrorism' to Joseph Stack Demonstrates How Cynically It Is Used," *Salon*, February 19, 2010, accessed June 15, 2015, http://www.salon.com/2010/02/19/terrorism_19.

4. Brian Stelter, "In Plane Crash Coverage, Networks Use the Word 'Terrorism' with Care," *New York Times*, February 18, 2010, accessed June 15, 2015, http://mediadecoder.blogs.nytimes.com/2010/02/18/in-plane-crash-coverage-networks-use-the-word-terrorism-with-care/?src=twt&twt=mediadecodernyt.

5. See FAIR's website, accessed April 1, 2002, at http://www.fair.org/extra/9812/buffalo-vaul.html.

6. From *The Public Papers of the Presidents* (William J. Clinton—1998, vol. 2), Government Printing Office, 2000.

7. See the *CBS Evening News* transcript of October 24, 1998, retrieved from the Lexis-Nexis database.

8. "Defending Abortion Rights," *New York Times*, March 31, 2001, A14.

9. *CBS Evening News*, February 25, 1994.

10. Reynold's report aired on *ABC World News Tonight*, March 8, 1994.

11. Brown's report aired on *ABC World News Tonight*, February 25, 1995.

12. Clinton's news briefing was broadcast in a CBS News Special Report on February 25, 1994.

13. *New York Times*, accessed June 20, 2015, http://www.nytimes.com/2015/06/19/opinion/killings-at-a-black-church-in-charleston.html?partner=rssnyt&emc=rss.

14. The table shows the number of stories about or mentioning terrorism, ISIS or Islamic State, health insurance, Medicare, and poverty.

15. Stephen J. Dubner, "'I do not want to live long. I would rather get the death penalty than spend the rest of my life in prison,'" *TIME*, October 18, 1999, accessed June 16, 2015, http://content.time.com/time/magazine/article/0,9171,992264,00.html.

16. These and other letters are available on the Smoking Gun website, accessed June 16, 2015, http://www.thesmokinggun.com/documents/crime/unabombers-media-pen-pals.

17. The interview with Sheik Nasrallah was aired on the ABC News *Nightline* program on October 19, 2000.

18. Malise Ruthven, "Inside the Islamic State," review of *Islamic State: The Digital Caliphate* by Abdel Bari Atwan, *New York Review of Books*, July 9, 2015.

19. Loren Coleman, "The Copycat Effect," *blogspot*.com, April 19, 2007, accessed June 15, 2015, http://copycateffect.blogspot.com.

6

Attack on America as Breaking News—a Case Study

While there were several major terrorist incidents before 9/11 and many more thereafter, the devastating attack on America by al-Qaeda was at the time and for a long time to come the most deadly strike against a nation-state by a non-state actor. For terrorists, the attacks of 9/11 and the unprecedented media coverage they received became the model they strove to replicate or even trump in terms of communication power and global public and elite attention. The 9/11 attacks were choreographed and staged like a sensational Hollywood thriller and reported as nonstop breaking news with the whole world watching. The following is a case study that describes and analyzes how the American news media covered the 9/11 events and whether this coverage helped al-Qaeda leaders to achieve the perennial publicity objectives of terrorists as described in chapter 2.

∾

Tuesday, September 11, 2001, began as a perfect day along the American East Coast. The sun was golden bright. The sky was blue and cloudless. On a clear day like this, the World Trade Center's twin towers resembled two exclamation marks above Manhattan's skyline, and they could be seen from many miles away in the surrounding counties of three states—New York, New Jersey, and Connecticut. At 8:48 a.m., when the workday began for thousands of employees in the offices of the 110 stories of the Center's towers, a hijacked Boeing 767 crashed into the North Tower. Eighteen minutes later, at 9:06 a.m., another Boeing 767 crashed into the South Tower. Just before 10:00 a.m., the South Tower collapsed, and twenty-nine minutes later, its twin fell. In between these events, at 9:40 a.m., a Boeing 757 dived into the Pentagon; at 10:10, another

Boeing 757 crashed in Somerset County near Pittsburgh, Pennsylvania. September 11, 2001 was forever America's "Black Tuesday."

Within eighty-two minutes, the United States suffered a series of synchronized attacks that terminated in the most deadly, most damaging case of terrorism in history. More than three thousand persons were killed, and the damage to properties, businesses, and the economy was incalculable. With the symbol of America's economic and financial power toppled in New York, the symbol of U.S. military strength partially destroyed near Washington, and a symbol of political influence—most likely the White House or Capitol—spared by courageous citizens aboard another jetliner that crashed near Pittsburgh, Pennsylvania, the impact was cataclysmic. America after the terror attack was not the same as it was before. Although the World Trade Center bombing of 1993 demonstrated that the United States was not immune to international terrorism on its own soil, and the Y2K terrorism alert reinforced that recognition, Americans were stunned by the ferocity and audacity of the 2001 strike.

Apart from the relatively small number of people who were alerted by relatives and friends via phone calls from the stricken WTC towers and those eyewitnesses who watched in horror, millions of Americans learned of the news from television, radio, or the Internet. In fact, minutes after the first kamikaze flight into Tower I, local radio and television stations as well as the networks reported first a possible explosion in the WTC, then a plane crash into one of the towers. Soon thereafter, the first pictures of the North Tower appeared on the screens, with a huge hole in the upper floors enveloped in a huge cloud of dark smoke. As anchors, hosts of morning shows, and reporters struggled to find words to describe what was indescribable, a mighty fireball shot out of Tower II—presumably the result of a second powerful explosion. The towering inferno was eventually replaced by another horror scene: one section of the headquarters of the Department of Defense engulfed in a large plume of smoke. With the cameras again on the WTC, the South Tower collapsed in what seemed like slow motion. Switching again to the Pentagon, the camera revealed a collapsed section of the facade. Amid rumors that a fourth airliner had crashed in Pennsylvania, the cameras caught the collapse of the World Trade Center's North Tower.

For at least part of this unfolding horror, many millions of Americans watched television stations or their related Internet sites. And, ironically, most Americans were familiar with the shocking images: the inferno in a skyscraper, the terrorist attack on a towering high-rise, the total destruction of a federal building in the nation's capital by terrorists, the nuclear winter landscape in American cities, Manhattan under siege after a massive terrorist attack. In search of box office hits, Hollywood had produced a steady stream of disaster movies and thrillers, often based on best-selling novels about ever more gruesome images of destruction. The entertainment industry's cavalier exploitation of violence was shockingly obvious following the terror strikes, when it was revealed that the "planned cover for a hip-hop album due to be released in November [2001] depicted an exploding World Trade Center."[1]

In a popular culture inundated with images of violence, Americans could not comprehend what was happening before their eyes and what had happened already. The horror of the quadruple hijack and suicide coup was as real as in a movie, but it was surreal in life. As Michiko Kakutani observed, "there was an initial sense of déjà vu and disbelief on the part of these spectators—the impulse to see what was happening as one of those digital special effects from the big screen."[2] The following quotations reflect the reactions of people who escaped from the World Trade Center, witnessed the disaster, or watched it on television:

I looked over my shoulder and saw the United Airlines plane coming. It came over the Statue of Liberty. It was just like a movie. It just directly was guided into the second tower.

—Laksman Achuthan,
managing director of the Economic Cycle Research Institute[3]

I think I'm going to die of smoke inhalation, because you know, in fires most people don't die of burning, they die of smoke inhalation. This cop or somebody walks by with a flashlight. It's like a strange movie. I grab the guy by the collar and walk with him.

—Howard W. Lutnick, chairman of Cantor Fitzgerald[4]

I looked up and saw this hole in the World Trade Center building. And I—I couldn't believe it. I thought, you know, this can't be happening. This is a special effect; it's a movie.

—Clifton Cloud, who filmed the disaster with his video camera[5]

It's insane. It's just like a movie. It's, it's actually surreal to me to see it on TV and see major buildings collapse.

—Unidentified man in Canada[6]

This is very surreal. Well, it's out of a bad sci-fi film, but every morning we wake up and you're like it wasn't a dream, it wasn't a movie. It actually happened.

—Unidentified woman in New York[7]

Witnessing the calamity from a tenth-floor apartment in Brooklyn, novelist John Updike felt that "the destruction of the World Trade Center twin towers had the false intimacy of television, on a day of perfect reception."[8] Many people who joined newscasts in progress thought that they were watching the promotion for one of several terrorism thrillers scheduled for release later in the month. Whether they realized it or not, and many did not, most people, even eye-witnesses at the disaster scenes, were far from sure whether movies had turned into life, or whether life was now a movie. Updike alluded to this sentiment, when he recalled the experience:

> As we watched the second tower burst into ballooning flame (an intervening building had hidden the approach of the second airplane), there persisted the notion that, as on television, this was not quite real; it could be fixed; the technocracy the towers symbolized would find a way to put out the fire and reverse the damage.[9]

In a seemingly inexplicable lapse of judgment, the German composer Karlheinz Stockhausen characterized the terror attacks on the United States as "the greatest work of art."[10] His remarks caused outrage in his country and the abrupt cancellation of two of his concerts in Hamburg. Perhaps this was a case of total confusion between the real world and the "pictures in our heads" that Walter Lippmann (1997 [1922]) described long before the advent of television. In particular Lippmann suggested that "for the most part we do not first see, and then define, we define first and then see."[11] While many people initially identified the horrors of "Black Tuesday" as familiar motion picture images, Stockhausen may have processed the real-life horror first as a symphonic Armageddon in his head, when he said: "That characters can bring about in one act what we in music cannot dream of, that people practice madly for 10 years, completely fanatically, for a concert and then die. That is the greatest work of art for the whole cosmos."[12] Following the uproar over his statement Stockhausen apologized for his remarks saying, "Not for one moment have I thought or felt the way my words are now being interpreted in the press."[13] One can only guess that the angry reactions to his statement brought him back from the pseudo-reality in his head to the real-life tragedy and its consequences.

When emotions gave way to rationality, the truth began to sink in. The most outrageous production of the terrorist genre was beyond the imagination of the best special effects creators. This was not simply two hours' worth of suspense. Real terrorists had transformed Hollywood's pseudo-reality into an unbearable reality, into real life. This time there was neither a happy ending to be enjoyed nor an unhappy ending that the audience could forget quickly.

Perhaps the temporary confusion was a blessing. Perhaps the fact that reality replaced media-reality in slow motion helped people cope with the unprecedented catastrophe within America's borders. Perhaps the delayed tape in people's heads prevented citizens in the stricken areas from panicking, helped citizens all over the country to keep their bearings.

The greatest irony was that the terrorists who loathed America's pop culture as decadent and poisonous to their own beliefs and ways of life turned Hollywood-like horror fantasies into real-life hell. In that respect, they

outperformed Hollywood, the very symbol of their hate for Western entertainment. After visiting the World Trade Center disaster site for the first time,
New York's Governor George Pataki said:

> It's incredible. It's just incomprehensible to see what it was like down there. You
> know, I remember seeing one of these Cold War movies and after the nuclear
> attacks with the Hollywood portrayal of a nuclear winter. It looked worse than
> that in downtown Manhattan, and it wasn't some grade "B" movie. It was life.
> It was real.[14]

The question of whether imaginative novelists and filmmakers anticipate
terrorist scenarios or whether terrorists borrow from the most horrific images
of Hollywood's disaster films was no longer academic. Shortly after the events
of September 11, an ongoing cooperation between filmmakers and the U.S.
Army intensified with the goal to predict the forms of future terrorist attacks.
The idea was that the writers who created Hollywood terrorism for the screen
might be best equipped to conceptualize terrorists' intentions. According to
Michael Macedonia, the chief scientist of the Army's Simulation, Training, and
Instrumentation Command, "You're talking about screenwriters and producers, that's one of the things that they're paid to do every day—speculate. These
are very brilliant, creative people. They can come up with fascinating insights
very quickly."[15] However, on the other hand, it was not farfetched to suspect
that the perpetrators of the 9/11 terror took special delight in borrowing from
some of the most horrific Hollywood images in planning and executing their
terrorist scheme.

The Perfect "Breaking News" Production

From the terrorists' point of view, the attack on America was a perfectly choreographed production aimed at American and international audiences. In the
past, terrorism has often been compared to theater because it is performed for
the people watching. While the theater metaphor remains instructive, it has
given way to that of terrorism as television spectacular, as breaking news that
is watched by record audiences and far transcends the boundaries of theatrical
events. And unlike the most successful producers of theater, motion picture,
or television hits, the perpetrators of the lethal attacks on America affected
their audience in unprecedented and lasting ways. "I will never forget!" These
or similar words were uttered over and over.

After President John F. Kennedy was assassinated in 1963, most Americans
and many people abroad eventually saw the fatal shots and the ensuing events
on television. But beyond the United States and other Western countries, far
fewer people abroad owned television sets at the time. When the Palestinian
"Black September" group attacked and killed members of the Israeli team during the 1972 Olympic Games in Munich, an estimated eight hundred million

people around the globe watched the unfolding tragedy. At the time, satellite TV transmission facilities were in place to broadcast the competitions into most parts of the world. But nearly thirty years later, a truly global television network, CNN, existed along with competitors that televised their programs across national borders and covered large regions of the world. Thus, more people watched the made-for-television disaster production "Attack on America," live and in replays, than any other terrorist incident before. It is likely, as many observers concluded, that the terrorist assaults on New York and Washington and their aftermath were the most watched made-for-television production ever.

From the perspective of those who produced this unprecedented, terrorism-as-breaking-news horror show, the broadcast was as successful as it could get. Whether a relatively inconsequential arson by an amateurish environmental group or a mass destruction by a network of professional terrorists, the perpetrators' media-related goals are the same in that terrorists strive for attention, for recognition, for respectability and legitimacy in their various target publics as described in chapter 2. It has been argued that contemporary religious terrorists (unlike secular terrorists, such as the Marxists of the Red Brigade/Red Army or the nationalists of the Palestinian Liberation Front during the last decades of the Cold War), want nothing more than to lash out at the enemy and kill and damage indiscriminately, to express their rage. But while all of these sentiments may well figure into the complex motives of group leaders and their followers, there is no doubt that their deeds were in the past and are today planned and executed with the mass media and their effects on the masses and governmental decision makers in mind. Unlike the typical secular terrorists, religious terrorists want to inflict the greatest possible pain, but they also want a whole country, and in the case of transnational terrorism the whole world, to see their attacks, to understand the roots of their rage, to solidify their esteem in their constituencies, and to win recruits or new sympathizers.

It is not hard to determine the short-term and long-term objectives of those who planned and executed the homicide-suicide missions against the United States. Even without the benefit of an immediate claim of responsibility, the mass media, decision makers, and the general public in the United States and abroad discussed the most likely motives for the unprecedented deeds. In the short term, the architects and perpetrators wanted to demonstrate the weakness of the world's only remaining superpower vis-à-vis determined terrorists, to frighten the American public, and to fuel perhaps a weakening of civil liberties and domestic unrest. No doubt, the long-term schemes targeted U.S. foreign policy, especially American influence and presence in the Middle East and other regions with large Muslim populations. More important, as communications from Osama bin Laden and his organization revealed, those who decided on these particular terror attacks regarded the anticipated strikes by the United States as the beginning of a holy war between Muslims and infidels. Bin Laden, in a fax to Qatar-based Al-Jazeera television, called the Muslims of Pakistan "the first line of defense . . . against the new Jewish crusader campaign

[that] is led by the biggest crusader Bush under the banner of the cross."[16] The bin Laden statement, which was widely publicized in the United States, left no doubt that he purposely characterized the confrontation as a battle between Islam and "the new Christian-Jewish crusade."[17]

Whatever else their immediate and ultimate goals were, those who planned the attacks were well aware that the mass media were central to furthering their publicity goals and even their political and religious objectives. Without the frightening images projected endlessly on television and computer screens, the impact on America and the rest of the world wouldn't have been as immediate and intense as it was.

When Terrorists Strike Hard, They Command Attention

In the past, media critics have documented and questioned the mass media's insatiable appetite for violence; they have explored the effects of this kind of media content on people who are regularly exposed to violence in the news and in entertainment (Gerbner and Gross 1976; Nacos 1996b; Bok 1998; Wolfsfeld 2001). While violence-as-crime and violence-as-terrorism tend to be grossly over-reported, the coverage of terrorist incidents that provide dramatic visuals is in a league of its own in terms of media attention. With few exceptions, ordinary criminals do not commit their deeds to attract cameras, microphones, and reporter's notebooks. But for terrorists, as previous chapters explain, publicity is their lifeblood and their oxygen. For decades, no other medium has provided more oxygen to terrorism than television because of its ability to report the news instantly, nonstop, and in visuals and words from any place to all parts of the globe, a facility that has affected the reporting patterns of other media as well. While the Internet was a source of news for a growing number of people, when the 9/11 incident took place, it was far from playing a role in terms of information and communication as it did years later (as described in chapter 4). Thus, this case study focuses on the traditional news media's coverage.

When commentators characterized the terrorist events of "Black Tuesday" as the Pearl Harbor of the twenty-first century or the second Pearl Harbor, they ignored one fundamental aspect that separated the surprise attack on December 7, 1941, from that on September 11, 2001: the vastly different communication technologies. Three hours passed from the time the first bombs fell on Pearl Harbor and the moment when people on the U.S. mainland first learned the news from radio broadcasts. More than a week lapsed before the *New York Times* carried the first pictures of the actual damage. Sixty years later, the terror attacks had a live global TV, radio, and Internet audience and many replays in the following hours, days, and weeks.

In September 1970, members of the Popular Front for the Liberation of Palestine (PFLP) simultaneously hijacked four New York–bound airliners carrying more than six hundred passengers. Eventually, three of the planes landed in a remote part of Jordan, where many passengers, most of them Americans and Europeans, were held for approximately three weeks. This was high drama. The media reported extensively, but the reporting paled in comparison to the great attention devoted to equally as dramatic or far less shocking incidents in later years. The communication technology at the time did not allow live transmissions from remote locations. Satellite transmissions were in their early stages and were very expensive. For the PFLP, the multiple hijacking episode ended in disappointment. While the tense situation resulted in media, public, and government attention, no news organization covered the events in ways that might have forced President Richard Nixon and European leaders to act under pressure.[18]

As television technology advanced further and competition among TV, radio, and print organizations became fiercer, the media became more obsessed with exploiting violence-as-crime and violence-as-terrorism in search of higher ratings and circulation. As a result, the contemporary news media have customarily devoted huge chunks of their broadcast time and news columns to major and minor acts of political violence by non-state actors supporting media critics' argument that the mass media, as unwitting as they are, facilitate the media-centered terrorist scheme.

There was no need to count broadcast minutes or measure column length to establish the proportion of the total news that dealt with the 9/11 attacks and their aftermath. For the first five days after the strikes, television and radio networks covered the disaster around the clock without the otherwise obligatory commercial breaks. Judging from the news content, there was no other news. Most sports and entertainment channels switched to crisis news, many of them carrying the coverage of one of the networks or suspending their suddenly irrelevant broadcasts altogether. For example, Fox cable's sports channel in New York simply showed the image of the U.S. flag. Newspapers and magazines devoted all or most of their news to the crisis. Given the dimension of the attacks on America, this seemed the right decision early on. Eventually one wondered, however, whether terrorism coverage needed to be curtailed so that other important news got the attention it deserved. *Newsweek* and *TIME*, for example, devoted all cover stories in the eight weeks following the events of 9/11 to terrorism and terrorism-related themes.

If not the perpetrators themselves, the architects of the operation surely anticipated the immediate media impact: blanket coverage not only in the United States but in other parts of the world as well. How could the terrorists better achieve their number one publicity objective: obtaining the attention of their targeted audiences? Opinion polls revealed that literally all Americans (99 percent or 100 percent according to public opinion surveys) followed the news of the attacks by watching and listening to television and radio broadcasts. While most adults identified television and radio as their primary sources for crisis information, nearly two-thirds also mentioned the Internet as one of their information sources. This initial universal interest did not weaken quickly. Nearly six weeks after 9/11, still more than 90 percent of the public kept on watching the news about terrorism "very closely" or "closely" according to polls. The volume of domestic and international media coverage and the level of global attention were remarkable achievements from the terrorists' perspective. Indeed, the architects of 9/11 were delighted. Referring to the kamikaze pilots as "vanguards of Islam," bin Laden marveled,

> Those young men (inaudible) said in deeds, in New York and Washington, speeches that overshadowed other speeches made everywhere else in the world. The speeches are understood by both Arabs and non-Arabs—even Chinese.[19]

With these remarks, bin Laden revealed that he considered terrorism a vehicle to dispatch messages—speeches in his words. And since he and his circle had followed the news of 9/11, they were sure that their message had been heard. Not surprisingly, from one hour to the next, the perpetrators set America's public agenda and profoundly affected most Americans' private lives. As soon as television stations played and replayed the ghastly scenes of jetliners being deliberately flown into the World Trade Center and the Pentagon, business as usual was suspended in the public and private sector. All levels of government and vast parts of the business community concentrated on the immediate rescue contingencies and on preventing further attacks rumored in the media. Within days, all levels of government and the business community began to implement new anti- and counterterrorist measures. All of this was thoroughly reported by the news media, as was the fact that most Americans no longer lived ordinary lives in one respect or another. There was a great deal of anxiety and fear—precisely what terrorists hope to achieve. In a videotaped message, Osama bin Laden said about the reactions of Americans to the terror of 9/11, "There is America, full of fear from north to south, from west to east. Thank God for that."[20]

Many Americans had trouble returning to their normal, everyday life routines. Many had trouble sleeping at night. And the news media did not help in this respect. When President George W. Bush, New York's Mayor Rudy Giuliani, and other public officials urged Americans to return to quasi-normal lives, the media's crisis coverage did not reflect that public officials in Washington had returned to normalcy. There were pictures of Washington's Reagan National Airport remaining closed because of its proximity to the White House and other government buildings. There was an image of a fighter jet over Washington escorting the presidential helicopter on a flight to Camp David. There were reports explaining Vice President Richard Cheney's absence when the president addressed a joint session of Congress and in the weeks thereafter, as a precaution, in case terrorists might strike again. And there were constant visuals of a tireless Mayor Giuliani as crisis manager before the daunting background of Ground Zero in Manhattan's financial district, at the funeral of yet another police officer or firefighter, at a mass at St. Patrick's Cathedral, or at a prayer service in Yankee Stadium.

Every public appearance by the president, New York City's mayor, New York Governor George Pataki, U.S. Senators, U.S. Representatives, members of the Bush administration; every hearing and floor debate in the two chambers of Congress; and every publicly announced decision was in reaction to the terrorist attack and was reported in the news. Even weeks after "Black Tuesday" and during the uproar over anthrax letters sent to several persons, CNN and other all-news channels interrupted their programs not only to report on President Bush's public appearances but on Mayor Giuliani's activities as well. And when the broadcast networks returned to their normal schedules, the around-the-clock news channels continued to report mostly on terrorism and counterterrorism, especially once military actions against targets in Afghanistan began less than one month after 9/11. When professional sports competition resumed after a voluntary moratorium of several days, watching sports broadcasts did not necessarily mean that fans could forget the horror of 9/11for a while. Unwittingly or not, the media transmitted constant reminders: Baseball fans in Chicago displaying a "We Love New York" banner; American flags placed on helmets and caps of competitors; a hockey game being interrupted so that players and fans could hear the presidential speech before Congress; players praising rescue workers at the terror sites and embracing members of a rival team in an expression of unity. The sports pages of newspapers captured the reactions of well-known sports stars and the American flag on the cover of *Sports Illustrated* signaled that the entire issue following 9/11 was devoted to patriotism.

Entertainment as well was in the grasp of the horrendous acts. When David Letterman resumed his late-night TV-show, he was unusually serious and made no attempt to be funny. Instead of offering hilarious punch lines, he found words of comfort for news anchor Dan Rather who was twice moved to tears when talking about the terror next door. *Saturday Night Live*, Comedy Central, and other entertainment shows were all less aggressive in provoking laughter at the expense of political leaders. Bill Maher of ABC's *Politically Incorrect* was the exception when he told his audience that the suicide bombers were not cowards but that the United States was cowardly when launching cruise missiles on targets thousands of miles away. Maher, who later apologized for his remarks, was criticized by White House spokesman Ari Fleischer and punished by some advertisers who withdrew their commitments; some local stations dropped the program. Even poking fun at bin Laden and the Taliban, as Jay Leno and the *Saturday Night Live* performers did, seemed not really funny. Indeed, cartoons in general seemed out of place for some publications, among them the *New York Times*, who suspended the paper's weekly cartoon section for a while. And when a star-studded cast of entertainers performed in a two-hour telethon to raise funds for the victims of terrorism, the celebrities told touching stories of innocent victims and real-life heroes. But nothing reminded the American audience more succinctly of the extraordinary circumstances behind the benefit than the sight of superstars Jack Nicholson, Sylvester Stallone, Meg Ryan, Whoopi Goldberg, and other show business celebrities relegated to answering telephone calls of contributors, since the producers had not found slots for them to perform in the program. Finally, even the most outrageous TV and radio talk show hosts toned down their personalities as they embraced the terror crisis story, albeit only for a short time. When the television series *The West Wing* postponed its scheduled season opener and replaced it with a special episode in which the White House dealt with the aftermath of a terrorist nightmare, the blur of fact and fiction, life and entertainment, came full circle.

As media organizations, star anchors, and public officials became the targets of biological terrorism and postal workers the most numerous victims of "collateral damage" in an unprecedented anthrax offensive by an elusive terrorist, the news devoted to terrorism multiplied—especially in the United States but abroad as well. The aftermath of the 9/11 terror—the anthrax cases, the debate of possibly more biological and chemical agents in the arsenal of terrorists, and the military actions against al-Qaeda and Taliban targets in Afghanistan—crowded out most other events and developments in the news.

In sum, by carrying out the most lethal and most spectacular terrorism mission, the 9/11 terrorists were super-successful in setting the media agenda, the government agenda, and the public agenda in America.

Why Do They Hate Us?

Sixteen days after the attacks on New York and Washington, the *Christian Science Monitor* published an in-depth article addressing a question that President Bush had posed in his speech before a joint session of Congress: "Why do they hate us?" Describing a strong resentment toward America in the Arab and Islamic world, Peter Ford summarized the grievances articulated by Osama bin Laden and like-minded extremists, but also held by many less radical people in the Middle East and other Muslim regions, when he wrote that

> the buttons that Mr. bin Laden pushes in statements and interviews—the injustice done to the Palestinians, the cruelty of continued sanctions against Iraq, the presence of US troops in Saudi Arabia, the repressive and corrupt nature of the US backed Gulf governments—win a good deal of popular sympathy.[21]

This lengthy article was but one of many similar reports and analytical background pieces tracing the roots of anti-American attitudes among Arabs and Muslims and possible causes for a new anti-American terrorism of mass destruction. Lisa Beyer (2001) offered this summary of grievances in her story in *TIME* magazine:

> The proximate source of this brand of hatred toward America is U.S. foreign policy (read: meddling) in the Middle East. On top of its own controversial history in the region, the United States inherits the weight of centuries of Muslim

bitterness over the Crusades and other military campaigns, plus decades of indignation over colonialism.

A former U.S. Ambassador at Large for Counterterrorism wrote,

> Certainly, the U.S. should reappraise its policies concerning the Israeli-Palestinian conflict and Iraq, which have bred deep anger against America in the Arab and Islamic world, where much terrorism originates and whose cooperation is now more critical than ever. (Wilcox 2001, 4)

While the print press examined the roots of the deeply seated opposition to U.S. foreign policy in the Arab and Islamic world extensively, television and radio dealt with these questions as well—in some instances at considerable length and depth. Thus, in the two and a half weeks that followed the terrorist attacks, the major television networks and National Public Radio broadcast thirty-three stories that addressed the roots of anti-American terrorism of the sort committed on September 11, 2001, the motives of the perpetrators, and, specifically, the question that President Bush had asked. In the more than eight months before the attacks on New York and Washington, from January 1, 2001 to 9/11, none of the same TV or radio programs addressed the causes of anti-American sentiments in the Arab and Islamic world.[22] This turnaround demonstrated the ability of terrorists to force the media's hand and in fact set the media agenda. Suddenly, in the wake of terrorist violence of unprecedented proportions, the news explored and explained the grievances of those who died for their causes and how widely these grievances were shared even by the vast majority of those Arabs and Muslims who condemned violence committed in the United States. With or without referring to a fatwa (religious edict) that Osama bin Laden and four other extremist leaders had issued in1998, or to the most recent communications from these circles, the news media now dealt with the charges contained in these statements as well as with additional issues raised by Muslims in the Middle East and elsewhere. The 1998 fatwa, posted on the website of the World Islamic Front, listed three points in particular:

> First, for over seven years the United States has been occupying the lands of Islam in the holiest places, the Arabian Peninsula. . . . If some people have in the past argued about the fact of the occupation, all people of the Peninsula have now acknowledged it. The best proof of this is the Americans' continuing aggression against the Iraqi people using the Peninsula as a staging post. . . .
>
> Second, despite the great devastation inflicted on the Iraqi people by the Crusader-Zionist alliance, and despite the huge number of those killed, which has exceeded 1 million . . . despite all this, the Americans are once again trying to repeat the horrific massacres. . . .

Third, if the Americans' aims behind these wars are religious and economic, their aim is also to serve the Jews' petty state and divert attention from its occupation of Jerusalem and murder of Muslims there.[23]

These specific accusations were among a whole laundry list of grievances that the media explored in the wake of the terrorism in New York and Washington. And the existence and content of bin Laden's various fatwa releases were reported as news although they were issued as far back as 1996 and 1998.

It has been argued that religious fanatics who resort to this sort of violence are not at all interested in explaining themselves to their enemies because their only conversation is with God. But it was hardly an accident that the leaders among the suicide attackers, who diligently planned every detail of their conspiracy, left behind several copies of their instructions in the hours before and during the attacks. By insuring that law enforcement agents would find the documents, the terrorists must have been confident that America and the world would learn of their cause. They were proven right when the FBI released copies of the four-page, handwritten document to the media for publication. Revealing the pseudo-religious belief that drove the hijackers to mass destruction and their own deaths, the instructional memorandum contained the following sentences:

Remember that this is a battle for the sake of God. . . .

So remember God, as He said in His book: "Oh Lord, pour your patience upon us and make our feet steadfast and give us victory over the infidels." . . .

When the confrontation begins, strike like champions who do not want to go back to this world. Shout, "Allah Akbar," because this strikes fear in the hearts of the non-believers. God said: "Strike above the neck, and strike at all their extremities."

Know that the gardens of paradise are waiting for you in all their beauty, and the women of paradise are waiting, calling out, "Come hither, friend of God."[24]

The intent here is not to criticize the media for publicizing such documents, for trying to answer why terrorists hate Americans and why many nonviolent people in the Arab and Islamic world hold anti-American sentiments, but rather to point out that this coverage and the accompanying mass-mediated discourse were triggered by a deliberate act of mass destruction terrorism. After 9/11 there was a tremendous jump in the quantity of news reports about one of the other aspects of developments in the Muslim and Arab world and even more so about Islam. Television news especially paid little attention to these topics before the terror attacks in New York and Washington. The switch from scarce or modest coverage before 9/11 to far more news prominence thereafter occurred in radio and the print press as well. While many of these news segments and stories focused on anti-American terrorism committed by Muslim and Arab perpetrators and the role of fundamentalist Islamic teachings, there were also many stories reporting on and examining the grievances of the mass of nonviolent Muslims and Arabs as well as the teachings of main-stream Islam.

Before "Black Tuesday," the news from the Middle East and other Islamic regions was overwhelmingly episodic and focused on particular, typically violent, events. Following the Iran hostage crisis, one critic noted, "Muslims and Arabs are essentially covered, discussed, apprehended either as oil suppliers or as potential terrorists. Very little of the detail, the human density, the passion of Arab-Muslim life has entered the awareness of even those people whose profession it is to report the Islamic world" (Said 1981, 26). Given the scarcity of foreign news in the post–Cold War era in the American mass media, especially television (Hickey 1998), there was even less contextual news or "thematic" stories (Iyengar 1991) from this part of the world. But it would have been precisely the thematic approach that should have addressed all along the conditions that breed anti-American attitudes in the Arab and Muslim world. It took the terror of "Black Tuesday" for the media to offer a significant amount of contextual coverage along with episodic reporting. In the process, the perpetrators of violence achieved their recognition goal: By striking hard at America, the terrorists forced the mass media to explore their grievances in ways that transcended by far the quantity and narrow focus of their pre-crisis coverage.

Making the News as Villain and Hero

What about the third goal that many terrorists hope to advance—to win or increase their respectability and legitimacy? Here, the perpetrators' number one audience is not the enemy or the terrorized public, in this case Americans, but rather the population in their homelands and regions. And in this respect, again, the terror of "Black Tuesday" was beneficial in the view of the architects and the perpetrators of violence. A charismatic figure among his supporters and sympathizers to begin with, Osama bin Laden was the biggest winner in this respect. Whether he was directly or indirectly involved in the planning of the terrorist strikes did not matter. The media covered him as "America's number one public enemy"[25] and thereby bolstered his popularity, respectability, and legitimacy among millions of Muslims. The American and foreign news publicized visuals and reports of the popular support for bin Laden following the terror attack against the United States. A lengthy bin Laden profile in the *New York Times*, for example, contained the following passage: "To millions in the Islamic world who hate America for what they regard as its decadent culture and imperial government, he [Osama bin Laden] is a spiritual and political ally."[26]

A page one article in the same edition of the *Times* reported from Karachi, Pakistan,

In every direction in this city of 12 million people, the largest city in a nation that has become a crucial but brittle ally in the United States' war on terrorism, there are cries and signs for Osama bin Laden, for the Taliban, for holy war.[27]

The Associated Press reported that a book about the terrorist-in-chief was a best seller in the Middle East. The volume contained the complete transcript of an interview with bin Laden that was broadcast in abbreviated form by Al-Jazeera television in 1998 and rebroadcast after the terror strike against the United States in September of 2001. Sold out in most bookstores of the region, readers were reportedly borrowing the book from friends and making photocopies.[28]

Bin Laden, his al-Qaeda group, and the closely related web of terror spanning from the Middle East into other parts of Asia, Africa, Europe, North America, and possibly South America, were no match for the American superpower in terms of political, economic, and military power. In the aftermath of the terrorist attacks on New York and Washington and up to the beginning of the bombing of Afghanistan on October 7, the U.S. television networks mentioned Osama bin Laden more frequently and the leading newspapers and National Public Radio only somewhat less frequently than President George W. Bush. A terrible act of terror turned the world's most notorious terrorist into one of the world's leading newsmakers. The fact that the American news media paid more attention to bin Laden than to the U.S. president, or nearly as much, was noteworthy, if one considers that George W. Bush made fifty-four public statements during this period (from major addresses to shorter statements to a few words during photo opportunities) compared to bin Laden, who did not appear in public at all, did not hold news conferences or give face-to-face interviews.[29]

Although the American media did not portray bin Laden as a sympathetic figure, he did share center stage with President Bush in the mass-mediated global crisis. Since the 1998 bombings of the U.S. embassies in Kenya and Tanzania, the American media devoted considerable broadcast time and column inches to bin Laden. But the celebrity terrorist's ultimate ascent to the world stage was more dramatic and forceful than that of Yasir Arafat in the 1970s, the Ayatollah Khomeini and Muammar Gadhafi in the 1980s, Saddam Hussein in the early 1990s, and bin Laden himself in the years and months preceding "Black Tuesday." And through all of this, bin Laden was in hiding. However, the Qatar-based Arab television network Al-Jazeera aired a videotape made available by al-Qaeda immediately after President Bush told America and the world that military actions had begun in the multifaceted hunt for bin Laden and his terror organization. All U.S. networks broadcast the tape as they received the Al-Jazeera feed. Bin Laden's shrewdly crafted speech received the same airtime as President Bush's speech. The same was true for a videotaped statement by bin Laden's lieutenant for media affairs who threatened that "Americans must know that the storm of airplanes will not stop, God willing, and there are thousands of young people who are as keen about death as Americans are about life."[30]

In the ten weeks following the attacks of 9/11, *TIME* magazine depicted Osama bin Laden three times and President George W. Bush twice on its cover. During the same period, *Newsweek* carried bin Laden twice on its cover and President Bush not at all. Finally, the cover of *Newsweek's* eleventh issue after 9/11 featured President George W. and First Lady Laura Bush.

From the terrorists' point of view, it did not matter that bin Laden earned bad press in the United States and elsewhere. Singled out, condemned, and warned by leaders, such as President Bush and British Prime Minister Tony Blair, Osama bin Laden was in the news as frequently as the world's legitimate leaders, or even more frequently. This in itself was a smashing success from the perspectives of bin Laden and his associates: The mass media reflected that bin Laden and his followers preoccupied not only America and the West but literally the entire world.

In sum, then, by attacking symbolic targets in America, killing thousands of Americans, and causing tremendous damage to the American and international economy, the architects and perpetrators of this horror achieved their media-centered objectives in all respects. This propaganda coup continued in the face of American and British counterterrorist military actions in Afghanistan and later on in Iraq that were, after all, provoked by bin Laden and his group.

Some High Marks for the News Media

In the days following the attacks, when most Americans kept their televisions or radio sets tuned to the news during most of their waking hours, the public gave the media high grades for its reporting. Nearly nine in ten viewers rated the performance of the news media as either excellent (56 percent) or good (33 percent). The Pew Research Center for the People & the Press (which keeps track of the relationship between the public and the news media) called this high approval rating "unprecedented."[31] This record approval came on the heels of increasing public dissatisfaction with the mass media and a number of journalistic and scholarly works that identified the degree of and reasons for the increasing disconnect between the public and the news media (Fallows 1996; Patterson 1993). The terrorism catastrophe brought Americans and the press closer together, closer than in recent times of normalcy and during previous crises, in particular, the Gulf War. Five aspects in particular seemed to effect these attitudinal changes:

First, the public appreciated the flow of information provided by television, radio, and print either directly or via media organizations' Internet sites. In the hours and days of the greatest distress, television and radio especially helped viewers and listeners feel as if they were involved in the unfolding news. Unconsciously, people took some comfort in seeing and hearing the familiar faces and voices of news anchors and reporters as signs of the old normalcy in the midst of an incomprehensible crisis. At a time when the overwhelming majority of Americans stopped their normal activities, watching television, listening to the radio, reading the newspaper, going online gave them the feeling of doing something, of being part of a national tragedy.

Second, people credited the news media, especially local television, radio, and newspapers in the immediately affected areas in and around New York, Washington, and the crash site in Pennsylvania, with assisting crisis managers in communicating important information to the public. For crisis managers, the mass media offered the only effective means to tell the public about the immediate consequences of the crisis—what to do (for example, donate blood of certain types, where to donate and when) and what not to do (initially, for example, not trying to drive into Manhattan because all access bridges and tunnels were closed). In this respect, the media served the public interest in the best tradition of disaster coverage (see chapter 11 on media and crisis management).

Third, Americans experienced a media—from celebrity anchors, hosts, and other stars to the foot soldiers of the fourth estate—that abandoned cynicism, negativism, and attack journalism in favor of reporting, if not participating in, an outburst of civic spirit, unity, and patriotism. From one minute to another, media critics and pollsters recognized a reconnection between the press and the public after years of growing division. As even the most seasoned news personnel couldn't help but show their emotions while struggling to inform the public during the initial hours and days of the crisis, audiences also forgot about their dissatisfaction with the media in a rare we-are-all-in-this-together sentiment. This explains the sudden high approval ratings for the fourth estate mentioned earlier. To be sure, there were some bones of contention. As Americans everywhere displayed the star-spangled banner, images of the American flag appeared on television screens as well. Many anchors and reporters wore flag pins or red, white, and blue ribbons on their lapels. Others rejected this display of patriotism. Barbara Walters of ABC-TV, for example, declared on the air that she would not wear any version of Old Glory.[32] When the news director of a cable station on Long Island, New York, issued a memo directing his staff not to wear any form of flag reproductions, there was a firestorm of opposition from viewers and advertisers. But even this incident seemed to fade after the news director issued an apology and it became obvious that the flag was not banned from the station's coverage.[33]

Fourth, the news provided public spaces where audience members had the opportunity to converse with experts in various fields and with each other, or witness question-and-answer exchanges between others. Whether through quickly arranged electronic town hall meetings or phone-in programs, television, radio, and online audiences wanted to get involved in public discourse. Many news organizations facilitated the sudden thirst for dialogue. While television and radio were natural venues for these exchanges, newspapers and news magazines published exclusively, or mostly, letters to the editors on this topic and reflected a wide range of serious and well-articulated opinions. Seldom, however, was the value of thoughtful moderators and professional gatekeepers more obvious than in the days and weeks after the terror nightmare. The least useful, often bigoted comments were posted on Internet sites and message boards.

Fifth, news consumers were spared the exasperation of watching reporters and camera crews chasing survivors and relatives of victims, camping on front lawns, shoving microphones in front of people who wanted to be left alone. In the 1980s, when terrorists struck against Americans abroad, the media often pushed their thirst for tears, grief, tragedy, and drama to and even beyond the limits of professional journalism's ethics in their hunt for pictures and sound bites. But this time around, neither the public nor media critics had reason to complain about the fourth estate's insistence on invading people's privacy and exploiting grief-stricken relatives of victims and survivors. This time, many husbands and wives, mothers and fathers, daughters and sons of disaster victims spoke voluntarily to reporters, appeared voluntarily, and in many instances repeatedly, on local and national television to talk about their traumatic losses. Many survivors described their ordeals and their feelings in touching detail. Most of these people were born and grew up in the era of television and seemed comfortable, in some cases even eager, to share their sorrow and their tears, their memories and their courage with anchors, hosts, correspondents—and many millions of fellow Americans.

Again, this was not the result of a changed and more restrained media but of a cultural change. Expressing one's innermost feelings, showing one's despair, controlled crying or sobbing before cameras and microphones seemed natural in the culture of so-called reality TV and talk shows with a human touch such as *The Oprah Winfrey Show* or *Larry King Live*. Thus, unlike past TV audiences who seemed exposed to ruthless exploits of grief during and after terrorist incidents, following the terror attacks of September 11, 2001, viewers participated in mass-mediated wakes, full of collective sadness and shared encouragement.

When the broadcast media played and replayed the recorded exchanges between victims in the World Trade Center and emergency police dispatchers, they exploited the unimaginable suffering of those who were trapped and soon died in the struck towers. Criticizing this practice as "primetime pornography," one commentator wrote,

> Can there be anybody on the planet who failed to immediately grasp the full horror of what went on Sept. 11 that they need to hear, over and over, the emotional mayhem of ordinary people trying to cope amidst overwhelming disbelief, fear and terror—not to mention grief? But in our show-and-tell culture there is nothing so private and sensitive that it can't be exposed and sensationalized—especially where ratings are involved.[34]

One can perfectly agree with this criticism and still wonder whether it should be mostly directed at the media or equally to an increasing segment of the public perfectly fine with dropping the boundaries between public and private. If anything, this trend toward public disclosure has intensified on social media networks.

Criticism of 9/11 Crisis News Aspects

Twelve days after the kamikaze attacks on the World Trade Center and Pentagon, media critic Marvin Kitman (2001, D27), commenting on the perhaps longest continuous breaking news event in the history of television, wrote:

> They [the TV people] kept on showing those same pictures of the planes hitting, the buildings crumbling. I'm sure if I turned the TV on right now, the buildings would still be crumbling. It never got any better. One picture is worth a thousand words, except in "live" television, where people felt compelled to constantly talk even when they knew very little about what they were talking about.

While the initial emergency coverage, especially in television and radio, deserved high marks, some of the infotainment habits that had increasingly made their way into television news crept rather soon into the presentations of what screen banners called the "Attack on America" or "America Attacked." Recalling the rather trivial headlines and cover stories before 9/11, one expert in the field suggested early on that "suddenly, dramatically, unalterably the world has changed. And that means journalism will also change, indeed is changing before our eyes" (Kurtz, 2001). As it turned out, this was wishful thinking. It is true that there was no longer the feeding frenzy on Congressman Gary Condit's private life, Mayor Rudy Giuliani's nasty divorce, or the meaning of Al Gore's beard for his political future, but that did not mean an end to the overkill and hype that characterized past reporting excesses, whether in the context of the O. J. Simpson murder case and trial or the accidental deaths of Princess Diana and John F. Kennedy Jr. Immediately after 9/11, when a series of unspeakable events were reported as they unfolded, and a day or two thereafter, when the enormity of the attacks and their consequences began to sink in, there was simply not enough genuine news to fill twenty-four hours per day. As a result, television networks and stations replayed the scenes of horror repeatedly, revisiting the suffering of people repeatedly, searching for emotions beyond the boundaries of good taste. As noted earlier, in their search for family members or friends who were among the thousands of missing in New York, many people pursued reporters and camera crews with photographs of their loved ones in the hope of some good information, some good news. While highlighting these photographs could be seen as serving a grieving community, dwelling on picture galleries of the victims was certainly not. One shocked observer recalled that "one of the yokels on Channel 2 showed pictures she had found in the street after the explosion and cheerfully pointed out 'that these little children may now be without parents'" (Kitman 2001, D27).

The shock over the events of 9/11 wore off rather quickly in the newsrooms, giving way to everyday routine. Some television anchors welcomed their audiences rather cheerfully to the "Attack on America" or "America's New War" and led into commercial breaks with the promise that they would be right back with "America's War on Terrorism" or whatever the slogan happened to be that day or week.

There were signs of bias that were especially upsetting to Arab and Muslim Americans who felt, for example, that the scenes of Palestinians rejoicing over the news of the attacks in New York and Washington were over-reported and too often replayed. In contrast to Palestinian celebrations, anti-American outbursts in Europe received little or no attention. For example, when fans of a Greek soccer team at the European Cup game in Athens jeered America during a minute of silence for the terrorism victims of 9/11 and tried to burn an American flag, no television news programs and only a handful of American newspapers (publishing only a few lines in reports about the soccer game on the sports pages) mentioned the incident.[35]

But the post–9/11 coverage raised far more serious questions about the proper role of a free press in a crisis that began with the suicide terror in New York, Washington, and near Pittsburgh and intensified when anthrax letters were delivered in states along the U.S. East Coast. Three areas, in particular, proved problematic.

The first of these issues concerned the videotapes with propaganda appeals by bin Laden and his lieutenants that al-Qaeda made available to the Arab language TV network Al-Jazeera. On October 7, shortly after President Bush informed the nation of the first air raids against targets in Afghanistan, five U.S. television networks (ABC, CBS, NBC, CNN, and Fox News) broadcast an unedited feed from Al-Jazeera that gave bin Laden and his inner circle access to the American public. Two days later, three cable channels (CNN, Fox News, and MSNBC) aired in full a statement by bin Laden's spokesman Sulaiman Abu Ghaith. Both tapes contained threats against Americans at home and abroad. Bin Laden said, "I swear to God that America will not live in peace before peace reigns in Palestine and before all the army of infidels depart [*sic*] the land of Muhammad, peace be upon him."[36] His spokesman warned that "the storms will not calm down, especially the storm of airplanes, until you see defeat in Afghanistan." He called on Muslims in the United States and Great Britain "not to travel by airplanes and not to live in high buildings or skyscrapers."[37] The Bush administration cautioned that these statements could contain coded messages that might cue bin Laden followers in the United States and elsewhere in the West to unleash more terror. But intelligence experts were unable to identify suspect parts in the spoken text or visual images. While the administration's argument that these tapes were vehicles for hidden messages was not credible, these videos contained terrorist propaganda. Students of propaganda have argued that propaganda of fear is most effective "when it scares the hell out of people" (Pratkanis and Aronson 1992, 165). But this is not what the administration argued. Prodded by National Security Adviser Condoleezza Rice, who warned that the hateful threats from the bin Laden camp could incite more violence against Americans, all American television networks agreed to edit future tapes and eliminate "passages containing flowery rhetoric urging violence against Americans."[38]

Not surprisingly, the networks' joint decision raised the question whether the networks had given in to pressure from the administration when they agreed to exercise this form of self-censorship. While the argument that the press in a democracy needs to fully inform citizens, especially in times of crisis and great danger, has most weight here, it is also true that the news media make decisions all the time about whom and what to include and exclude, or whom and what to feature more or less prominently in their broadcasts. In the case of the al-Qaeda tapes, after the first ones were aired excessively by some cable networks, subsequent tapes were under-covered. All of these videotapes should have been broadcast fully, and their transcripts should have been published in the press. The mistake was made initially when passages of the first bin Laden video were broadcast so many times with full screen or split screen exposure, when bin Laden and al-Qaeda loomed too large in the overall news presentations compared to other news sources and news developments. First overkill and then under-coverage in reaction to White House pressure were wrong calls.

A similar controversy arose over CNN's decision to join Al-Jazeera in submitting questions to Osama bin Laden following an invitation by al-Qaeda and the promise that bin Laden would respond to them. While a face-to-face interview with the man who openly praised the terrorism of 9/11 perhaps could have yielded valuable information—especially for U.S. decision makers—the exchange of written questions and answers was a far more questionable journalistic exercise under the circumstances. It was not even clear whether bin Laden himself or someone else would answer the questions. Nor was it clear whether all or selected questions would be answered. The better argument was on the side of critics. Why would an American TV network give Osama bin Laden airtime to present his propaganda? Why treat him as if he were a legitimate political actor?

Another issue concerned the media's sudden obsession with endlessly reporting and debating the potential for biological, chemical, and nuclear warfare in the wake of 9/11. As real and would-be experts filled the airwaves, some hosts and anchors were unable to hide their preference for guests who painted doomsday scenarios. This was common in broadcasts even before the first anthrax case in Florida made the news on October 4, 2001, about four weeks after 9/11. It was as if anchors and news experts expected the other shoe to drop as they went out of their way to report to the public that the public health system and other agencies were ill prepared to deal with bioterrorism and other catastrophic terrorism.

When the news of a Florida man dying of anthrax and subsequent cases validated these predictions, anthrax terrorism and other forms of bioterrorism moved higher up on the agenda of TV, radio, and print news. In less than a month, from the discovery of the first case on October 4 to October 31, the television networks and leading newspapers covered or mentioned the anthrax terror in hundreds of segments and stories.

The most serious bioterrorism attacks in the United States deserved headlines and serious, regular, in-depth coverage, but the attacks did not merit an army of talking heads who beat the topic to death many times over. In the process, public officials who tried to mask their own confusion, experts who scared the public, and media stars who overplayed the anthrax card contributed to a general sentiment of public fear and uncertainty. By shrewdly targeting major news organizations and two of the most prominent television news anchors, Tom Brokaw of NBC and Dan Rather of CBS (and perhaps Peter Jennings of ABC, considering that the baby son of one ABC news producer was diagnosed with exposure to anthrax bacteria following his visit at ABC News headquarters in New York), the perpetrator was assured massive attention even before the first anthrax letter hit Washington. Along the way, mass-mediated advice about whether to buy gas masks, take antibiotics, and avoid public places, and speculations over the next form of bioterrorism (smallpox?) or chemical terror warfare (sarin gas attacks, such as Aum Shinrikyo's attack in Tokyo's subway system?) fueled the nightmares of those citizens who could not switch off their television sets.

This concern was not lost on a few people inside the media. The political columnist Robert Samuelson (2001, A29) identified the greatest danger of journalism—"our new obsession with terrorism will make us its unwitting accomplices. We will become (and have already partly become) merchants of fear. Case in point: the anthrax fright. Until now, anthrax has been a trivial threat to public health and safety." Samuelson (ibid.) warned furthermore,

> The perverse result is that we may become the terrorists' silent allies. Terrorism is not just about death and destruction. It's also about creating fear, sowing suspicion, undermining confidence in public leadership, provoking people—and governments—into doing things that they might not otherwise do. It is an assault as much on our psychology as on our bodies.

Not many in the media listened. At the height of the anthrax scare, the media kept publicizing far more scary scenarios for terrorism of mass destruction. *Newsweek*'s November 5, 2001, edition was a case in point. The issue's extensive cover story, "Protecting America: What Must Be Done," described the most vulnerable targets for terrorist attacks as "airports, chemical plants, dams, food supplies, the Internet, malls, mass transit, nuclear power plants, post offices, seaports, skyscrapers, stadiums, water supplies." Collapsed into ten priorities "to protect ourselves" in the actual cover story, the described vulnerabilities read more like a target description for terrorist planners than useful information for a nation in crisis.

Finally, in taking a cooperative stand vis-à-vis the president, administration officials, members of Congress, and officials at lower levels of government during the immediate management of the 9/11 disaster response, the news media made the right choice. After all, the nation had to deal with problems it had never faced before. But suspending the adversarial stance for a limited time is one thing; to join the ranks of cheerleaders is another. While comparing the hands-on and very effective crisis-managing mayor of New York City with Winston Churchill during World War II was understandable under the circumstances, likening President George W. Bush (on the basis of his speech before a joint session of the U.S. Congress) to Abraham Lincoln during the Civil War and Winston Churchill during WWII, as some media commentators and many cited sources did, was quite a stretch. But nothing demonstrated more clearly that some reporters and editors had lost their footing than an article about Laura Bush as "a very different" first lady after the terrorist crisis began. When Mrs. Bush visited New York in her "new role of national consoler," a reporter concluded, "As the need for a national hand-holder has made itself evident, Mrs. Bush's role as a kind of Florence Nightingale at least comes as a natural one."[39] Even more farfetched was a comparison by presidential scholar Michael Beschloss, a frequent guest on political talk TV, who, according to the *New York Times*, compared "the first lady's sang-froid to that of Queen Elizabeth the Queen Mother during World War II. (The queen mother refused to leave London, against the wishes of her advisers.)"[40] Given this kind of hyperbole, even in the most respected media, it was hardly surprising that the news media's most important role in the democratic arrangement—that of acting as a governmental watchdog—took a backseat after the 9/11 terror attacks and during the anthrax scare.

When the Republican-controlled House of Representatives stopped its work after anthrax spores were found in Senator Tom Daschle's office (but were not yet found in the lower chamber of Congress), the *New York Post*, a conservative daily, called members "Wimps" in a huge front-page headline and chided representatives because they had "chicken[ed] out" and "headed for the hills yesterday at the first sign of anthrax in the Capitol."[41] Even for a tabloid, this choice of words was perhaps not the best; however, the substance proved on the mark in the following days, when government offices from Capitol Hill to the Supreme Court were closed while thousands of fearful postal workers in Washington, New York, and New Jersey were told by their superiors to continue working because anthrax spores in their buildings and on their mail sorting machines did not pose any danger to their health. At the time, two postal workers in Washington had already died of anthrax inhalation and several others had been diagnosed with less lethal cases. Yet, by and large, the news media did not question what looked like a double standard.

In late October and early November, when public opinion polls signaled that the American public was far less satisfied with the Bush administration's handling of homeland defense in the face of anthrax bioterrorism than with its military campaign against bin Laden, al-Qaeda, and the Taliban in Afghanistan, some in the media asked questions that needed to be answered and voiced criticism that needed to be expressed. In an in-depth piece in the *New York Times*, for example, John Schwartz wrote, "[If] there's one lesson to be learned from the Bush administration's response to the anthrax threat, it's this: People in the grip of fear want information that holds up, not spin control."[42] He cited critics who enumerated the reasons for the administration's "lackluster" performance, "Lack of communication between agencies, a lack of preparedness on the part of the Health and Human Services Secretary, Tommy G. Thompson, a former governor of Wisconsin with little background in medicine or science, and officials' tendency to respond in the same way they would respond to a mere political problem."[43]

If observers hoped that this piece, similar news stories, and commentary signaled that the news media began to slowly reclaim their watchdog role, especially on policies related to terrorism and, just as important, the administration's responses to terrorism, they were in for a bitter disappointment as described in chapter 10.

Notes

1. Quoted from Amy Harmon, "The Search for Intelligent Life on the Internet," *New York Times*, September 23, 2001, Week in Review, 2.

2. Michiko Kakutani, "Critic's Notebook: Struggling to Find Words for a Horror beyond Words," *New York Times*, September 13, 2001, E1.

3. "A Day of Terror: The Voices," *New York Times*, September 12, 2001, 10.

4. "After the Attacks: One Man's Account," *New York Times*, September 15, 2001, 10.

5. Cloud described his reaction as a guest on NBC's *Today* program on September 12, 2001.

6. The unidentified Canadian made the remark on the Canadian Broadcasting Corporation's program *The National*, September 11, 2001.

7. From *CNN Money Morning*, September 14, 2001.

8. John Updike, untitled contribution in "Talk of the Town," *The New Yorker*, September 24, 2001, 28.

9. Ibid.

10. Stockhausen's remarks and the reactions they caused in Germany were reported in "Attacks Called Great Art," *New York Times*, September 19, 2001, accessed April 1, 2002, http://www.nytimes.com/2001/09/19/arts/music/19KARL.html.

11. Lippmann explores the idea of environment and pseudo-environment (or reality and pseudo- or media-reality) especially in chapters 1 and 6 of his book.

12. Ibid.

13. Stockhausen is quoted here from Bill Carter and Felicity Barringer, "In Patriotic Times, Dissent Is Muted," *New York Times*, September 28, 2001. According to

the article, the Eastman School of Music's Ossia Ensemble canceled a planned performance of Stockhausen's work "Stimmung" scheduled for early November at New York's Cooper Union.

14. Governor Pataki made these remarks on ABC News' *Nightline* on September 14, 2001.

15. Quoted here from Associated Press reporter Robert Jablon, "Hollywood Think Tank Helping Army," accessed April 1, 2002, http://dailynews.yahoo.com/h/ap/20011009/us/attacks_hollywood_1.html.

16. The statement was written in Arabic, but an English translation was carried by the wire services and widely publicized in the media. See, for example, MSNBC, accessed September 26, 2001, http://www.msnbc.com/news/633244.asp.

17. Ibid.

18. Eventually, the hijackers released most of their hostages. Afterward, some European governments did free several terrorists from prison as demanded by the PFLP and thereby resolved the standoff.

19. The quote is taken from the translated transcript of a videotape, presumably recorded in mid-November 2001, and retrieved from the *Washington Post*, accessed December 13, 2001, http://www.washingtonpost.com/wp-srv/nation/specials/attacked/transcripts/binladentext_121301.html.

20. Ibid.

21. For the full text, see Peter Ford, "Why Do They Hate Us?" *Christian Science Monitor*, accessed April 1, 2002, http://www.csmonitor.com/2001/0927/p1s1-wogi.html.

22. To retrieve relevant transcripts from the Lexis-Nexis database, the following search words were used: "why they hate us"; "roots" and "terrorism"; and "terrorism" and "motivation." Each transcript was examined as to the relevancy of its content. While all transcripts retrieved for the post-attack period (September 11, 2001–September 29, 2001) addressed the reasons for anti-American sentiments in the Arab and Muslim world, those retrieved for the pre-attack period (January 1, 2001–September 10, 2001) did not include a single record that dealt with this problem.

23. For the full text of the document, visit Federation of American Scientists, accessed April 5, 2002, http://www.fas.org/irp/world/para/docs/980223-fatwa.html.

24. The document was written in Arabic. This translation was taken from "Full Text of Notes Found after Hijackings," *New York Times*, accessed April 3, 2002, http://www.nytimes.com/2001/09/29/national/29S/FULL-TEXT.html.

25. Quoted here from *People* magazine on CNN, September 29, 2001.

26. Robert D. McFadden, "Bin Laden's Journey from Rich, Pious Boy to the Mask of Evil," *New York Times*, September 30, 2001, B5.

27. Rick Bragg, "Streets of Huge Pakistan City Seethe with Hatred for U.S.," *New York Times*, September 30, 2001, 1.

28. The sudden bestseller was Jamal Abdul Latif Ismail's *Bin Laden, Al-Jazeera—and I*. For more on this book, see Donna Abu-Nasr, "Bin Laden's Past Words Revisited," accessed April 12, 2002, http://dailynews.yahoo.com/htx/ap/20010928/wl/bin_laden_s_words_2.html.

29. George W. Bush's fifty-four public statements during the period were retrieved from the Lexis-Nexis database in the political transcript category.

30. This statement by al-Qaeda's spokesman Sulaiman Abu Ghaith was aired by Al-Jazeera TV and U.S. networks. The quote was taken from the Associated Press's version, accessed April 1, 2002, as publicized on http://dailynews.yahoo and retrieved on October 10, 2001.

31. See the Pew Research Center for the People & the Press, accessed 1 April 2002, http://www.people-press.org/files/2001/09/3.pdf, which states: "Overwhelming support for Bush, military response, but . . ."

32. Walters revealed her "no flag" decision on *The View*, a talk show she cohosted. See Rita Ciolli, "Flags Raise among Media," *Newsday*, September 23, 2001, A39.

33. The station was Long Island Cablevision. See Warren Strugatch, "Patriotism vs. Journalistic Ethics," *New York Times*, October 7, 2001, section 14, p. 1.

34. "Comment: Broadcast News," *Wall Street Journal*, October 8, 2001, A25.

35. The *New York Times*, for example, mentioned the Palestinian celebrations in nine articles following the 9/11 terrorism; the anti-American incident in Athens received twenty lines of an Associated Press dispatch on its sports pages. See "Fans in Athens Try to Burn U.S. Flag," *New York Times*, September 23, 2001, sports section, 9.

36. Quoted here from John F. Burns, "A Nation Challenged: The Wanted Man," *New York Times*, October 8, 2001, A1.

37. Quoted in Susan Sachs and Bill Carter, "A Nation Challenged: Al Qaeda. Bin Laden Spokesman Threatens Westerners at Home and in the Gulf," *New York Times*, October 14, 2001, section 1B, 1.

38. Bill Carter and Felicity Barringer, "A Nation Challenged: The Coverage," *New York Times*, October 11, 2001, A1.

39. Alex Kuczynski, "A Very Different Laura Bush," *New York Times*, September 30, 2001, sect. 9, 1 and 7.

40. Ibid.

41. Deborah Orin and Brian Blomquist, "Anthrax Plays to Empty House," *New York Post*, October 18, 2001, 5.

42. John Schwartz, "Efforts to Calm the Nation's Fears Spin out of Control," *New York Times*, October 28, 2001, section 4, 1 and 2.

43. Ibid.

7

Terrorism and Mass-Mediated Gender Stereotypes

In 1994, after a worldwide manhunt and numerous escapes, the notorious "Carlos the Jackal" (Ilich Ramirez Sanchez) was caught and sentenced to prison for life, following several already incarcerated members of his "harem," his many female lovers (some of whom were aware of his exploits—and each other—and some of whom weren't). Carlos is believed responsible for as many as 90 murders in the name of insurgent causes. . . . Meanwhile, this year, at age 52, Carlos announced plans to wed his attorney, Isabelle Coutant-Peyre, at the La Sante State Prison in Paris; she confirmed the plans, saying, "It is a meeting of hearts and of minds."

—Robin Morgan (2001, xv)

On the morning of January 27, 2002, more than a thousand Palestinian women came to hear Yasser Arafat speak in his compound in Ramallah. It was an address intended specifically for them. To thunderous applause and cheers, Arafat stressed the importance of the woman's role in the Intifada. . . . "Women and men are equal," he proclaimed with his hands raised above his head and his fingers forked in a sign of victory. "You are my army of roses that will crush Israeli tanks. . . ." What made this particular speech different—and changed forever the nature of the Palestinian-Israeli conflict—was a phrase he used, words that would become his mantra in the weeks and months ahead. "Shahida all the way to Jerusalem," he said, coining on the spot the feminized version of the Arab word for martyr, shahide, which previously existed only in the masculine form. . . . That very day, Arafat found his first shahida. On the Afternoon of January 27, 2002, Wafa

Idris, a twenty-six-year-old Palestinian woman, blew herself to pieces in a downtown Jerusalem shopping mall, killing one Israeli and wounding 131 bystanders.

—Barbara Victor (2003, 19–20)

In the second decade of the twenty-first century, many people in the West were surprised about the growing number of young Muslim men leaving the Western diaspora and traveling to the Middle East to become ISIS jihadists. Many people were shocked, not merely surprised, when increasingly Muslim girls and young women left Europe and the United States, making their way to Syria and the Islamic State. That most people reacted differently to the news about the growing recruitment of females than to reports about male recruits was hardly surprising. Although women have been among the leaders and followers of terrorist organizations throughout the history of modern terrorism, the mass media typically depicted in the past and continue to depict women terrorists as interlopers in an utterly male domain, framing them differently from their male counterparts. According to an article in *Newsweek* magazine published in 2002, "Testosterone has always had a lot to do with terrorism, even among secular bombers and kidnappers like Italy's Red Brigades and Germany's Baader-Meinhof gang [also known as Red Army Faction]" (Dickey and Kovach 2002). Here, the reader was explicitly told that terrorism is the domain of men, not of women.

Such claims ignore that throughout the history of modern terrorism, females have been among the leaders and chief ideologues (e.g., in the American Weather Underground, in Italy's Red Brigades, and Germany's Red Army Faction) and among followers of many terrorist groups. According to Christopher Harmon (2000, 212), "more than 30 percent of international terrorists are women, and females are central to membership rosters and operational roles in nearly all insurgencies." Other estimates range from 20 percent to 30 percent for many domestic and international terrorist groups. Typically, left-wing organizations have far more females in leadership roles and as rank-and-file members than conservative violent extremist groups. Yet, whenever a woman carries out an act of terrorism, most people react with an extra level of shock and horror.

These sorts of public perceptions dovetail with gender stereotypes in the news that are not found only in the coverage of terrorists; instead, gender frames are common in all kinds of reports, most of all in those depicting candidates for political office and elected or appointed public officials. Whether print or television, the media tend to report the news along explanatory frames that cue the reader, listener, and viewer to put events, issues, and political actors into contextual frameworks of reference. Framing can and does affect the news in many ways, for example, in the choice of topics, sources, language, and photographs. According to Entman (1996, 77–78), "a frame operates to select and highlight some features of reality and obscure others in a way that tells a consistent story about problems, their causes, moral implications, and remedies." Accordingly, reporters, editors, producers, and others in the news media make constant decisions as to what and whom to present in the news and how.

More than a generation ago, Gans (1980, 61) concluded that in the United States "the news reflects the white male social order." Although contemporary newsrooms are more diverse than twenty-five years ago, entrenched prejudices and stereotypical perceptions have not disappeared. As one newsman observed, "Newsrooms are not hermetically sealed against the prejudices that play perniciously just beneath the surface of American life" (Shiper 1998, 28). The result is that the media continue to use different framing patterns in the news about women and men. Research by Pippa Norris (1997, 6) revealed, for example, that "journalists commonly work with gendered 'frames' to simplify, prioritize, and structure the narrative flow of events when covering women and men in public life." She found evidence for the prevalence of sex stereotypes, such as the female compassionate nature and the male natural aggressiveness, that affect people to expect men and women to behave differently. As a result, "Women in politics are commonly seen as compassionate, practical, honest, and hardworking, while men are seen as ruthless, ambitious, and tough leaders" (ibid., 7). Moreover, by perpetuating these sorts of stereotypes, the news magnifies the notion that the softness of female politicians qualifies them for dealing capably with social problems and policies, such as education and welfare, but not with national security and foreign relations—areas best left to tough males. Although preferring "stereotypes of women politicians as weak, indecisive, and emotional," the news sometimes reflects the opposite image of the mean and tough female politician, the "bitch," who does not fit the conventional profile of the soft woman. Or female politicians are portrayed as "outsiders," the exception, not the norm (Braden 1996, chapter 1). Moreover, it seems that women are "most newsworthy when they are doing something 'unladylike'" (ibid., 4).

In the early 1980s, Crenshaw (1983a, 24) noted that there was "considerable speculation about the prominent position of women in terrorist groups" and that it would be "interesting to find out if female participation in violence will have an effect on general social roles or on the stereotyping of women." To what extent the roles and images of women in social, political, and professional settings have been affected by the significant number of female terrorists is difficult to assess but one doubts that there have been such effects. The growing literature on women terrorists puts forth a number of explanations why women join terrorist organizations and why they carry out political violence. Some of these explanations reflect reality and others are rooted in conventional gender stereotypes.

The same stereotypical patterns prevalent in the coverage of politics are also present in news reports about female and male terrorists (Nacos 2005;

Conway and McInerney 2012). Conway and McInerney (2012) contributed significantly to our understanding of these particular gender stereotypes by analyzing and comparing the news coverage of one American woman (Colleen LaRose, also known as Jihad Jane) and two American men (Farooque Ahmed and Daniel Patrick Boyle) who were arrested in 2009–2010 before they could carry out their unrelated terrorist plots. To begin with, the researchers found that newspapers in the United States and in the United Kingdom paid far more attention to the female would-be terrorist than to the male plotters, publishing a total of 267 articles about Jihad Jane, fifty-two about Ahmed, and twenty-two about Boyle. Obviously, for decision makers in newsrooms Jihad Jane was more newsworthy because she did not fit the conventional female stereotype and was certainly not "ladylike." Among the most persistent female news frames in the terrorist context are those devoted to a woman's appearance, her family ties, and, most of all, her love life (Nacos 2005; Conway and McInerney 2012). In the following I discuss each of these gender frames.

The Appearance Frame: More than thirty years ago, Leila Khaled of the Popular Front for the Liberation of Palestine was described as a trim and dark-eyed beauty with sex appeal. Even three decades after Khaled's involvement in terrorism, reporters dwelled on the attention she received as the first female hijacker because of her "beauty," her "pin-up" looks, and her "delicate Audrey Hepburn face" (Viner 2001). One interviewer told Leila Khaled three decades after her career as a hijacker ended, "You were the glamour girl of international terrorism. You were the hijack queen."[1] And well after Khaled had retired from active terrorist duty, a Norwegian newspaper made jokes about her "bombs" (Norwegian slang for breasts). Nothing changed in the following decades. A 2002 front page story in a leading U.S. newspaper about a female would-be suicide terrorist began with the following sentence, "Her nails manicured and hair pulled back from her face, the Palestinian woman asks that she be called by an Arabic name for a faint star—Suha." The next paragraph revealed that Suha, a future suicide bomber for the Al Aqsa Martyrs Brigade, "is barely 5 feet tall, fair-skinned and pretty, with a quick smile and handshake" (Zoroya 2002, A1). The up-front sketch of a beautiful young woman, determined to become a human bomb in order to kill others, was contrasted with the description of her bodyguard as "grim-looking." Whether intended or not, the reader of this article published in one of the leading U.S. newspapers, was left with the paradox of a pretty girl as suicide terrorist and a tough-looking male as presumably content to live.

A newspaper article about the first female Palestinian suicide bomber, Wafa Idris, began with the sentence, "She was an attractive, auburn haired graduate who had a loving family and likes to wear sleeveless dresses and make-up" (Walter, 2002). In another report Idris was described as a woman with "long, dark hair tied back with a black-and-white keffiyeh."[2] Concerning the wave of "Palestinian women strapping explosives to their bodies and becoming martyrs" the website of the Christian Broadcasting Network headlined its report, "Lipstick Martyrs: A New Breed of Palestinian Terrorists." The *New York Times*

(Greenberg 2002, A1) emphasized the similarities between a Palestinian suicide bomber and her Israeli victim, both girls in their teens, with the following
lead, "The suicide bomber and her victim look strikingly similar. Two high
school seniors in jeans with flowing black hair."

In their content analysis of 150 U.S. newspapers, Conway and McInerney
(2012) produced 251 appearance frames for LaRose, the female plotter, but
merely fifteen for Ahmed and eight for Boyle, the two male would-be terrorists. To be sure, at times news stories do mention details about the physical characteristics of male terrorists—most of the time in order to explain a
particular facet of their actions or of police investigations. When a report on
a male terrorist's prison breakout says that he is very slim, this information
may explain how he could escape through a small window. Information about
a male terrorist's hair color is most likely discussed in the context of color
change on the part of a fugitive or captured perpetrator.

The Family Ties Frame: When women terrorists are pretty, reporters wonder why they are not married or engaged. The young Leila Khaled preempted
such questions when she declared that she was "engaged to the revolution"
(Weintraub 1970, 19). This statement was often cited in reports about the
"glamorous" Palestinian terrorist. In the case of the unmarried ETA terrorist
Idoia Lopez Riano, the media linked the fact that this beauty was single to her
"mythical sexual prowess" (McElvoy 1995) and her alleged habit of "picking up
police officers, normally ETA targets, in bars and having one-night stands with
them" (Tremlett 2002, 13). But just as common are reporters' references to and
explorations of female terrorists' family backgrounds that might explain, or
not explain, their violent deeds. One instructive example is the catchy sound
bite "Black Widows" that the news media coined and repeated over and over
again, when reporting on female Chechen terrorists. By invoking the image of
the widow, clad from head to toe in black, the news perpetuated the image of
the vengeance-seeking widow who becomes a terrorist because Russian troops
killed her husband—a woman with a strong personal rather than political motive. To be sure, some of these women lost their husbands and others reacted
to the violent death or disappearance of their sons, brothers, or fathers. But
by lumping them together as "Black Widows" with personal grievances, the
media ignored that some, perhaps many, of these women were not at all motivated by personal but political grievances.

Returning to Conway and McInerney's research, they found 269 family ties
frames for LaRosa in the U.S. press although she had no close family members. Instead, there were many references to her boyfriend, her boyfriend's
father, her ex-boyfriends, and her ex-husbands. There were thirty-five such
news frames for Ahmed and 165 for Boyd. The large number of family ties
frames for Boyd was the result of frequent references to his two sons, who were
arrested with him and thus part of the same case.

The flip side of the for-the-sake-of-love coin is the girl or woman who acts
because of a lost love. When a twenty-year-old Palestinian student was recruited as a suicide bomber, she was reportedly "out to avenge the death of

her fiancé, a member of a terrorist group" (Bennett 2002, A1). She was said to believe that the young man had been killed by the Israeli military even though the Israelis reported that he had blown himself up in an accident. When reporting on one of ETA's leaders, Maria Soledad Iparraguirre, the news media rarely failed to mention that she allegedly became a brutal terrorist after the police shot her boyfriend in the early 1980s.[3]

The Love Life Frame: Related to the previous category is the popular image of the woman terrorist for the sake of love—not for deeply held political reasons. Supporting the notion that females are drawn to terrorism by the men they love, Robin Morgan has argued that most women do not want to admit to such a love connection. According to Morgan (2001, 2004), "These women would have died—as some did—rather than admit that they had acted as they did for male approval and love." Surveying a host of female terrorists and their relationships with male colleagues as well as the many affairs enjoyed by Ilich Ramirez Sanchez, better known as "Carlos, the Jackal," Morgan (2001, 208) concluded that women in terrorist organizations, whether followers or leaders, are involved in a "rebellion for love's sake [that] is classic feminine—not feminist—behavior." She told an interviewer that female terrorists are "almost always lured into it by a father, a brother or most commonly by a lover" (Mann 2001). For Morgan "Carlos, the Jackal" is the perfect example of a pied piper attracting females as a free man, fugitive, and prisoner. As Morgan (2001, xv) described it, "In 1994, after a worldwide manhunt and numerous escapades, the notorious 'Carlos, the Jackal' was caught and sentenced to prison for life, following several already incarcerated members of his 'harem,' his many female lovers (some of whom were aware of his exploits—and each other—and some of whom weren't)." Just as telling was the fact that the Jackal's attraction did not wane behind bars: In 2002, he announced his engagement to and soon thereafter married his French attorney Isabella Coutant-Peyre, a high-society figure, who characterized their love according to news accounts as a "meeting of hearts and of minds."

To explain the large number of female members of the German Red Army Faction in the 1970s, the news media also noted the love connection, citing typically male criminologists who said that "a few male terrorists and extremist lawyers in West Germany have had the fanatical devotion of female gang members" and that women join because they "admire someone in the terrorist movement" (Getler 1977).

Female members in white supremacy organizations, such as the Ku Klux Klan, themselves spread the word that most of them joined because of their husbands or boyfriends. According to one longtime female KKK member, a woman who uses the pseudonym Klaliff, "My introduction into the White Pride Movement (WP Movement) was in college where I fell in love with another college student, a man who had been an activist in the WP Movement." She reveals that many women got involved because they had a boyfriend in the movement. "I cannot speak for all women in the WP Movement," she wrote, "but I see the men in the WP Movement as manly men with strong ideals and courage."[4] The writer notes furthermore that she married her husband because of "his [WP] beliefs."[5] In the recent case of a young woman in Boston, accused of participating in a white supremacy bomb plot, the media reported that it was her romantic involvement with a former prison inmate that pushed her into a federal conspiracy (Cambanis 2002).

While often used to explain the motives of female terrorists, the love life frame is rarely present in the coverage of male terrorists. This discrepancy was confirmed by Conway and McInerney's research that found forty-two such frames for Colleen LaRose in the 150 U.S. newspapers they examined but none for the two male plotters Ahmed and Boyd. The researchers pointed to one editorial as "the most egregious example of 'terrorist for the sake of love'" framing with respect to LaRose, citing the following sentences:

> Colleen LaRose put a weird, midlife twist on the stereotype of the sixth-grade girl stuffing her bra with Kleenex in hopes boys will notice her. Except LaRose stuffed her hair under a hijab and sashayed onto the Internet as JihadJane. But she seemed more intent upon domestic bliss than domestic terrorism, the founder of My Pet Jawa told *The New York Times*. She used his site and others almost as a dating service, he said, "like she was looking for a soul mate."[6]

Deborah M. Galvin (1983) recognized both motivations guiding females making their way into terrorist groups, the-political-conviction path, and the-pull-of-a-lover scenario. According to some observers, these different motivations matter in the treatment of women within the group in that the politically motivated woman is treated "more professionally by her comrades than the one who is perceived lacking in this regard."[7] Thus, there have always been female terrorists who joined violent groups because of their love for a man, while others were motivated by political grievances and objectives. It is entirely possible that there were significant differences in the motivations of women from the Middle East and other Muslim majority countries when it came to their joining the Islamic State. As Nimmi Gowrinathan argued,

> ISIS' particularly inhumane violence can obscure the fact that the conflict in Iraq is also rooted in identity: at its base, the fight is a sectarian struggle between Sunni and Shiite Muslims, with several smaller minorities caught in between. It makes sense, therefore, that the all-female al Khansaa Brigade of ISIS relies heavily on identity politics for recruitment, targeting young women who feel oppressed as Sunni Muslims.[8]

Gowrinathan compared ISIS women with females in countries like El Salvador, Eritrea, Nepal, Peru, and Sri Lanka who joined terrorist groups because "they faced constant threats to their ethnic, religious, or political identities— and it was typically those threats, rather than any grievances rooted in gender that persuaded them to take up arms." Her point was that these women joined for the same reasons their male comrades did.

Yet, in the second decade of the twenty-first century, when young Muslim girls and women left Western countries to join the Islamic State, the motivation scale seemed to tilt in favor of the "for the sake of love" side.

ISIS Women Different from Females in Other Terrorist Groups?

Nobody knew for sure why a growing number of Western girls and young women traveled to a territory controlled by the terrorist organization ISIS. Nobody knew for sure why young women, used to the stability and comfort of Western societies, left their families and friends for lives in a faraway war zone to become the brides of ISIS fighters. Some observers suggested that these young females, just like young men, were the victims of online propaganda and brainwashing, turning the seemingly "normal" persons next door into religious zealots; others believed that young women, just like young men, were bored and sought adventure; still others thought that these young females came to admire Islamic warriors who were willing to die for their faith and for their religious brethren and that some of them fell in love with particular jihadists before meeting them in person.

ISIS's clever use of the Internet's many paths to spread their propaganda was certainly instrumental in convincing young Muslim men in the West to join the jihad (see chapter 4). Unlike Hamas, the religious Palestinian group that enlisted female suicide bombers for tactical reasons, ISIS did not invite women to become actual fighters in the so-called holy war or jihad. Like al-Qaeda before, ISIS appealed to Muslim women to marry a jihadist and bear his children. Commenting on the increasing number of young Western women joining ISIS, Melanie Smith of the International Centre for the Study of Radicalization told an interviewer, "Most of the women fit into two groups, those who travel with their husbands to jihad, and those who travel to Syria or Iraq to get married."[9] This was a drastic departure from the roles of women in Western Marxist groups as well as in other secular terrorist and insurgent groups, including the Colombian FARC and other Latin American groups. These women were involved in planning and/or carrying out terrorist attacks. Also, these women members of terrorist groups were well versed in the ideology of their respective movements, whereas many ISIS girls and women had little or no knowledge of Islam and ISIS's use of the Quran as justification for their reign of terror. After interviewing radicalized Muslim teenagers in the suburbs of Paris, a French journalist concluded, "They knew very little about religion. They had hardly read a book and they learnt jihad before religion. They'd tell me, 'You think with your head, we think with our hearts.' They had a romantic view of radicalism. I wondered how that happened" (Driscoll 2015).

ISIS Online Magazine without Women

Soon after al-Qaeda in the Arabian Peninsula began publishing the online magazine *Inspire*, the same group put out a glossy women's magazine titled *Al-Shamikha* (The Majestic Woman). The cover photograph shows a huge AK-47 machine gun and a woman covered by a niqab. Whereas *Inspire* was an English-language publication, *Al-Shamikha* was published in Arabic. But both online magazines were official al-Qaeda media projects. In their explanation as to why there was a need for a magazine for Muslim women, the editors wrote,

> Because women constitute half of the population—and one might even say that they are the population since they give birth to the next generation—the enemies of Islam are bent on preventing the Muslim woman from knowing the truth about her religion and her role, since they know all too well what would happen if women entered the field of jihad. . . . The nation of Islam needs women who know the truth about their religion and about the battle and its dimensions and know what is expected of them.[10]

By mentioning the prospect of women entering "the field of jihad," the editorial did not mean to signal the coming of female jihadists but rather the importance of their support of their men. Accordingly, the magazine's stories were full of advice for female readers along the lines of advice columns in Western magazines and newspapers. For example, there were articles about how to find the right husband (marrying a mujahideen), how to protect one's beauty (staying inside; covering the face), and, most importantly, how to play vital roles in the jihadist movement (encourage the jihadists to fight and become martyrs).[11]

The glossy online magazine *Dabiq* was established by ISIS as its official publication with the stated mission of communicating to Muslims factual and truthful information contrary to the content of the "Satanic" international media. Reviewing the first eight issues of *Dabiq*, I found that each was heavily illustrated with photographs but each one of these visuals depicted males only. When the images of children were shown, they were of boys in different age groups. In issue five there was a photograph of children, among them two little girls with head scarves—the only exception to the male-only rule.

So, in the official press organ of ISIS women did not exist. *Dabiq* was exclusively about brothers, muhajids, (male) martyrs, soldiers, warriors, and Muslims in general. The few times the typically long articles mentioned females they referred to women and children as victims of apostates or Crusaders. Then there were threats, explanations, and justifications concerning the role of female slaves and in passing a reference or two to "wives" as expressed in the following passage:

We will conquer your Rome, break your crosses, and enslave your women, by
the permission of Allah, the Exalted. . . .

Allah ta'āla said, "Successful indeed are the believers who are humble in their
prayers, and who shun vain conversation, and who are payers of the zakāh, and
who guard their modesty except from their wives or the [female slaves] that
their right hands possess, for then they are not blameworthy, but whoever craves
beyond that, such are transgressors."[12]

While ignoring women in their flagship publication, ISIS "brothers" out-
sourced the indoctrination and recruitment of Western girls and young wom-
en to some of the "sisters" already living in the self-proclaimed Caliphate.
Western ISIS women in Syria must have known fairly soon about the Islamic
States' views about the roles of wives and female slaves as expressed in the citation above but they did not mention this in their online posts. Instead, they
glorified ISIS's religious cause, the courage of jihadists and male martyrs, and
the responsibility of women to marry holy warriors and give birth to and edu-
cate future jihadists. For the ISIS leaders it was an important organizational
goal to attract and recruit women because "the presence of females provides
incentive to young male fighters high in testosterone but low on opportunities
to engage with the opposite sex" (Neer and O'Toole 2014, 149).

When Western females were ready to join, they asked for information
and received answers from women who were willing to give advice based on
their own experiences and decisions. One of the most often asked questions
was posted by teenagers whose parents were either in the dark about their
daughters' plans to join ISIS or refused to give their permission. In literally
all of these cases, the advice was categorical: Follow the wishes of Allah and
the Prophet, not the pleas of your parents (see chapter 4). It is noteworthy
that questions concerned the availability of beauty care in the Caliphate. Are
there hair blowers? Can I get makeup supplies? One teenager wanted to know
whether jihadists were only interested in beautiful girls. Obviously, these girls
and young women wanted to look their best for their men.

Communication, Para-Social Interaction, and Fandom

Six decades ago Donald Horton and R. Richard Wohl (1956, 215) coined the
term "para-social interaction" based on their observations about the relationship between mass media personalities and their audiences. "One of the most
striking characteristics of the new mass media—radio, television, and the
movies—is that they give an illusion of face-to-face relationship with the per-
former," they wrote. While for most people para-social interactions take place
side by side with actual social relationships, for some persons they become
their sole social life. As the authors (223) explained, for socially inept or isolated persons the media persona "is readily available as an object of love—especially when he succeeds in cultivating the recommended quality of 'heart.'"

Admiring audience members "play a psychologically active role which, under some conditions, but by no means invariably passes over into the more formal, overt, and expressive activism of *fan behavior*"[emphasis added] (Horton and Wohl, 228).

In the Internet age, social media platforms offer groups, movements, and individuals ample opportunities for mass self-communication (Castells 2009, chapter 2) and for the establishment and cultivation of para-social relationships with online audiences and particularly susceptible persons. The fans that today's originators of para-social interactions win over are no longer mere spectators but participants in virtual interactions tying them even closer to their idols and whole fan communities. Noting that "fan communities have long defined their membership through affinities rather than localities," Henry Jenkins characterized "fandoms" as "virtual communities, 'imagined' and 'imagining' communities."[13] While Jenkins wrote this with fan communities in the pop culture milieu in mind, his observations might be equally useful to explain female ISIS fans. Some news reporters and terrorism researchers recognized fan characteristics in female ISIS sympathizers and recruits. After interviewing Muslim girls in France who were devoted fans of ISIS in general and of ISIS fighters in particular, a French journalist concluded, "To them jihadists are like Brad Pitt, only better because Brad Pitt is not religious" (Driscoll 2015).

Social media posts revealed that young ISIS fans expressed great admiration for the Islamic State and its jihadists, not unlike the sentiments displayed by their secular peers' devotion to pop music stars or sports clubs. As for the young women, Melanie Smith called them ISIS-fangirls.[14] The Merriam-Webster online dictionary defines "fan" as "an enthusiastic devotee (as of a sport or a performing art) usually as a spectator" and "an ardent admirer or enthusiast (as of a celebrity or a pursuit)." When adding, according to the same dictionary source, that the term fan is probably a short form for "fanatic," it makes sense to consider these young Muslim women in the West as part of a virtual fandom community similar to fanatic fan groups devoted to sports teams, pop bands, or Hollywood celebrities. Based on their analysis of Twitter data concerning the 2012 edition of Eurovision's Song Contest, Tim Highfield, Stephen Harrington, and Axel Bruns (2013, 315) characterized "Twitter as an important new medium facilitating the connection and communion of fans." We can assume that the same is true for other social media platforms.

According to Gayle S. Stever (2009, 5), "People use media relationships to relieve boredom, fight loneliness, or give focus and direction to their lives. They look for romance, understanding, inspiration, communion and identity, meeting these needs through mediated relationships." Mareike Herrmann (2008, 81), who interviewed girl fans of popular music performers in post-unification Germany of the 1990s, argues that "fandom can empower girls because it offers a sense of control over and adds pleasure to people's everyday lives." She also found that actual encounters with fellow fans are far more potent than virtual community. To that end, Herrmann (2008, 97) writes, "My participants'

Boredom and the Quest for Adventure as Motives for Joining ISIS?

In early 2015, as more young Muslims made their way from the Western diaspora to the territory controlled by the Islamic State, questions about the motivations of these young women and men were asked in mass-mediated public debates. *Bloomberg View* columnist Eli Lake rejected the most commonly made explanations concerning economic deprivation, social discrimination, and the like. "Some young people—particularly those born far away from the conflict in the Middle East and North Africa—are just bored," he wrote.[a] In this respect, the pull of ISIS was nothing terribly new according to Lake, who explained,

> Radical Islam is hardly the first movement to take advantage of bored young people. Think of all the dreamers who flocked to both sides of the Spanish Civil War, or the utopians who volunteered to fight against great odds to create Israel. Then there was the first generation of holy Muslim warriors and foreign fighters who fought against the Soviet occupation of Afghanistan in the 1980s. Today the big historical draw for many bored young people is the promise of the caliphate.[b]

Interestingly, the notion of boredom leading to anger and aggression is supported by scholarly inquiry. As the authors of one research project concluded, "this study contributes to an improved understanding of how boredom proneness is associated with aggression, anger expression, and anger control. The propensity to experience boredom due to a lack of external stimulation was associated with aggressive behavior, dysfunctional anger expression, and impaired anger control independent of impulsiveness and sensation seeking" (Dahlen et al. 2004, 1626).

During a 2015 White House conference on violent extremism, President Obama also mentioned boredom in the context of young Muslim Americans who are targeted by the propaganda of terrorist organizations abroad. At one point he told the representatives of Muslim communities from around the country, "And by the way, the older people here, as wise and respected as you may be, your stuff is often boring—compared to what they're [ISIS and the like] doing. You're not connected. And as a consequence, you are not connecting."[c]

Notes

a.   Eli Lake, "State's Best Recruiting Tool is Youth Boredom," *Bloomberg View*, February 17, 2015, accessed February 25, 2015, http://www.bloombergview.com/articles/2015-02-18/islamic-state-of-boredom-how-jihadis-recruit-western-youth.
b.   Ibid.
c.   White House, "Remarks by the President in Closing of the Summit on Countering Violent Extremism," February 18, 2015, accessed June 2, 2015, https://www.whitehouse.gov/the-press-office/2015/02/18/remarks-president-closing-summit-countering-violent-extremism.

comments indicate that the fan experiences they have in public, when they go on ritualistic pilgrimages to material places that will place them in physical proximity to the stars, affect them differently than symbolic pilgrimages to imaginary places." One of the girls Herrmann interviewed described her attendance of a concert by her favorite band as "a kind of out-of-body experience" (ibid.). Some experts in the fandom field (e.g., Reeves, Roders, and Epstein 1996) have likened the strong fan attachment to cult communities and as quasi-religious, while others (e.g., Jenkins 2006) reject any association between fandom and religion. Still others (Herrmann 2008, 83) divorce fandom devotion from organized religious institutions but see relevance in "certain aspects of fandom to religious experiences."

These aspects of fandom seem to apply to the devotees of ISIS, their strong feelings for and commitment to the Islamic State, their admiration of jihadists, and the religious fanaticism they share with the objects of their love. Just as fans of pop entertainment get their "out-of-body" highs at actual fan gatherings, the most devoted ISIS fans tend to move from their virtual or para-social interactions to the actual and their ultimate fandom community—the Islamic State.

At first glance, there is seemingly no difference between young females and males who became involved in ISIS's cleverly staged para-social interactions. But whereas Muslim males enjoy a considerable degree of freedom and independence even in the most devout families and communities, their female counterparts, even when they are born and live in the West, are typically more restricted by religious edicts and cultural tradition in observant Muslim families. Strange as it may sound, by coming under the spell of ISIS and the prospect of becoming the brides of the group's devoted fighters, Muslim girls and young women make something like a declaration of independence by no longer obeying their parents and the moderate clergy in their local mosques.

Take the example of Hoda, a Muslim girl growing up near Birmingham, Alabama, who left her family and joined ISIS in Syria. She grew up in a household where the father was far stricter with his wife and daughter than with his sons. For example, while her father and brothers set up social media accounts, the females in the family were not allowed the same. But after her father gave her a smartphone, Hoda secretly utilized social media sites, established her own accounts, and became a fanatic ISIS fan. This and the flight of the twenty-year-old to the ISIS Caliphate rejected the influence of the authority figures around her; it was a decision to finding her own identity and determining her own social interactions. In the eyes of her father, the daughter was brainwashed but the young woman herself claimed in an interview from Syria that she had a religious awakening and that life was no longer "bland," but has now "much more meaning."[15] And then there may have been the allure of romance. Instead of letting her parents choose her husband, the young woman made her own decision. It was reported that she married an Australian jihadist and soon thereafter became his widow, the widow of a martyr in the eyes of ISIS women.[16] Becoming the widow of a martyr is not reason for grief and mourning but rather for joy and celebration. As one female ISIS devotee tweeted, "Allah Ah-kbar, there is no way to describe the feeling of sitting with the akhawat [sisters] waiting on the news of whose husband has attained shahadah [martyrdom]" (Neer and O'Toole 2014, 150).

As for Hoda, a spokesman for her distraught parents said in a public statement,

> It's often young, naive, impressionable, ignorant troubled youth who are dis-satisfied with their life and are seeking a sense of belonging. And it's frankly the same social factors that lead to youth joining various gangs. I think ISIS is just another gang.[17]

The characterization of ISIS as a street gang may not explain Hoda's attrac-tion to the Islamic Caliphate. While street gangs in the American setting tend to draw their rank-and-file members typically from the lowest social strata (Bell 2009, 365), Hoda grew up in a middle-class family and community. In one respect, though, the gang metaphor was appropriate in that female mem-bers of street gangs tend to defer to their male counterparts. As Steffensmeier and Allan (1996, 464) concluded,

> The aggressive rhetoric of some female gang members notwithstanding, their actual behavior continues to display considerable deference to male gang members, avoidance of excessive violence, and adherence to traditional gender-scripted behaviors. . . . The most common form of female gang involvement has remained as auxiliaries or branches of male gangs.

This arrangement within gangs seems quite similar to that within ISIS. As noted above, ISIS women acted increasingly as Internet recruiters and online jihadists who displayed threatening rhetoric. Hoda was among the circle of ISIS women who expressed their commitment to and fanaticism for the jihad. According to one report,

> "Terrorize the kuffar [derogatory term for non-Muslims] at home," she tweeted. "Americans wake up! Men and women altogether. You have much to do while you live under our greatest enemy, enough of your sleeping! Go on drive-bys and spill all of their blood, or rent a big truck and drive all over them. Veterans, Patriot, Memorial etc Day parades . . . go on drive by's + spill all of their blood or rent a big truck n drive all over them. Kill them."[18]

At the height of RAF terrorism in the 1970s, German security forces consid-ered female RAF terrorists more violent and brutal than their male comrades and allegedly advised each other, "Shoot the women first." Unlike those RAF females, ISIS girls and women were not directly involved in terrorist attacks, what the early anarchists called "propaganda by deed," but they are among the extreme online jihadists that spread what I call "propaganda by word." On that count, they may be as tough and convincing as male Internet-jihadists. Moreover, there were reports of female moral police squads whose members made sure that women in areas controlled by ISIS obeyed the strict dress and behavior codes laid down by the powers that be in the Islamic State. More shockingly, ISIS "established an all-female unit responsible for forcing captured Iraqi women into sexual slavery. Known as the al-Khannsaa Brigade the unit is reportedly comprised of Muslim converts from the UK who believe the mistreatment of Iraqi captives is justified because they are non-Muslims" (Neer and O'Toole 2014, 150). Like their other violent deeds ISIS propagandists justified this capture and abuse of female slaves with passages from the Quran.

Speaking at the 2015 White House Summit on Combating Violent Extremism, President Barack Obama said,

> Terrorist groups like al Qaeda and ISIL deliberately target their propaganda in the hopes of reaching and brainwashing young Muslims, especially those who may be disillusioned or wrestling with their identity. That's the truth. The high-quality videos, the online magazines, the use of social media, terrorist Twitter accounts—it's all designed to target today's young people online, in cyberspace.[19]

Not surprisingly, neither the president nor representatives of American Muslim communities provided new answers to the question why some of the young women and men in the Western Muslim diaspora are more susceptible to jihadist propaganda than are others. Nor was there a discussion of possible gender differences in this respect. After all, there are no uniform explanations that fit all.

Notes

1. Philip Baum interviewed Khaled for *Aviation Security International*, accessed January 3, 2005, http://www.avsec.com/leila_khaled__in_her_own_words/.

2. National Public Radio's program "All Things Considered," February 7, 2002.

3. See, for example, Giles Tremlett, "ETA Brings Women Fighters to the Fore." *The Guardian* (London), August 27, 2002, 13.

4. Klaliff, "Women in the White Pride Movement," accessed October 20, 2003, https://www.stormfront.org/writings/women.htm.

5. Ibid.

6. Conway and McInerney mention and cite here from Gwen Florio, "Women Tripped Up by Their Search for Love." *Philadelphia Inquirer*, April 25, 2010.

7. Library of Congress: Federal Research Branch, "The Sociology and Psychology of Terrorism: Who Becomes a Terrorist and Why?" September 1999, accessed June 1, 2015, http://www.loc.gov/rr/frd/pdf-files/Soc_Psych_of_Terrorism.pdf.

8. Nimmi Gowrinathan, "The Women of ISIS: Understanding and Combating Female Extremism," *Foreign Affairs*, August 21, 2014, accessed June 1, 2015, https://www.foreignaffairs.com/articles/middle-east/2014-08-21/women-isis.

9. Cassandra Vinograd, "Jihadi Brides Swap Lives in the West for Front Line with Syria Militants," NBC News, July 8, 2014, accessed April 15, 2015, http://www.nbcnews.com/storyline/iraq-turmoil/jihadi-brides-swap-lives-west-front-line-syria-militants-n150491.

10. Julius Cavendish, "Al-Qa'ida Glossy Advises Women to Cover Up and Marry a Martyr," *The Independent*, March 14, 2011, accessed May 20, 2015, http://www.independent.co.uk/news/world/asia/alqaida-glossy-advises-women-to-cover-up-and-marry-a-martyr-2240992.html.

11. Ibid and Anti-Defamation League, "Terrorism," accessed May 20, 2015, http://archive.adl.org/main_terrorism/as_shamikha.html#.VVo-WpNcA89.

12. "The Revival of Slavery before the Hour." *Dabiq* 4: 14, accessed April 14, 2015, http://media.clarionproject.org/files/islamic-state/islamic-state-isis-magazine-Issue-4-the-failed-crusade.pdf.

13. Henry Jenkins, "Interactive Audiences? The 'Collective Intelligence' of Media Fans," accessed May 21, 2015, http://labweb.education.wisc.edu/curric606/readings/Jenkins2002.pdf.

14. Vinograd, "Jihadi Brides Swap Lives," n2.

15. Ellie Hall, "Gone Girl: An Interview with an American in ISIS," Buzzfeed, April 17, 2015, accessed May 20, 2015, http://www.buzzfeed.com/ellievhall/gone-girl-an-interview-with-an-american-in-isis#.pwVlarMwA.

16. Ibid.

17. "Desperate Alabama Family: Woman, 20, Left to Join ISIS." CBS News, April 21, 2015, accessed May 20, 2015, http://www.cbsnews.com/news/desperate-alabama-family-woman-20-left-to-join-isis.

18. Hall, "Gone Girl," cit. n6.

19. White House, accessed April 20, 2015, https://www.whitehouse.gov/the-press-office/2015/02/18/remarks-president-closing-summit-countering-violent-extremism.

8

Political Violence as Public Entertainment

At 7:12:30 o'clock this morning, Leon Frans Czolgosz, murderer of President William McKinley, paid the extreme penalty exacted by the law for his crime. He was shocked to death by 1,700 volts of electricity. He went to the chair in exactly the same manner as have the majority of murderers in this State, showing no particular sign of fear, but, in fact, doing what few of them have done—talking to the witnesses while he was strapped in the chair. He said he was not sorry for having committed this crime.

New York Times, October 30, 1901

In a late-night appearance in the East Room of the White House, Mr. Obama declared that "justice has been done" as he disclosed that American military and C.I.A. operatives had finally cornered Bin Laden, the leader of Al Qaeda, who had eluded them for nearly a decade. American officials said Bin Laden resisted and was shot in the head. He was later buried at sea. The news touched off an extraordinary outpouring of emotion as crowds gathered outside the White House, in Times Square and at the ground zero site, waving American flags, cheering, shouting, laughing and chanting, "U.S.A., U.S.A.!" In New York City, crowds sang "The Star-Spangled Banner." Throughout downtown Washington, drivers honked horns deep into the night.[1]

New York Times, May 2, 2011.

News reports of Czolgosz's execution were extensive and quite detailed but they were tame in comparison to the ghastly images in the short docudrama "Execution of Czolgosz, with Panorama of Auburn Prison" that Edison Studios produced shortly after Czolgosz's death. Since he was not permitted to film the actual execution, producer Edwin S. Porter had actors reenact the capital punishment scenes. As film historian Tony Shaw (2015, 12) wrote about one of the earliest silent films about terrorism,

> It was a refined piece of work for its time, in other words, one that combined purposeful elaboration of plot with changes of scene, focus, and tone. It was also, to quote industry parlance, a sure money earner. Executions were a macabrely popular subject during the very earliest, novelty phase of cinema and few murderers had greater pulling power than Leon Czolgosz."[2]

Before long, movie producers discovered the allure of fictional terrorist melodramas that hyped the threat of violent extremists within the United States. "Few such films purported to explain the terrorists' behaviour [*sic*]," wrote Shaw (2015, 13). "Why should they when most people viewed cinema as a form of entertainment rather than education and when, by necessity, actions, not words or exposition, drove silent cinema?" Yet, even when produced and viewed as pure entertainment, these silent films exaggerated the actual terrorist threat and promoted the harshest punishment for actual terrorists.

News reports of bin Laden's end were extensive, detailed, and prominently placed in print and electronic media, but they were tame in comparison to the dramatization of the hunt for the 9/11 villain-in-chief and his violent demise as depicted in the Hollywood action thriller *Zero Dark Thirty*. The film opened in late 2012, received wide critical acclaim, and was a box office hit, but it also became controversial because it contributed to the idea that torture works in that tortured terrorists will spill the beans about crucial information, which will stop evil plots and plotters. The movie starts with the torture of a major al-Qaeda figure and the implication that information gained during that violent interrogation was instrumental in finding and neutralizing bin Laden. Among those who immediately protested against what they considered a non-factual association between information gained through torture and the capture of bin Laden were Senate Intelligence Committee chairperson Dianne Feinstein, a Democrat, and Senator John McCain, a Republican. But for those arguing for the efficiency of torture in the "war against terrorism," this movie provided welcome support for their position.

After reviewing terrorism-related Hollywood movies Thomas Riegler (2010, 43–44) concluded that Hollywood productions cannot be separated from the political realities of particular times. More specifically, he wrote,

> Although as exaggerated and deformed as Hollywood's interpretation of terrorism may be, the movies can be "read" in an insightful way: as a sort of "snapshot" of the cultural context from which they originate, what the cinematic texts tell us about prevailing mass fears, fantasies, and projections about terrorism. They represent the status quo of the public discourse at that time, reproducing hegemonic ideas promoted by many politicians, the media, or think tank experts.

Thus, both the meaning of terrorism and what is projected into it cannot be understood, without paying close attention to what is happening on the cinema screen. This "mirror(ed) image" of terrorism is revealing because ultimately it expresses certain dimensions we prepare to confront in real life: the specter of unspeakable atrocities, the notion of extra-legal violence to be employed against terrorists, or the establishment of a "state of siege" ending all civil liberties.

In this respect, there were no meaningful differences between motion picture blockbusters and TV entertainment. While Hollywood embraced all along the notion that extraordinary events, including heinous crimes and terrorism, call for extraordinary responses, this conclusion manifested itself in the dramatic proliferation of brutality and torture in prime-time network television following the 9/11 attacks.[3] Moreover, before 9/11 the bad guys were the ones displaying brutality; after 9/11 the good guys tortured—allegedly for the common good in the so-called war against terrorism. Typically, there was a ticking time bomb or some other kind of imminent attack and a captured suspect who knew of the plot. By torturing the villain, the episode's hero and his team would extract information that would be crucial in preventing another man-made catastrophe. Whether in fictitious TV episodes or in real life, Hollywood assumed that this was precisely what Americans wanted—protection from further attacks by evil terrorists.

Entertainment as "Adult Education"

Screen heroes, their successful ways of "tuning up" terrorists, and the fictitious ticking-time-bomb scenario influenced America's post–9/11 debate about homeland security and in particular about the treatment of captured terrorists or suspected terrorists—perhaps more than news reports (Kamin 2007; Downing 2007; Nacos 2011). Commenting on a tidal wave of motion pictures "so viciously nihilistic that the only point seems to be to force you to suspend moral judgments altogether," David Edelstein (2006) coined the term "torture porn" and recognized the possible impact of these sorts of movies in post–9/11 America. "Fear supplants empathy and makes us all potential torturers, doesn't it?" he wrote. "A large segment of the population evidently has no problem with this. Our righteousness is buoyed by propaganda like the TV series *24*, which devoted an entire season to justifying torture in the name of an imminent threat: a nuclear missile en route to a major city. Who do you want defending America? Kiefer Sutherland [Jack Bauer] or terrorist-employed civil-liberties lawyers?"

With few exceptions media and communication researchers tend to focus either on the news or on entertainment, not both concerning the same research project and topic. Yet, both observations and research findings suggest that film and television fiction are as potent as news media in affecting audiences' information about and views of public affairs. Nearly a century ago, based on his observations, Walter Lippmann (1997 [1922], 61) hypothesized that links exist between film images and movie-goers' perception of reality, when he wrote,

> The shadowy idea becomes vivid; your hazy notion, let us say of the Ku Klux Klan, thanks to Mr. Griffiths, takes vivid shape when you see *The Birth of a Nation*. Historically, it may be the wrong shape, morally it may be a pernicious shape, but it is a shape, and I doubt whether anyone who has seen the film and does not know more about the Ku Klux Klan than Mr. Griffiths, will ever hear the name again without seeing those white horsemen.

Seeing the tortured villain providing the information needed to prevent a catastrophic attack may equally become part of audiences' memories and reference points. As the Intelligence Science Board, a group of expert advisers to the U.S. intelligence community noted in its extensive 2006 report on interrogation,

> Prime time television is not just entertainment. It is "adult education." We should not be surprised when the public (and many otherwise law-abiding lawyers) applaud when an actor threatens the "hostile *du jour*" with pain or mayhem unless he or she answers a few, pointed questions before the end of the episode.[4]

Research confirms such observations. Michael Delli Carpini and Bruce Williams (1994, 793) found that participants in focus groups referred slightly more often to fictitious TV shows than news programs in political discourse about the environment. They concluded that "understanding the full impact of television on political conversations and on the public opinions formed during them requires expanding the definition of politically relevant television to include both fictional and nonfictional programming" because "when subjects draw on media in their conversations, they make few distinctions between fictional and nonfictional television." In their extensive and systematic examination of all kinds of media, Robert Entman and Andrew Rojecki (2000, 208) found, "Although we have distinguished between news, entertainment, and advertising, there is little reason to believe that such distinctions significantly shape people's responses. The *overall patterns* of images and information establish the mental associations, the schemas, used to process the social world. The most relevant differentiation is not between genres but between different patterns of communicated information and prototypes they construct."

The blurred lines between entertainment and news in audience perceptions exist as well with respect to terrorism and counterterrorism. Based on their research of post–9/11 television news and Hollywood entertainment like the American *24* and the British *Spooks* TV dramas Andrew Hoskins and Ben O'Loughlin (2007, 148) reckoned that "it is not surprising that when our audiences talk about news and actual events in the War on Terror, they lapse into dialogue about movies and TV drama."

In the twenty-first century, even more so than in the last decades of the previous century, the division line between news and entertainment media continues to get less sharp than some people still tend to assume—perhaps because of some obvious differences in the way the press and electronic media organize themselves. Typically, newspapers had in the past and still have today different sections for hard news and entertainment/art news; some print presses and some TV programs offer predominantly serious news—others, see tabloids and tabloid programs, provide mostly infotainment or entertainment. Television and radio networks, too, have news and entertainment divisions. In the golden years of television news, the three American TV networks ABC, CBS, and NBC tried in fact to separate news and entertainment by establishing a firewall of dos and don'ts between the two. The idea was that news divisions were charged with presenting public affairs news in the public interest and were not expected to be profitable; news divisions were rather financed by their well-earning entertainment brethren.

In this climate, the head of CBS News Richard Salant established rules that would be unimaginable in contemporary news divisions. One rule, for example, disallowed the use of music in a news report to make it more dramatic or more entertaining nor was it allowed to give in to television's need for visuals by recreating scenes to clarify what had happened if no such real images existed. According to Peter Boyer (1988, 15), Salant explained in his memos to the newsrooms,

> All of television's efforts, high and low, tumble into the American living room from the same tube, with no physical dividing line between *The Evening News* and *The Beverly Hillbillies*. Television journalists, therefore, had to make the distinction themselves, in their work. "This may make us a little less interesting to some," said Salant, "but that is the price we pay for dealing with fact and truth."[5]

When 9/11 happened, this understanding of television news was already a closed chapter in TV history. Thus, lacking compelling images of actual torture scenes, newsrooms used visuals of brutality as depicted in Hollywood motion pictures and television series to give viewers an idea of torture. For example, during a "live" TV town hall meeting on the pros and cons of torturing terrorists a few months after 9/11, anchorman Ted Koppel showed the audience a scene from the TV series *NYPD Blues* in which detective Andy Sipowicz brutally "tuned up" a suspect to make him talk. He was not the only news anchor hyping the then seemingly hypothetical debate about torture. On March 4, 2003, *World News Tonight with Peter Jennings* opened with a segment on "torture or persuasion" by showing a torture scene from the motion picture *The Siege* with Bruce Willis. The clip underlined that, as correspondent Jackie Judd said, "Hollywood's version of torture knows no limits."

While the distinction between news and entertainment and the avoidance of infotainment were probably never fully achieved, such efforts had fallen by the wayside to make room for the overriding corporate profit imperatives of giant media companies. As James Hamilton (2004, 7) has noted, "News is a commodity, not a mirror image of reality. To say that the news is a product shaped by forces of supply and demand is hardly surprising today." Not surprisingly, then, discussions concerning "the role of entertainment in news coverage all end up pointing to the market as likely media outcomes" (ibid.).

In his book *Amusing Ourselves to Death* Neil Postman (1986, 87, 88) was not at all concerned with market forces or the proportion of hard or public affairs news versus soft or infotainment news. Instead, he wrote that television "has made entertainment itself the natural format for the representation of all experience." This, in Postman's view, is the case for television entertainment and news. In Postman's words,

> Entertainment is the supra-ideology of all discourse on television. No matter what is depicted or from what point of view, the overarching presumption is that it is there for our amusement and pleasure. That is why even on news shows which provide us daily with fragments of tragedy and barbarism, we are urged by the newscasters to "join them tomorrow." . . . A news show, to put it plainly, is a format for entertainment, not for education, reflection or catharsis.

Similarly, after comparing life to a movie and recognizing that movies draw much of their material from real life, Gabler (1998, 4, 5) concluded that "the two are now indistinguishable from each other." Gabler characterized newscasts as

> "lifies"—movies written in the medium of life, projected on the screen of life and exhibited in the multiplexes of the traditional media which are increasingly dependent upon the life medium. The murder trial of former football star O. J. Simpson, the life and death of Diana, the Princess of Wales . . . the bombing of the federal office building in Oklahoma City by right-wing dissidents, . . . to name only a handful of literally thousands of episodes life generates—these are the new blockbusters that preoccupy the traditional [news] media.

Postman's and Gabler's characterization of television news as entertainment were echoed by communication scholars. Michael Delli Carpini and Bruce Williams (2001, 162–63), for example, wrote about the interchangeable characteristics of news and entertainment. "Despite the seeming naturalness of the distinction between news and entertainment media, it is remarkably difficult to identify the characteristics upon which this distinction is based," they wrote. "In fact, it is difficult—we would argue impossible—to articulate a theoretically useful definition of this distinction. The opposite of *news* is not *entertainment*, as the news is often diversionary or amusing (the definition of entertainment) and what is called 'entertainment' is often neither . . . all of the usual characteristics we associate with news of public affairs media can be found in other media, and those we associate with popular or entertainment media can be found in the news."[6]

The majority of Americans are not aware or do not want to admit that entertainment programs affect their understanding of public affairs, including terrorism and counterterrorism. A few months after 9/11, when pollsters asked survey respondents whether they "learn something about terrorist attacks or the war on terrorism from late night TV shows such as David Letterman and Jay Leno," 17 percent answered "regularly" or "sometimes," 23 percent "hardly ever," and 63 percent "never." Among eighteen- to thirty-four-year olds the result was different in that 24 percent told pollsters that they learned regularly or sometimes from late-night comedian shows about terrorism and counterterrorism, whereas 22 percent said hardly ever and 53 percent never.[7]

Hollywood as Supporting Cast for Washington's War Against Terrorism

Rejecting the conservative argument that Hollywood is "a den of leftist shills" Michael Parenti (2010, x) characterizes the films and TV productions of what he calls "make-believe media" as providing "political entertainment [that] makes political propagation all the more insidious" (1992, 3). Concentrated corporate ownership and the influence of the Pentagon, CIA, NASA, and other government agencies on war movies in particular ensure according to Matthew Alford (2010a, 4) that "Hollywood generates considerable sympathy for the status quo and, indeed, frequently glorifies US institutions and their use of political violence."

What Hoskins and O'Loughlin (2010) and others (e.g., Westwell 2010; Frank 2010) concluded after analyzing post–9/11 TV dramas and films is consistent with Alford's (2010b) "propaganda model for Hollywood" borrowed from Edward Herman and Noam Chomsky's (2002) propaganda theory designed for analyzing and explaining mainstream news media in the United States. After examining post–9/11 motion pictures Alford concluded that the propaganda model "is equally applicable to mainstream US cinema" and that, thanks to Hollywood entertainment "a cultural framework was laid for the war against terrorism that fitted neatly with the broader objectives and narratives of the US government" (2010b, 88).

One does not have to embrace the propaganda model to recognize that Hollywood's movie community reacted to the events of 9/11 like most Americans by rallying behind the flag and President George W. Bush's efforts to fight the terrorist threat abroad and at home. Given the popularity of television shows that dramatized the efficacy of "enhanced interrogations" in the war against terrorism, it was hardly surprising that the American public bought to one degree or the other into the fiction that torture could be used for a good end, namely the extraction of information to prevent terrorism; merely a minority rejected torture categorically. Indeed, the public's pro-torture sentiment was highest after bin Laden's death in May 2011 and after the release of the movie *Zero Dark Thirty* in late 2012 (see table 8.1).

Table 8.1
Torturing Terrorists and the Public

Do you think *the use of torture against suspected terrorists in order to gain important information* [emphasis added] can often be justified, sometimes be justified, rarely be justified, or never be justified?*

Date	Source	Often justified %	Sometimes justified %	Rarely justified %	Never justified %	DK/ refused %
2004	PEW	15	28	21	32	4
2005	PEW	15	31	21	30	5
2006	PEW	18	28	19	32	3
2007	PEW	16	31	23	28	3
2008	PEW	17	31	20	30	2
2009	PEW	17	32	19	27	5
2011	PEW	19	34	18	24	4
2013	AP/NORC**	18	32	22	25	3

Source: Author

*When the question was asked more than once per year by Pew, we present a yearly average (for 2005, 2007, and 2009).

** AP/NORC question's wording: *"How do you feel about the use of torture against suspected terrorists to obtain information about terrorism activities? Can that often be justified, sometimes be justified, rarely be justified, or never be justified?"*

Jack Bauer, the protagonist of *24*, became not merely a superhero in the eyes of many Americans but among Washington's decision makers as well. John Yoo, the lead author of the Justice Department's infamous "torture memos," wrote in defense of his role in the Bush administration's war on terrorism, "What if, as the popular Fox television program *24* recently portrayed, a high-level terrorist leader is caught who knows the location of a nuclear weapon in an American city. Should it be illegal for the President to use harsh interrogation short of torture to elicit this information?" (Yoo 2006, 172). His and the administration's answer, as reflected in the "torture memos" was in favor of torture, not "short of torture" although they called it "enhanced interrogation techniques."

Or take U.S. Supreme Court Justice Antonin Scalia. In a 2007 panel discussion on terrorism and the law in Ottawa, a Canadian judge said, "Thankfully, security agencies in all our countries do not subscribe to the mantra 'What would Jack Bauer do?' Scalia disagreed and argued forcefully, 'Jack Bauer saved Los Angeles. . . . He saved hundreds of thousands of lives. Are you going to convict Jack Bauer? Say that criminal law is against him? Is any jury going to convict Jack Bauer? I don't think so!'"[8]

It would be wrong to believe that merely conservative officials were fans of *24* and Jack Bauer. The truth is that he was a big hit with liberals, conservatives, and moderates; with Democrats, Republicans, and Independents. He was the hero who got the better of the "bad guys" in the best tradition of Hollywood narratives. As Carl Boggs and Tom Pollard (2006, 348) noted, in Hollywood terrorism is "reduced to the diabolical work of certain designated groups: Visual images, plot lines, musical scores, and sound effects merge to convey an epochal 'clash of civilizations' thematic, as shady personality types (irrational, fanatical, sadistic) hostile to the US occupy center stage." The embrace of this good-versus-evil cliché transcended partisan and ideological convictions.

Ex-president Bill Clinton is a good example for a liberal Jack Bauer admirer. During one of the Democratic Party's presidential primary debates, moderator Tim Russert of NBC News described the same unreal time bomb case that Britt Hume had posed to Republican presidential hopefuls and then asked U.S. Senator Hillary Clinton, "Don't we have the right and responsibility to beat it out of him [the terrorist]? You could set up a law where the president could make a finding or could guarantee a pardon."[9] Senator Clinton rejected the idea categorically. Russert countered that her husband, ex-president Clinton, had expressed support for torture in the case of a ticking time bomb threat.

A few days later, during his appearance on the NBC news program *Meet the Press*, Bill Clinton tried to dance around his previous position. When pressed by Russert to voice his opinion, Clinton said,

> The more I think about it, and the more I have seen that, if you have any kind of formal exception, people just drive a truck through it, and they'll say "Well, I thought it was covered by the exception." I think, I think it's better not to have one. And if you happen to be the actor in that moment which, as far as I know, has not occurred in my experience or President Bush's experience since we've been really dealing with this terror, but I—you actually had the Jack Bauer moment, we call it, I think you should be prepared to live with the consequences. And yet, ironically, if you look at the show, every time they get the president to approve something, the president gets in trouble, the country gets in trouble. And when Bauer goes out there on his own and is prepared to live with the consequences, it always seems to work better.[10]

Bill Clinton mentioned Jack Bauer no fewer than seven times in response to a multitude of questions about his wife's different position on torturing terrorists. Like many others in the general public and in the political class he bought into the "ticking time bomb" justification according to which an imminent threat of catastrophic terrorism calls for an otherwise illegal response—torture. As the comprehensive expert report on interrogation methods by the above-mentioned Intelligence Science Board noted:

> Most observers, even those within professional circles, have unfortunately been influenced by the media's colorful (and artificial) view of interrogation as almost always involving hostility and the employment of force—be it physical or psychological—by the interrogator against the hapless, often slow-witted subject. This false assumption is belied by historic trends that show the majority of sources (some estimates range as high as 90 percent) have provided meaningful

answers to pertinent questions in response to direct questioning (i.e., questions posed in an essentially administrative manner rather than in concert with an orchestrated approach designed to weaken the source's resistance).[11]

Whereas most Americans are familiar with Hollywood heroes fighting the war on terrorism effectively, few have read the 372-page report of the Intelligence Science Board or the 500-page executive summary of a shocking torture report released by the U.S. Senate's Select Committee on Intelligence.[12]

In post–9/11 America, even those explicitly charged with preventing terrorists from striking the homeland seemed in awe of Jack Bauer's successful on-screen fight against terrorists. After his failed attempt to bomb New York's Times Square on May 1, 2010, Faisal Shahzad was in police custody before he could leave the country. When New York City's Police Commissioner Raymond Kelly announced the arrest, he drew a comparison with his fast-moving fictitious colleague Jack Bauer. During a news conference, Kelly said, "Fifty-three hours and 20 minutes elapsed from the time Faisal Shahzad crossed Broadway in his Pathfinder to the time he was apprehended at Kennedy Airport. Jack Bauer may have caught him in '24.' But in the real world, 53's not bad."[13] Then Homeland Security Secretary Michael Chertoff spoke in his opening remarks at a Washington panel discussion (topic: 24 *and America's Image in Fighting Terrorism: Fact, Fiction or Does It Matter?*) about the difficult choices that Jack Bauer faced in his fights against terrorists, the need for Bauer to make risk assessments in the TV show, and how that "reflects real life."[14]

That seemed a stunning statement. But then, both episodes were reminders of how fact and fiction in news and entertainment intertwine in the minds of many Americans—including top officials in the homeland security and law enforcement communities. When film producers are asked about real-life consequences of their work, they tend to insist that they deal in fiction, not reality. Joel Silver, for example, defended violence in his movies (e.g., *Lethal Weapon*, *Die Hard*, and *Predator*) by arguing, "I mean, it's a western, it's entertaining, it's good guys versus bad guys. In that scene in 'The Searchers' when John Wayne went after all those Indians, was that genocide? Was that racist? When James Bond dropped the guy in a pond of piranhas, and he says, 'Bon appetite,' we loved that. That's a great moment. Movies are not real."[15] Howard Gordon, the lead writer of *24*, told an interviewer, "I think people can differentiate between a television show and reality."[16] And Richard Walter, the chair of the graduate screenwriting program at UCLA, rejected the notion that soldiers were getting training from television dramas. "Viewers are able to draw a distinction between entertainment and reality. It's pretend," he said.[17] Bok (1998, 37) rejects such arguments; she insists that "a killing in a movie is watched by real people on whom it may have real effects."[18] Similarly, one could argue that Jack Bauer and his brethren in their all-out fight against terrorists are watched by real people on whom it may have real effects.

Indeed, real people attested to real effects after personally witnessing reactions to Hollywood's favorite narratives concerning terrorists who reveal crucial information during brutal interrogation. Tony Lagouranis, a U.S. military interrogator in Iraq including the Abu Ghraib prison, revealed that he "definitely saw instances where people took specific ideas from TV shows . . . what we took from television was the idea that torture would work."[19] Diane Beaver, the top military lawyer at Guantanamo, said that in the search for an interrogation model that worked, Jack Bauer of *24* "gave people lots of ideas."[20] Concerned about his soldiers' admiration for action-hero Jack Bauer, Brigadier General Patrick Finnegan of the West Point Military Academy traveled to Hollywood and met with producers of the show. He told them that promoting illegal behavior in the series was having a damaging effect on young troops in an effort to get them to tone down those torture scenes.[21] The general got his hearing but was not successful at all.

Entertainment in the Service of Radical Extremism

In the summer of 2014, when a successful British rapper uploaded a photograph on Twitter that showed him holding a severed head before the background of the Syrian city of Raqqa, it was his disturbing message to friends and foes that he had joined the Islamic State or ISIS and in fact promoted the group's unspeakable cruelty. "Chillin' with my homie or what's left of him," he wrote underneath the shocking image. It shouldn't have come as a surprise that a rapper like Abdel-Majed Abdel Bary made his way to the Islamic State and became part of the organization's reign of terror. After all, even before the emergence of ISIS, Islamic hip-hop groups and rappers had spread their music and lyrics of hate and violence—mostly via the Internet.

While Islamic fundamentalists condemned Western popular culture for a long time as decadent, "radical Islamic groups have harnessed the influence of hip-hop in American and Western culture by producing their own [hip-hop] bands" that try to indoctrinate young listeners (Gruen 2006, 16). Terror rap is the most extreme form of this phenomenon and the British group Soul Salah Crew and their soloist Sheik Terra were one of the first performing in support of Arab terrorist groups. On and off available on the YouTube site, the group's first post–9/11 terror rap video was "Dirty Kuffar," which lauded the 9/11 attacks, Osama bin Laden, and terrorist groups calling for violence against Western leaders with lyrics like the following:

> Peace to Hamas and the Hezbullah
> OBL [Osama bin Laden] pulled me like a shining star
> Like the way we destroyed them two towers ha-ha
> The minister Tony Blair, there my dirty Kuffar [infidel]
> The one Mr. Bush, there my dirty Kuffar
> Throw them on the fire.[22]

"By current rap standards, Sheikh Terra and Co are not amazing; in fact, they are not even very good, just barely average. But the quality of the rapping is not an issue; it is the message they are conveying," the musician and writer Mehrak Golestan (2004, 10) wrote. "'Dirty Kuffar' is aimed at Muslim youths who reside in the West and walk the difficult line between the two worlds: a sensationalist piece of propaganda designed to further confuse the confused."

> The chorus to Yasser & Ozman's rap song "An alle Brüder" concludes with the line: "Together we fuck the shitty Americans." Yasser Gowayed begins the rap with the explanation: "This is to all Americans, who have something against us; to all Zionists, dude; only the ones who don't like us . . . and fuck Israel!" Austrian authorities incarcerated the young Egyptian man for inciting terrorist activities based on the lyrics of this song. This is the most recent, and perhaps most shocking, development within the youth groups of Brigittenau and other working-class districts in Vienna and elsewhere in Austria and Europe: Hundreds of them are attracted to terrorism, Salafatism, and jihadism. During the summer of 2014 some teenagers attempted to provoke the stuffy and tame Viennese soul by publically stating "Once Ramadan is over, we'll come and get you infidels!" and similar confrontational avowals.

With the sentences above Barbara Franz (2015, 177) described the dark side of the European and especially Austrian underground hip-hop scene. But in her in-depth study of second-generation immigrants in a working-class district of Vienna, Franz (2015, chapter 4) found also a brighter side of the hip-hop underground culture where young men and women found communality in creative meet-up spaces that ignored ethnic and religious differences. Here rappers created a community where young minority members found their self-worth and an acceptance of their identity. This was achieved because hip-hop devotees met and worked with members of other minorities and Austrian natives in a cooperative spirit that transcended multi-culturalism and embraced what one social worker and rapper described as "'a new interculturalism' in which cultures share a common space and associate respectfully with each other" (Franz, 199).

Arab Mickey Mouse as Voice of Hate

Long before terror rock came onto the scene terrorist groups discovered the power of entertainment as a tool to indoctrinate the youngest members of the communities they operated in. For many years, Hezbollah's global satellite TV network Al Manar and Hamas's Al Aqsa television have produced and aired entertainment programs for Arab children at home and abroad that encouraged boys and girls to hate Israelis, hate Jews, hate Christians, and prepare to become martyrs. An instructive example is Al Aqsa's program *The Pioneers of Tomorrow* that borrows from Western children's favorites, such as Mickey

Mouse, Donald Duck, Barney, and other popular figures to indoctrinate the young audience. Typically, when one of those lovable animals is killed by evil Israelis, the mourning children believe the propaganda narratives they are spoon-fed. One particularly manipulative program shown by Al Aqsa TV glorified a real female suicide bomber pretending to show her young daughter and son. First the daughter laments the death of the mother who cannot hold her in her arms; but eventually the girl praises her mother's sacrifice and pledges to follow her example doing even more harm to the enemy than her mom.

No wonder that a vast majority of Palestinian children want to be martyrs when they grow up.[23]

White Power Rock as Tune of Hate

Extremists in the Arab and Muslim world are not the only ones who use entertainment for spreading their ideology in order to win supporters and new members. Hundreds of white supremacists and neo-Nazi bands and rockers in Europe, North and South America, Australia, and elsewhere have disseminated for many decades their messages of hate targeting all non-Caucasians but most of all Jews, blacks, and more recently Muslims in what they consider "our" countries.

Take the case of Wade Michael Page, who in the summer of 2012 shot to death six people and injured four others as they worshipped at a Sikh temple in Oak Creek, Wisconsin. The forty-year-old Page shot himself after the lethal shooting spree. Obviously, he wrongly believed that his Sikh targets were Muslims. According to one account, Page "was so furious after the Sept. 11 attacks that he thought the U.S. should just bomb Middle Eastern countries to smithereens. Most of his hate rhetoric, though, was directed toward Jews and blacks."[24] Page was a white supremacist and a member of the most notorious skinhead organization Hammerskin Nation, a longtime promoter of white power rock bands, and an organizer of neo-Nazi music festivals.[25] Most of all, it was white power rock music and its violent lyrics that drew Page into violent extremism. As one source described it, Page "played on the festival circuit with racist skinhead bands including 13 Knots and Definite Hate. Definite Hate produced an album called "Violent Victory," whose cover showed a disembodied white arm punching a black man in the face, with blood spurting out. Page formed End Apathy in 2005 and promoted it, along with Definite Hate, on Stormfront, the largest neo-Nazi Web forum."[26]

One of the first and most popular white power rock bands was Skrewdriver, founded by Ian Stuart Donaldson, who took his band from playing non-political punk rock to extreme neo-Nazi songs. Although Donaldson's death in 1993 was the beginning of the end for his band, Skrewdriver videos and CDs remained best sellers of several labels specializing in white power rock. Anti-Semitic, anti-black, and anti-non-white-immigrants vitriol was and remains the most common theme in the lyrics. Here are some descriptions of typical lyrics:

> *Anti-Semitic Themes:* One song by the group Final War (California), for ex-
> ample, condemns a "feeble minded fool" who has hung up his skinhead boots
> "to join the Zionist rule." Many songs perpetuate anti-Semitic stereotypes. A
> song by the hate music group Squadron (Australia), "Our Time Will Come,"
> uses such stereotypes as a call to action: "Sick and tired of watching the Zionists
> control and gain/Rich men on our TV screens looking so vain/Raping our na-
> tions, They take what they want/Join up now, join in the fight, it's time that they
> were stopped." Others are even more explicit, such as the Nokturnal Mortum
> (Ukraine) song, "The Call of Aryan Spirit," whose English translation reads:
> "Everything I own/Is given to the damned Jewish tribe /My Blood is calling me,
> and I won't calm down /Until I taste the smell of their blood."

> *Racist Themes:* All non-whites are potential subjects for hate music, but hate
> music especially targets African Americans and non-white immigrants. "Re-
> patriation," a song from Final War, rages against such immigrants by stating
> that "One way or another the evil has crept in/They are pouring through the
> floodgates again and again/It's time to close them up and shut them out/We are
> here to put an end to it, so we shout!" Some songs are crudely brutal, such as
> the Grinded Nig (Texas) song "Splatterday, Nigger Day": "Drive around in my
> van/We want to kill a nigger/They are in the city/Follow one into the alley/We
> all attack the nigger/He has seen his last day."[27]

After demand for this sort of music declined and several of the white power rock labels folded in the early twenty-first century, the digital marketplace kept selling the hate voices of these bands. The Southern Poverty Law Center (SPLC), which investigates and exposes hate groups, reported that in Septem-ber 2014 Apple's iTunes offerings "included at least 54 racist bands . . . across the spectrum of hate music, ranging from established acts like Skrewdriver, the Bully Boys and Max Resist to little-known, DIY groups."[28] Soon after the SPLC report was published, iTunes began to remove the most offensive white power rock products from its services but at the time other online retailers did not follow Apple's example. In mid-2015, CDs of bands like Skrewdriver and The Bully Boys were still sold by Amazon and a host of other e-retailers.

Poet and Propagandist for the Islamic State

In spite of the Islamic State's male supremacy culture the organization elevated a Syrian woman, Ahlam al-Nasr, to its much admired and promoted poet in residence. A selection of her poems, all written in Arabic, was published in a book titled *The Blaze of Truth*. These poems were also sung a cappella and, for a while, in video form available on YouTube. Whatever her talents as a poet were, al-Nasr was most of all a pop artist in the service of ISIS propaganda. As Robyn Creswell and Bernard Haykel (2015, 102) wrote,

Al-Nasr fled [from Assad's Syria] to one of the Gulf states but returned to Syria last year, arriving in Rappa, the de-facto capital of ISIS, in early fall. She soon became a kind of court poet, and an official propagandist for the Islamic State. She has written poems in praise of Abu Bakr al-Baghdadi, the self-styled Caliph of ISIS, and in February, she wrote a thirty page essay defending the leadership's decision to burn the Jordanian pilot Moaz al Kasasbeh alive. In a written account of her emigration, al-Nasr describes the caliphate as an Islamist paradise.

Whether poetry, lyrics of songs, beats of music, television series, or films, literally all entertainment forms can and are exploited to serve violent extremist ideologies and politics.

Notes

1. Peter Baker, Helene Cooper, and Mark Mazetti, "Bin Laden Is Dead, President Says," *New York Times*, May 2, 2011, accessed February 25, 2015, http://www.nytimes.com/2011/05/02/world/asia/osama-bin-laden-is-killed.html.

2. The short, silent film is available on YouTube, accessed February 26, 2015, https://www.youtube.com/watch?v=FFbUVYWkbOA.

3. Whether dealing with terrorists or criminals, television drama series became far more violent and torture scenes far more numerous after the events of 9/11. In the four years before 2001 (1997 through 2000) there were forty-seven torture scenes in prime-time network television; in the four years after 9/11 (2002–2005) there were 624 such scenes, according to Human Rights First, accessed August 3, 2010, http://www.workersrights.humanrightsfirst.org/us_law/etn/primetime/index.asp.

4. Intelligence Science Board, "Educing Information," May 2006, ix, accessed August 10, 2010, http://www.fas.org/irp/dni/educing.pdf.

5. Peter J. Boyer, *Who Killed CBS? The Undoing of America's Number One News Network* (New York: Random House, 1988), 15.

6. Delli Carpini and Williams 2001, 162, 163.

7. Survey by Pew Research Center for the People & the Press, conducted by Princeton Survey Research Associates, November 13–November 19, 2001 and based on 1,500 telephone interviews. Retrieved April 6, 2014 from the iPOLL Databank, The Roper Center for Public Opinion Research, University of Connecticut, http://www.ropercenter.uconn.edu.ezproxy.cul.columbia.edu/data_access/ipoll/ipoll.html.

8. Reported on the *Wall Street Journal*'s Law Blog, accessed February 12, 2009, http://blogs.wsj.com/law/2007/06/20/justice-scalia-hearts-jack-bauer.

9. The debate took place at Dartmouth College, New Hampshire, on September 26, 2007, accessed 20 July 2010, http://www.cfr.org/publication/14313/democratic_debate_transcript_new_hampshire.html.

10. Excerpts taken from the Lexis/Nexis transcript of NBC News *Meet the Press*, aired on September 30, 2007.

11. Intelligence Science Board, "Educing Information," 95.

12. U.S. Senate Select Committee on Intelligence, accessed March 13, 2015, http://www.intelligence.senate.gov/study2014.html.

13. A transcript of Kelly's remarks is available at silive.com, accessed August 12, 2010, http://www.silive.com/news/index.ssf/2010/05/transcript_of_police_commissio.html.

14. Audio- and videotapes of the event are available at the Heritage Foundation, accessed February 25, 2015, http://www.heritage.org/events/2006/06/24-and-americas-image-in-fighting-terrorism-fact-fiction-or-does-it-matter.

15. Bernard Weinraub, "For This Movie Producer, Violence Pays," *New York Times*, June 14, 1992, accessed August 4, 2010, http://www.nytimes.com/1992/06/14/movies/film-for-this-movie-producer-violence-pays.html.

16. Jane Mayer, "Whatever It Takes," *The New Yorker*, February 27, 2007.

17. Barry Bergman, "Prime-Time Torture Gets a Reality Check," http://www.berkeley.edu/news/berkeleyan/2008/03/05_torture.shtml.

18. Bok 1998, 37. Howard Gordon, the lead writer of *24*, insisted, however, that people are able to differentiate between a television show and reality.

19. Bergman, "Prime-Time Torture."

20. Jane Mayer, *The Dark Side* (New York: Doubleday, 2008), 196.

21. Think Progress, accessed February 12, 2009, http://thinkprogress.org/2007/02/13/torture-on-24.

22. Available on YouTube, accessed May 30, 2015, https://www.youtube.com/watch?v=pWZd088e2Lg.

23. A pediatrician practicing in Gaza told me so. See also "ISLAM: Brainwashing Palestinian Children," accessed June 9, 2015, https://www.youtube.com/watch?v=FT6iKFQDEP4.

24. Marilyn Elias, "Sikh Temple Killer Wade Michael Page Radicalized in Army," Intelligence Report 148 (Winter 2012), accessed June 8, 2015, http://www.splcenter.org/get-informed/intelligence-report/browse-all-issues/2012/winter/massacre-in-wisconsin.

25. The Anti-Defamation League described Hammerskins as "the United States' best-organized neo-Nazi skinhead group, with the Hammerskin Nation website boasting six chapters in the United States and chapters existing in Canada, France, Italy, Germany, Hungary, Portugal, Spain, Sweden, Switzerland, New Zealand and Australia. The Hammerskins also have supporter chapters, known as Crew 38, in most of these countries, for those who do not seek membership but wish to show their appreciation."

26. Ibid.

27. Anti-Defamation League, accessed June 15, 2015, http://archive.adl.org/nr/exeres/32be45ea-7300-477d-bf3e-d01c0c56b809,db7611a2-02cd-43af-8147-649e26813571,frameless.html.

28. Keegan Hankes, "Music&Money&Hate," Intelligence Report 156 (Winter 2014).

9

Terrorism, Counterterrorism, and Freedom of Expression

In 2013, soon after Edward Snowden had left the United States for Hong Kong where he spilled the beans about the National Security Agency's (NSA) massive post–9/11 eavesdropping program to journalists, federal prosecutors filed a criminal complaint against the former NSA contractor and asked the authorities in Hong Kong to detain him. Snowden was charged with stealing "unauthorized communication of national defense information" and the "willful communication of classified communications intelligence information to an unauthorized person" under the 1917 Espionage Act. The same charges were repeated in a letter that U.S. Attorney General Eric Holder sent to his Russian counterpart Vladimirovich Konovalov when Snowden was negotiating for asylum in Russia.[1] While Holder assured the Russian minister of justice that Snowden would not face the death penalty upon his return to the United States, others wanted him tried and if found guilty executed for treason. Former CIA Director James Woolsey, for example, said on FOX News, "He should be prosecuted for treason. If convicted by a jury of his peers, he should be hanged by his neck until he is dead."[2]

∽

Calling Snowden a hero, Daniel Ellsberg, the leaker of the Pentagon Papers wrote, "In my estimation, there has not been in American history a more important leak than Edward Snowden's release of NSA material. . . . Snowden's whistleblowing gives us the possibility to roll back a key part of what has amounted to an 'executive coup' against the US constitution. Since 9/11, there has been, at first secretly but increasingly openly, a revocation of the bill of rights for which this country fought over 200 years ago. . . . That is what Snowden has exposed, with official, secret documents. The NSA, FBI, and CIA have, with the new digital technology, surveillance powers over our own citizens that the Stasi—the secret police in the former 'democratic republic' of East Germany—could scarcely have dreamed of. Snowden reveals that the so-called intelligence community has become the United Stasi of America."[3] *Jay Rosen defined what he called "the Snowden effect" as "direct and indirect gains in public knowledge from the cascade of events and further reporting that followed Edward Snowden's leaks of classified information about the surveillance state in the U.S." Media critic Rosen pointed to "journalists who were not a party to the transaction with Snowden" but who were now beginning to report on these matters.*[4]

∼

While Snowden was considered a traitor by some and a hero by others, there was no denying that he had laid bare U.S. intelligence agencies' widespread eavesdropping programs that violated basic civil liberties, among them the right to privacy and freedom of expression. Indeed, according to the leaked information the NSA broke into communications links of major data centers around the globe, enabling the agency to spy on hundreds of millions of American and foreign user accounts. What agents learned from intercepted conversations resulted in certain instances to charges of assisting terrorist organizations, plotting terrorist acts, or planning other terrorist-related wrongdoings and thus threatening America's national security.

In the post–9/11 era, the American news media contributed to a public debate and climate in which the tradeoff between protecting national security and safeguarding civil liberties tilted in favor of security at the expense of civil liberties, among them freedom of expression. Based on their research Douglas McLeod and Dhavan Shah (2015, 164) concluded that the framing patterns in the news and their effects on the public paint "a troubling picture of media's role in reducing tolerance and eroding support for civil liberties in an era of limited domestic terrorist threat and expanded government surveillance." In this case, there was no censorship or self-censorship involved; the reporting was the result of inherent news frames that favor the narratives of government officials—especially in perceived crisis periods; in other instances censorship or self-censorship affect media content; and in still other scenarios, journalists and other media personnel become the targets of threats and attacks.

This chapter discusses how different actors with roles in terrorism, counterterrorism, and media utilize different means to curb freedom of speech and expression. Some of the following cases and examples are drawn from the American setting; others concern liberal democracies elsewhere in the West as well as non-democratic systems in various parts of the world. While starting out with terrorists and how they target individual journalists and media organizations, most of the discussion deals with governments' efforts to curb terrorist propaganda and hate speech to control information, and with media organizations' self-censorship.

Terrorists against the Mainstream Media

As described in previous chapters, even in the age of social media the tradition-al news media continue to play a central role in the propaganda strategies and tactics of terrorist groups. As long as newspapers, news magazines, radio, and television as well as their online offerings remain for the majority of people the most important sources for public affairs news, terrorists need the mainstream media to further their propaganda objectives. Most of all, terrorists want to frame their narrative, their causes, their goals. While the mainstream media, simply by reporting about terrorism, unwittingly help terrorists to frame their narratives, they never satisfy those extremists. That is one reason that journal-ists, editors, cartoonists, photographers, and other media personnel are pre-ferred targets. Moreover, terrorists know that journalists held hostage or killed will guarantee extra media, public, and government attention.

In 2014 and 2015, when ISIS posted videos on social media showing the gruesome beheadings of American, British, and Japanese journalists, the world was shocked. That terrorists were singling out reporters as their vic-tims shouldn't have come as a surprise; it was nothing new. After all, in 2002 al-Qaeda operatives in Pakistan had kidnapped and decapitated *Wall Street Journal* correspondent Daniel Pearl. Or think of the dozens of hostages held by Hezbollah in and around Beirut through most of the 1980s; six of them were journalists. Whereas two American reporters, Charles Glass and Jerry Levin, two British journalists, Jonathan Wright and David Hirst, and one French TV reporter, Jean-Marc Sroussi, were able to escape, AP correspondent Terry An-derson, held for six years and nine months, became the longest-held captive and the last one to be released.

The kidnappings and killings occurred in the Middle East and South Asia, not in the journalists' homelands. But starting with the Danish cartoon con-troversy of 2005, cartoonists and editors and media organizations in the West who were responsible for creating and publishing material deemed blasphe-mous by many Muslims became the targets and victims of lone wolves and cells with or without direct ties to jihadist organizations.

The Danish cartoon controversy began when in September 2005 the news-paper *Jyllands-Posten* published a dozen cartoons most of which depicted the Prophet Mohammad. Editor Flemming Rose had commissioned the cartoons to highlight the European press's abrogation of freedom of expression in order not to offend Muslims. Cartoonist Kurt Westergaard had depicted the Prophet wearing a bomb in his turban. In the following years, Rose, Westergaard, the editorial offices of *Jylland-Posten*, and other newspapers that reprinted these cartoons became repeatedly the targets of terrorist attacks and plots. Even a dozen years after the cartoons were published Westergaard in particular con-tinued to live under police protection.

Among those presses that republished the Danish cartoons was the French satirical magazine *Charlie Hebdo*. Muslim groups sued the magazine for in-citing hatred but *Charlie Hebdo* was acquitted of those charges. In 2011, the magazine's offices were fire-bombed and several of its staffers along with Flemming Rose and Kurt Westergaard were put on a hit list that al-Qaeda in the Arabian Peninsula publicized. In January 2015, two gunmen shot their way into *Charlie Hebdo*'s headquarters, killing twelve staffers and injuring eleven others—in revenge for the magazine's repeated depiction of the Prophet Mohammad. Unlike other media in Europe, *Jylland-Posten* did not publish a single *Charlie Hebdo* cartoon. In 2005, the newspaper justified the publishing of the cartoons as taking a stand for freedom of expression; a decade of attacks and threats had made *Jylland-Posten* risk averse.

Several weeks after the massacre in Paris, in February 2015, a lone gunman attacked a cultural center in Copenhagen during a Free Speech event featuring the Swedish cartoonist Lars Vilks, another artist threatened by jihadists for satirizing the Prophet. The bullets did not hit Vilks but killed another man and injured three police officers, two of whom were Vilks's bodyguards.

For Muslims, insulting the Prophet is blasphemy punishable by death. And for many, not all Muslims, any illustration of the Prophet Mohammad is prohibited. Islamic values collide with civil liberties in Western democracies, namely, freedom of expression and press freedom. These opposing views have led to heated disagreements and in some cases to terrorist attacks.

Governments, Counterterrorism, and Free Speech

According to Article 19 of the UN Universal Declaration of Human Rights, "Everyone has the right to freedom of opinion and expression; this right includes freedom to hold opinions without interference and to seek, receive and impart information and ideas through any media and regardless of frontiers." While press freedom and freedom of expression are widely recognized fundamental civil liberties in democratic systems, neither constitutions nor laws nor declarations guarantee that these liberties are absolutist; instead, literally all nation-states take the right—in many cases supported by court rulings—to censor for the sake of national security, the protection of public safety, and privacy. While such curbs are more likely during times of war (in the American context, censorship measures were implemented most of all during the Civil War, World War I, and World War II), issues of freedom of expression can and do come into play in the context of terrorist violence and efforts to prevent further strikes. In particular, governments can and often do (1) censor terrorists' direct communications; governments can and sometimes do (2) limit communications carried by legitimate news organizations; governments can and do (3) suppress knowledge-based speech; governments can and do (4) withhold information from the press. Finally, news media can and sometimes decide to (5) exercise self-censorship.

Government Efforts to Censor Direct Terrorist and Hate Speech

Given the centrality of communication and media in the terrorist calculus as described in the previous chapters, silencing the voices of terrorists ranked high on the list of law enforcement. In nineteenth- and early-twentieth-century Europe and America anarchist newspapers were banned and some editors jailed. For example, after President William McKinley's assassination in 1901, Johann Most, the editor of the anarchist newspaper *Freiheit*, was convicted for publishing an article and thereby committing "an act endangering the peace and outraging public decency."[5] The article was a reprint of Karl Heinzen's fifty-year-old essay "Murder," which justified terrorism and had appeared in the September 7, 1901 issue—just one day after Leon Czolgosz shot the president. Although the defense claimed that no copy of the newspaper had been sold before the assassination, the judge ruled against Most, writing in his opinion:

> It is in the power of words that is the potent force to commit crimes and offenses in certain cases. No more striking illustration of the criminal power of words could be given, if we are to believe the murderer of our President, than that event presents. . . . It is impossible to read the whole article without deducing from it the doctrine that all rulers are enemies of mankind, and are to be hunted and destroyed through "blood and iron, poison and dynamite." It shows a deliberate intent to inculcate and promulgate the doctrine of the article. This we hold to be a criminal act.[6]

This was a remarkable ruling in that it made a direct connection between inflammatory, written words and somebody else carrying out a violent act. But ever since, different actors with roles in terrorism, anti-terrorism, and counter-terrorism utilized different means to curb freedom of speech and expression.

In the United States, the First Amendment to the Constitution prohibits the Congress from making laws that abridge freedom of the press and expression. Yet, during times of internal and external threats there was the adoption of sedition and espionage acts and a multitude of court decisions that did not rule out limits on those freedoms. The litmus test was established by the U.S. Supreme Court in a 1919 ruling according to which "*the most stringent protection of free speech would not protect a man falsely shouting fire in a theater and causing a panic. . . . The question in every case is whether the words used are used in such circumstances and are of such a nature as to create a clear and present danger that they will bring about the substantive evils that Congress has a right to prevent.*"[7] In the following decades, it became more difficult but not impossible for the government and other plaintiffs to satisfy the "clear and present danger" test.

The one case of censorship in the context of political violence/terrorism in recent times arose from the so-called Nuremberg Files—data of abortion providers and of politicians, judges, and other officials that support legalized abortions posted on the website of anti-abortion extremists or anti-abortion terrorists. Framed by animated dripping blood, the registry listed working "baby butchers" (names printed in black font), "wounded" abortion providers (names of those injured in anti-abortion actions grayed out) and "fatalities" (names of doctors assassinated by anti-abortion terrorists struck out). In essence this was a hit list that kept score of physicians killed and injured by anti-abortion extremists. The site encouraged visitors to "search for the office address of the baby butchers listed above" and lists the URL of the American Medical Association as a source of such information. In addition to physicians, the site showed lists with the names of clinic owners and workers, judges ("their shysters"), politicians ("their mouthpieces"), law enforcement officials ("their bloodhounds"), and of "miscellaneous spouses & other blood flunkies." If the inflamed language that accompanied the list was not enough to stir hate and militancy in supporters of radical anti-abortion actions, the gruesome images of the picture gallery of aborted babies may have done so. In the United States, abortion clinics have been the targets of hundreds of attacks, eight abortion providers were killed, and there were more than a dozen assassination attempts.

A Planned Parenthood organization on the West Coast sued the group responsible for the Nuremberg Files and the distribution of "Wanted" leaflets with the pictures of abortion providers in the area. A district court recognized the material as "clear and present danger" to the lives of those whose names were publicized, awarded the plaintiffs one hundred million dollars in actual and punitive damage, and ordered the removal of the website. However, a small panel of judges of the Ninth Circuit Court of Appeals set aside the verdict and ruled that the publication of the Nuremberg Files on the Internet fell within constitutionally protected free speech. The court held that abortion foes could not be held responsible for the possibility that their inflammatory Internet postings and leaflets might encourage some persons to commit violence against abortion providers and clinics. "If defendants threatened to commit violent acts, by working alone or with others, then their statements could properly support the [guilty] verdict. But if their statements merely encouraged unrelated terrorists, then their words are protected by the First Amendment. Political speech may not be punished just because it makes it more likely that someone will be harmed at some unknown time in the future by an unrelated third party."[8]

The full appeals court, however, ruled in a six-to-five vote that the website material amounted to serious threats and was not protected by the First Amendment; the court reinstated the original verdict including the order to remove the Nuremberg Files from the web. The U.S. Supreme Court refused to hear the case—although the very close six-to-five appeals court decision left doubts about the issues central in this case.

It did not take long for the same material and more drastic encouragements to kill "baby-killers" and the glorification of anti-abortion terrorism to reappear on the web (see chapter 4). Obviously, the close ruling discouraged further legal action by targeted groups—and the government did not take up the case either.

Nor did the U.S. government make efforts to challenge any publicized material that seemed to inspire terrorist violence. Take the example of neo-Nazi/ white supremacist William Pierce, who authored two novels. *The Turner Diaries* about white American supremacists' all-out war against non-white minorities and against the so-called the Zionist-Occupied (Federal) Government (ZOG) was the blueprint for Oklahoma City bomber Timothy McVeigh, who modeled his attack on the fictional bombing of the Washington FBI headquarters as described in Pierce's book. The book that Pierce wrote under the pseudonym Andrew Macdonald was for many years readily available at some bookstores and the leading online booksellers. The cover carried the publisher's warning, "This book contains racist propaganda. The FBI said it was the blueprint for the Oklahoma City bombing. Many would like it banned. It is being published to alert and warn America." More than a dozen years after Pierce's death, his book still sold well enough that in January 2015, the second edition of *The Turner Diaries* was according to Amazon "temporarily out of print."

Skimming through readers' reviews of *The Turner Diaries* at the Amazon site reveals that readers either hate or love the narrative of whites fighting and winning an existential war to protect the purity and dominance of their race against all non-Caucasians.

Other democracies do not have to overcome the same high constitutional hurdles as the United States to make laws against hate speech and what often comes down to the inciting of violence. Over the years, German authorities threatened and in some cases took legal action against Internet service providers that carried neo-Nazi websites. In France two interest groups won a court judgment against Internet portal Yahoo that ordered the American company to deny French web surfers access to e-auctions of Nazi memorabilia. When threatened with a fine of $13,000 per day, Yahoo obeyed the order by filtering out these sites for French Internet users.

A number of Internet service providers denied service to the most offensive among the many hundreds of hate sites originating in the United States and Canada without known government action. Thus, one U.S.-based neo-Nazi voice on the Internet complained that Geocities and other web hosting services as well as America Online "adopted policies censoring pro-White pages as soon as they can find them."[9] Kahane.org, the U.S.-based website of the extremist Jewish Kahane movement, whose political organizations Kach and Kahane Chai were outlawed in Israel as terrorist groups and designated by the U.S. State Department as foreign terrorist organizations, was dropped by its site's American server as well.[10]

But rejects can and do find alternative servers. Typically, these sites disappear when their content happens to catch the eyes of law enforcement and/ or hate site watch-groups but reappear with new domain names. But in many cases the driving forces behind the most offensive sites with terrorist speech are clever enough to refrain from *direct* calls for political violence against the targets of their hate and seem to stay in their public statements just within the parameters of their constitutional right to free expression.

Governments can enforce restrictions on free speech when actors operate in domestic and even regional settings; it is sheerly impossible to censor effectively even the most direct calls for violence when they come from transnational organizations and global networks of leaderless cells that use Internet service providers in remote jurisdictions.

While the appeal for violence is often implicit, the call to kill Americans and other Westerners has been explicit in many of al-Qaeda's and similar groups' communications. Take the fatwa or religious verdict signed by Osama bin Laden and four other radical Islamic leaders in February 1998. The document that was posted in several languages and on many websites—including American ones—contained the following call to violence: "The ruling to kill the Americans and their allies—civilians and military—is an individual duty for every Muslim who can do it in any country in which it is possible to do it, in order to liberate the Aqsa Mosque and the holy mosque [Mecca] from their grip, and in order for their armies to move out of all lands of Islam, defeated and unable to threaten any Muslim. This is in accordance with the words of the Almighty God."[11] More recently, ISIS and al-Qaeda affiliates have issued regularly direct death threats against infidels and appeals to followers to kill the enemies in their homelands.

There were not in the past and there are not today sure measures for governments to effectively ban this sort of material from all media—whether distributed via manuals, books, DVDs, or websites. As for social media, governments heightened their efforts to have content removed and to get information about accounts.

In the second decade of the twenty-first century, governments pushed for tougher counterterrorism laws in reaction to lethal terrorist attacks and foiled plots by jihadists in the West. Thus, following the attack on *Charlie Hebdo* staffers, the French government reacted almost immediately by writing broader new laws on phone tapping, planning to hire 3,000 new employees for the surveillance of persons with suspected ties to jihadists, and ordering prosecutors to crack down on hate speech and the glorification of terrorism.

But increased phone tapping and surveillance are problematic, as a project of the New York Police Department (NYPD) demonstrated. An NYPD cyber intelligence unit monitored for six years the blogs, websites, online forums, and phones of Muslim student groups in the Northeast. The unit produced several reports describing group activities, religious instruction, and the frequency of prayer by the selected organizations. None of those groups, none of those students had done anything to suspect them of sympathizing with terrorists or having extremist views. In all those years, the NYPD unit did not find any evidence of activities even remotely related to terrorist propaganda. So, the only reason for eavesdropping on group members was their religion.

What exactly does "glorifying terrorism" or the "glorification of terrorism" mean? In response to political violence carried out by the Red Army Faction in the 1970s and 1980s, Germany adopted legislation that criminalized the glorification of terrorism. Greece adopted a law prohibiting reporting on terrorists' communications during terrorist incidents. In the post–9/11 period the United Kingdom adopted a law that made the glorification of terrorism a crime. And in reaction to the October 2014 killing of a soldier in Ottawa the Canadian government proposed the 2015 Anti-Terrorism Act designed to criminalize the promotion of terrorism. The proposal was borrowed from the UK's prohibition of "glorifying terrorism." In France a law to rein in speech supporting and glorifying terrorism was adopted in late 2014 and aggressively enforced after the deadly attacks on *Charlie Hebdo*'s headquarters and a Jewish supermarket in Paris. The most prominent individual charged was the provocative French comedian Dieudonne M'bala M'bala, who wrote on his Facebook page, "As far as I am concerned, I feel I am Charlie Coulibaly." This was obviously a play on the popular slogan "Je suis Charlie" in support of the fallen *Charlie Hebdo* staffers. However, Amedy Coulibaly, a self-described jihadist, was the lone terrorist gunman who shot his way into the kosher market, killing three of his hostages. A court in Paris found M'bala M'bala guilty and gave him a suspended two-month prison sentence.[12]

In the United States, no law criminalizes the glorification of terrorism or speech that sympathizes with terrorists. When tried for terrorism-related offenses defendants typically are accused of either plotting and/or carrying out attacks but hate speech, justifying, and glorifying terrorism tend to play a role as well. Here are two examples:

- March 5, 2015: Khaled al-Fawwaz was convicted by a jury in a New York Federal Court of conspiracy in the 1998 deadly bombings of U.S. embassies in Kenya and Tanzania. Arrested in London in 1998, he was extradited from Great Britain in 2012. Featured prominently in court was that in the 1990s al-Fawwaz was al-Qaeda's media liaison in London where he established on bin Laden's order the group's media office, promoted motives and objectives, and made sure that bin Laden's declarations of war against the West were publicized.
- May 2014: Cleric Abu Hamza al-Masri was found guilty in federal court in New York for aiding kidnappers during a 1998 hostage-taking in Yemen; sending a recruit to jihadists in Afghanistan; trying to establish an al-Qaeda training camp in the United States; and other terrorist activities. "The defendant stands convicted, not for what he said, but for what he did," said U.S. Attorney Preet Bharara, describing al-Masri as "not just a preacher of faith, but a trainer of terrorists." But during the trial the prosecution emphasized the defendant's hate speech by playing video clips of al-Masri endorsing suicide missions and saying the killing of non-believers is permissible, comparing them to cows or pigs. In January 2015 he was sentenced to

life in prison. Before his extradition from the UK al-Masri was convicted there for inciting racial hatred and soliciting murder with his fiery sermons.

So far, the discussion focused on liberal democracies and their governments' efforts to censor terrorists' speech. What about non-democratic countries in this respect? As Freedom House data show, freedom of speech and press freedom continue to be curbed in a growing number of countries. Often this is done in the name of counterterrorism and national security. The 2015 report "Freedom in the World" noted, "More aggressive tactics by authoritarian regimes and an upsurge in terrorist attacks contributed to a disturbing decline in global freedom in 2014. Freedom in the World 2015 found an overall drop in freedom for the ninth consecutive year."[13]

Almost all states have constitutions and/or laws that support freedom of expression and press freedom but in reality in authoritarian countries these liberties are restricted for political expediency and/or religious and cultural traditions, and values.

Typically, opponents, critics, and protesters are labeled terrorists, arrested, tried, and found guilty. In Turkey, for example, the government considered Gezi Park protesters who opposed the removal of parkland in order to make room for building projects "terrorists" and the most common offense journalists were charged with was their alleged support of terrorism even though they merely voiced criticism of the government.

Or take a case from Jordan: In early 2015, using an amendment to the Anti-Terrorism law, a military court—not a civil court—sentenced Zaki Bani Rushaid, a Muslim Brotherhood official, to eighteen months in prison after convicting him of disturbing Jordan's ties with a foreign country. Rushaid had criticized the United Arab Emirates (UAE) in social media posts for designating the Muslim Brotherhood as a terrorist group. The UAE is one of Jordan's main financial backers and a close ally of Jordan. Rushaid's lawyers said in reaction to the verdict, "It's the death of freedom of speech and a sword that hangs over anyone who dares express his personal view."[14] It was interesting that the attorney for the Muslim Brotherhood, not a guarantor for freedom of expression, invoked precisely that.

The Freedom House 2015 Report documented that under the pretense of fighting terrorism and/or cybercrime authoritarian governments tightened their grip on freedom of expression and warned that "many governments have exploited the escalation of terrorism as a justification for new and essentially unrelated repressive measures. While a vigorous debate over how democracies should respond to terrorism at home and abroad is under way in Europe, Australia, and North America, leaders elsewhere are citing the threat as they silence dissidents, and shutter critical media."[15]

Information Potentially Useful to Terrorists

Less than two months after 9/11, the November 5, 2001 edition of *Newsweek* carried a cover story entitled "Protecting America: What Must Be Done?" that described the most vulnerable targets for terrorist attacks as "airports, chemical plants, dams, food supplies, the Internet, malls, mass transit, nuclear power plants, post offices, seaports, skyscrapers, stadiums, water supplies." The ten priorities "to protect ourselves" was just as much a list of attractive targets for terrorist planners.

Citing a list of similar articles with particularly alarming headlines, national security expert Dennis Pluchinsky condemned this kind of investigative reporting in an article published by the *Washington Post*. "I say the following with a heavy heart, but if there were an 'Osama bin Laden' award given out by al-Qaeda, I believe that it would be awarded to the U.S. news media for their investigative reporting," he wrote. "This type of reporting—carrying specifics about U.S. vulnerabilities—must be stopped or censored.[16] A week later, the *Post* responded to Pluchinsky's criticism and editorialized in his support:

> Mr. Pluchinsky correctly notes that reputable media organizations and highly skilled reporters are unwittingly doing the legwork for terrorists in identifying security vulnerabilities and interviewing expert sources to whom terrorists would be unlikely to have access. When national security is at stake, the media should not view the promotion of public awareness of security problems as an end in itself.[17]

In these cases and similar ones, no government actions were taken. Nor were there actions against the spread of detailed information about devastating methods of attack. A variety of potent homemade explosives is described in easily available books, such as *The Anarchist Cookbook* or *Home Workshop Explosives*. One customer reviewer of *The Anarchist Cookbook* wrote the following on Amazon.com's website:

> Almost all (with the exception of a few) of the things in here are accurate in the sense that they show you BASICALLY how to do something, but also in the sense that the way it tells you how to do it is so dangerous that it will most likely fail. . . . If you really want to know how to make homemade exploseives [*sic*] try "Home Workshop Explosives" by Uncle Fester, now that book is a real deal. This books [*sic*] techniques are tooken [*sic*] from military handbooks that date back to about 30 years ago!

But one doesn't even have to buy a book; instructions for putting together bombs were easy to come by in the past and still easier today. Following the pipe bomb explosion in the Centennial Olympic Park in Atlanta in July 1996, the CNN.com website carried a story that detailed in its text and an accompanying illustration how such a device is put together. Years after the initial posting, the same story was still available on CNN's website. However, while the CNN story seemed to provide basic information about the nature of pipe bombs unwittingly, other websites carried wittingly explicit instructions on building explosives such as Molotov cocktails and bombs consisting of fertilizer and fuel. It is amazing that this sort of information did not vanish altogether after a federal statute made unlawful the transmission of "information about how to build conventional and WMD explosive devices" as part of the 1996 Antiterrorism and Effective Death Penalty Act. The act was adopted in reaction to the 1995 Oklahoma City bombing. As noted in earlier chapters, in the age of al-Qaeda and ISIS, bomb making instructions are readily available in online magazines and found via links posted on social media.

What Laura Donohue has called knowledge-based speech goes to the heart of "information on its face innocuous, but which can be used for good or ill."[18] This is in particular information about biological, chemical, and nuclear research that could have devastating consequences if falling into the hands of terrorists. There are a number of laws on the books designed to prevent this sort of information falling into the hands of enemies going back to the Cold War era. One can only hope that these statutes can do the job.

Mainstream Media and Curbs in the Name of Counterterrorism

Following the Iran hostage crisis (1979–1981), Middle East expert Gary Sick observed that the situation "was the longest running human interest story in the history of television, in living colors from the other side of the world. Commercially it was a stunning success." Furthermore, he wrote, "It may never be known how many pairs of pantyhose and how many tubes of toothpaste were sold to this captive audience as a direct result of the hostage crisis, but the numbers are substantial." Far more troubling was that during the 444 days of that crisis and subsequent incidents in the 1980s during which Americans were held hostage, the news media provided terrorists unlimited access to print and airwaves to publicize their propaganda, whether they staged press conferences, gave interviews, provided their own film footage, or released communiqués.

The widely respected journalist and columnist David Broder suggested at the time that "the essential ingredient of any effective antiterrorist policy must be the denial to the terrorist of access to mass media outlets. The way by which this denial is achieved—whether by voluntary means of those of us in press and television, self-restraint, or by government control—is a crucial question for journalists and for all other citizens who share our beliefs in civil liberties."[19] But Katharine Graham, the publisher of the *Washington Post* and Broder's boss, did not agree. She argued strongly in favor of no press restraint at all when she wrote,

Publicity may be the oxygen of terrorists. But I say this: News is the lifeblood of liberty. If the terrorists succeed in depriving us of freedom, their victory will be far greater than they ever hoped and far worse than we ever feared. Let it never come to pass.[20]

While there was criticism of and self-criticism by the media in the United States after each so-called terrorist spectacular and while media insiders promised to heed the appeals for self-restraint, when the next terrorist incident occurred, there were no changes in the reporting patterns and no government efforts to curb this coverage.

This was different in other liberal democracies. As noted earlier, Germany was the first country to outlaw the glorification of terrorist violence. But as for the mainstream media, it was never defined what kind of reporting would be prohibited under that law. Greece enacted an antiterrorism law that gave prosecutors the power to ban the communications from terrorists following violent incidents. Editors who violated the law were indicted, convicted, and served prison terms.

But while some of these restrictions worked before the more recent advances in global communication and media networks, in the twenty-first century even governments with tough press laws cannot stop this sort of material from being publicized.

Take the following example: In October 2002, several dozen armed Chechen separatists took over a Moscow theater and held 850 people hostage—obviously, to put pressure on the Kremlin to listen to and give in to their demands. The Russian government moved quickly to deny the hostage holders access to the Russian media and particularly the airwaves. According to one observer, "the Russian Media Ministry issued warnings to several Russian news providers, and shut down the Moskoviya television station for its 'flagrant violations of the existing legislation' by broadcasting an interview with a hostage who called for an end to the war in Chechnya. The station was allowed to resume its broadcasts the next day."[21]

Yet, in spite of the press ministry's overall success in preventing the domestic media from carrying terrorist communications, the Chechens got their message across because comrades of the hostage holders delivered a pre-produced videotape to the Moscow bureau of Al Jazeera, not to a Russian media organization. On the tape, the Chechens demanded the immediate withdrawal of Russian troops from their territories and threatened to blow themselves and the hostages up, if their demand was denied. Shortly after it was delivered, the video was not only aired by the Arab satellite network but soon by other TV networks around the world as well; the text was available in many forms on the websites of legitimate news organizations. In one form or the other, the Russian public was soon informed about the very information that their government tried to suppress in Russia's mainstream media.

Germany has a blasphemy law that makes punishable by up to three years in prison public expression that discredits religions and/or religious institutions and thereby threatens public peace. Some other European countries have similar laws. In Germany, the *Charlie Hebdo* case triggered a debate about the law with three different views, namely, repealing the law, strengthening the law, or leaving the law as is.

Free speech advocates argued that not some satirical cartoon or criticism of religions but rather religious fanatics threaten public peace. They wanted to do away with the law altogether. The conservative Bavarian wing (Christian Social Union) of Chancellor Merkel's Christian Democratic Party (CDU) wanted a new blasphemy law with more muscle to prohibit ridiculing and insulting a religion (one suspects they had especially their own Catholic faith in mind). But the CDU and the Social Democratic Party (SPD), the governing coalition, decided to leave the existing law in place. There were similar debates in other European Union countries.

Media Self-Censorship

In the case of the theater takeover in Moscow, most of the Russian news media heeded the press ministry's warning that terrorist communication could play into the hands of the hostage holders by voluntarily "measuring out" this sort of information. While Western observers were quick to criticize this case of self-censorship in response to government warnings, governments in liberal democracies are also known to pressure news organizations to exercise self-censorship.

Following a series of bloody attacks and hostage takings by the Red Army Faction (RAF) in the 1970s, German media agreed to deny the terrorists access and to buy into the government's news management. After industrialist Hans Martin Schleyer was kidnapped in 1977, for example, this news management/self-censorship model worked. Although the RAF managed to get out more than a hundred messages with their demands and threats, the news media ignored almost all of them. Moreover, news organizations agreed to the government's request to publicize false reports designed to misinform the RAF about Bonn's true counterterrorist measures. For the duration of the hostage situation there was a news blackout of the incident.

Or a more recent example: A month after 9/11 and following a request that National Security Adviser Condoleezza Rice made during a conference call with leading news executives of ABC, CBS, CNN, Fox, and NBC, the networks agreed to edit future videotapes released by Osama bin Laden and to omit inflammatory passages and hate speech. Rice expressed concern that the videotapes contained secret messages for al-Qaeda operatives inside the country and could inflame Muslims abroad. There was apparently no resistance by the networks. According to one report, the agreement "was described by one network executive as a 'patriotic' decision."

It did not matter that no secret codes had been found to justify curbs on bin Laden's communications and that the Arab news network Al Jazeera and other foreign satellite networks showed the complete videotapes in the Arab and Muslim world. If there was opposition to the voluntary curbs, it was not reported and therefore not heard by the public. Dan Rather seemed to speak for many in the media when he said that this was an extraordinary time and therefore it was a reasonable solution for both sides.

More importantly, the U.S. media self-censored themselves in the months and even years after 9/11 by paying little or no attention to legitimate voices that challenged the Bush administration's counterterrorism policy, most of all, the lack of sound evidence for the false justifications for the invasion of Iraq. Nor did the influential media challenge the administration's propaganda campaign designed to overblow the threat of further terrorism as a means to enlist public support for the "war against terrorism." But that was a dramatic story for comprehensive books (Bennett, Lawrence, and Livingston 2007; Nacos, Bloch-Elkon, and Shapiro 2011; McLeod and Shah 2015).

Withholding of Information from or Denial of Access

Finally, in modern times, censorship has the meaning of withholding information on the part of governments and denial of access to the press from certain sites. Freedom of information tends to be curbed during times of crisis—including in the wake of major terrorist attacks and in the face of terror threats.

Much has been said and written about media access before and during military deployment and during occupation—mostly in the context of war, and, of course, including the "war on terrorism." But access issues arise also during hostage situations when news reports could (and have) tipped off hostage takers and endangered hostages and rescuers. Here, too, the technological advances have made it much more difficult to seal up areas because even an emergency responder may be tempted to use his or her cell phone to provide information to the outside world in this era of "citizen journalism." (For details about access issues during or after terrorist attacks or other disasters, see chapter 11.)

In conclusion, then, when it comes to terrorism and counterterrorism not only authoritarian governments but liberal democracies as well try to curb news deemed to be harmful to the national security in one way or the other. At times, such threat does not exist but is used to enlist support to particular counterterrorist policies (see chapter 10). In times of perceived crisis, the majority of the public tends to support government censorship rather than press freedom. Thus, at the end of November 29, 2001, according to a Pew Center for the People & the Press survey, 53 percent of Americans agreed that the government should be able to censor news deemed to threaten national security. But the globalization of communication and media systems has made it far more difficult to restrain the press altogether: Even if domestic media are forced or volunteer to refrain from publicizing certain information, global media networks with headquarters abroad and/or Internet sites will spread the news across all borders. In short, censorship or self-censorship in today's global media/communication landscape is far more difficult to carry out and thus far less likely to succeed.

Notes

1. Text of the Attorney General's letter, accessed March 18, 2005, is available at http://news.bbc.co.uk/2/shared/bsp/hi/pdfs/26_07_13_attorney_general_letter_to_russian_justice_minister.pdf.

2. See Fox News, accessed March 17, 2015, http://www.foxnews.com/politics/2013/12/17/ex-cia-director-snowden-should-be-hanged-if-convicted-for-treason.

3. Daniel Ellsberg, "Edward Snowden: Saving Us from the United Stasi of America," *The Guardian*, June 10, 2013, accessed March 20, 2015, http://www.the guardian.com/commentisfree/2013/jun/10/edward-snowden-united-stasi-america. For the "hero" remark, see Huffington Post, accessed March 20, 2015, http://www.huffingtonpost.com/2013/06/10/edward-snowden-daniel-ellsberg-whistleblower-history_n_3413545.html.

4. Jay Rosen, "The Snowden Effect: Definition and Examples." PressThink, July 5, 2013, accessed March 17, 2015, http://pressthink.org/2013/07/the-snowden-effect-definition-and-examples.

5. Quote is taken from "Anarchy at the Turn of the Century," University Libraries, Pan-American Exposition Exhibit Group, University of Buffalo, accessed March 27, 2003, http://ublib.buffalo.edu/libraries/exhibits/panam/copyright.html.

6. Ibid.

7. Schenck v. United States 249 U.S. 47 (1919).

8. Planned Parenthood of the Columbia/Willamette Inc. v. American Coalition of Life, No. 99-35320.

9. See "Links to other web sites" at http://www.stormfront.org.

10. While site server Scorpion Communications canceled its contract with the Kahane organization, another firm, McMurtrey/Whitaker & Associates, struggled with the decision of whether to let Kahane.org use its software to sell merchandise on its site. See Dean E. Murphy, "Ugliness Online Isn't Terrorism," *New York Times*, January 7, 2001, Week in Review.

11. See, for example, http://www.emergency.com. Most sites that posted the so-called fatwa were neither associated with bin Laden or his allies nor shared their views.

12. For more on the case, see WBUR, accessed March 21, 2015, http://www.wbur.org/npr/261059230/dieudonne-m-bala-m-bala.

13. The report is available at Freedom House, accessed March 21, 2015, https://freedomhouse.org/report/freedom-world/freedom-world-2015#.VQxvo-FcA89.

14. The description of the Jordanian case is based on several news accounts.

15. See note 13.

16. Dennis Pluchinsky, "They Heard It All, and That's the Trouble," *Washington Post*, June 16, 2002, B03.

17. "Tipsheets for Terrorists?" *Washington Post*, June 23, 2002, B06.

18. Laura K. Donohue, Terrorist Speech and the Future of Free Expression," *Cardozo Law Review* 27, no. 1 (2005): 271.

19. Broder made his remarks during a seminar on "The Media and Terrorism," sponsored by the Center for Communication, Inc., October 23, 1985.

20. Katharine Graham, "The Media Must Report Terrorism," in *Terrorism: Opposing Viewpoints*, ed. Bonnie Szumski (St. Paul: Greenhaven), 81.

21. Reported by PBS's *News Hour Report*, accessed July 2, 2008, http://www.pbs.org/newshour/media/media_watch/july-dec02/putin_11-25.html.

10

Indexing, Propaganda Model, and Counterterrorism News

How the News Media Cover Counterterrorism

Tom Brokaw, anchor, NBC News (September 11, 2001): Twenty-four hundred people were killed when the Japanese attacked Pearl Harbor sixty years ago this year. This attack on America, this terrorist war on America, could be more consequential in terms of lives lost. And it could be, as well, consequential in other ways in terms of getting this country involved around the world. Pearl Harbor, of course, triggered World War II, one of the epic events in the history of mankind.

Dan Rather, anchor, CBS News (September 11, 2001): Terror hits home. In the history of our country, we had "Remember the Alamo," then "Remember the Maine" during the Spanish-American War. We had "Remember Pearl Harbor," and now, "Remember the twin towers."

Peter Jennings, anchor, ABC News (September 11, 2001): As you look at these scenes, you can feel absolutely clear that you are looking at the results of the United States at war with angry and vicious people who will do in the future as they have in the past. . . . And so in fairness, without being too carried away with it, we are looking at pictures from a war zone this morning. Not a picture of something that look [sic] like a war zone—looks like an old war zone, but it's a picture of a current war zone in this endless battle between the United States and its enemies.

~

On September 11, 2001, even before President George W. Bush spoke of America's "war against terrorism" late that day in his address to the nation, the attack was cast by the mainstream media as an act of war, a Pearl Harbor–like event, and the likelihood of military responses. On the day of the attack, with the horrific images of the burning and collapsing World Trade Center towers and with the destroyed part of the Pentagon shown constantly on full or split screens, anchors, correspondents, and reporters of the three TV networks ABC, CBS, and NBC mentioned the term "war" fifty-seven times; "Pearl Harbor" forty-one times, and "war zone" eleven times. In addition, experts, public officials, historians, and other sources used the term "war" a total of twenty-nine times and "Pearl Harbor" seventeen times.

The enormity of the 9/11 strikes by itself resulted in a patriotic rally-round-the-flag reaction and record approval ratings for President George W. Bush. But the equally patriotic reporting patterns of the mainstream media in the weeks, months, and even years after 9/11 contributed to the Bush administration's ability to find overwhelming support by the U.S. public and in the political elite for its "war against terrorism," including the Iraq War (Bennett, Lawrence, and Livingston 2007; Nacos, Bloch-Elkon, and Shapiro 2011). And then there were outright signs that media personnel shared the emotions of politicians and the public. Nothing attested more to this than the emotions of Dan Rather who had the reputation of a hard-nosed newsman: Six days after the attacks, as guest on the *Late Show with David Letterman*, an emotional Rather shed tears as he discussed 9/11 and said, "George Bush is the president, he makes the decisions, and, you know, as just one American, he wants me to line up, just tell me where."[1]

Because of the constitutionally guaranteed freedom of press and expression, the American press has been characterized as an extra force or branch in the governmental system of checks and balances between the administrative, legislative, and judicial branches. Indeed, the American Society of News Editors (formerly the American Society of Newspaper Editors), the professional organization that pioneered codified journalism ethics, declares in its "Statement of Principles" that "freedom of the press belongs to the people" and, most important, that "the American press was made free not just to inform or just to serve as a forum for debate but also to bring an independent scrutiny to bear on the forces of power in the society, including the conduct of official power at all levels of government."[2]

But contrary to those ideals, which are shared by other journalistic organizations, the mainstream media do not always exercise their declared freedom and independence when reporting on public affairs. W. Lance Bennett's (1990) "indexing" theory speaks to the media's tendency to make news decisions based on their assessments of the power dynamics inside government, especially as these dynamics can be discerned at the major news beats in the administration (the White House, Departments of Defense and State) and in Congress. Decisive here is that the levels of agreement or disagreement among Washington's most influential officials will be reflected in the news. While the "indexing" theory recognizes the influence of government insiders to frame the news and shape mass-mediated policy debates and ultimately policies themselves, it does not go as far as the propaganda or hegemony model. The latter explains the American news media as an instrument of the power elite, among them the upper crust in politics, business, and the military. In C.

Wright Mills's (2000 [1956], 215) view the media are important instruments of power in the hands of the powerful with some in the media either part of those elites or in prominent roles among their hired hands. In their initial explanation of the "propaganda model" Edward Herman and Noam Chomsky (2002, xi) write that "among their other functions, the media serve, and propagandize on behalf of, the powerful societal interests that control and finance them." While the propaganda model assumes media dominance of a power elite that transcends the influence that the indexing framework assigns to government officials, the two explanations are actually more compatible than they seem to be at first sight. Whereas Herman (1995, 43) argues that "the mainstream media tend to follow a state agenda in reporting on foreign policy," the "indexing" school, too, recognizes the media's vulnerability to governmental news management and "spin," especially when it comes to foreign policy and international crisis.

Media scholars tend to distinguish between news of foreign/international politics and policies on the one hand and domestic politics and policies on the other. But in the age of globalization the once distinct domestic-international demarcation has become increasingly blurred in a multitude of areas, including trade, environment, health, and financial markets (Deese 1994; Huntington 1997). This convergence of the domestic and international spheres has been particularly compelling with respect to transnational terrorism and counterterrorism—even before the beginning of rapid globalization processes in the 1990s. Thus, whether we consider the wave of anti-American terrorism incidents in the 1980s or the catastrophic attacks of 9/11, the actions by transnational terrorist groups and American reactions to those had dramatic effects on U.S. domestic politics and policies as well as on international relations and foreign policy. For this reason, the propaganda and indexing models or a synthesis of both seem suited to examine counterterrorism reporting, to what extent this news takes its lead from government insiders, and how this is reflected in public opinion data.

Counterterrorism: Limited Military Deployments

In the face of an international crisis that involves the United States and challenges the president, Americans tend to rally around the flag and their president in what seem nearly automatic reflexes of patriotic passions. But scholars (Mueller 1985; Brody and Shapiro 1989; Hugick and Gallup 1991) found that not all such crises trigger "rallies-'round-the-flag." Even quite similar incidents, for example the 1968 seizure of the USS *Pueblo* by North Korea and the 1975 seizure of the SS *Mayaguez* by the Khmer Rouge resulted in different reactions by the American public. While President Lyndon Johnson's approval dropped after the *Pueblo* incident, President Gerald Ford's public approval increased after the *Mayaguez*. After studying such discrepancies Richard Brody and Catherine Shapiro (1989; Brody 1991) explained that rallies occur when the news reflects that "opinion leaders," such as administration officials and members of Congress, support the president or refrain from voicing criticism. However, when the news reflects disagreement on the part of "opinion leaders," the public will not rally. To be sure, leading media voices qualify as opinion leaders as well and thus contribute to news content that determines public reactions in this respect.

The rally phenomenon is most likely in the face of a major national security crisis, such as the events of 9/11, wars, and limited military deployment. Scholars suggest a range of minimum approval increases in the first post-incident surveys to qualify as rallies with percentages between 3 percent and 5 percent (Hugick and Gallup 1991; Edwards 1983). Moreover, robust rallies require further approval gains in the second poll after the particular event. In the following, I examine three cases in which presidents Ronald Reagan, Bill Clinton, and Barack Obama deployed the U.S. military for quick strikes abroad against transnational terrorists and terrorist sponsors in the name of counterterrorism.

The 1986 Bombing of Libya: Immediately after taking office in January 1981 and with an implicit reference to the just resolved 444-day Iran hostage crisis, President Reagan warned, "Let terrorists beware that when the rules of international behavior are violated, our policy will be one of swift and effective retribution."[3] But in the following years, as terrorist attacks against Americans increased, especially in the Middle East, there was no "swift and effective retribution." By the mid-1980s, the Reagan administration was eager to respond. While the Lebanese Hezbollah was involved in a wave of bombings, hijackings, and kidnappings, Washington did not target its sponsor, Iran, but rather the not quite as strong Libya and its ruler Muammar Qaddafi. Indeed, Qaddafi was, according to President Reagan and his administration's propaganda, what Osama bin Laden became in the wake of the 9/11 attacks for President George W. Bush, the world's number one evildoer. The opportunity to finally do something arose in April 1986, when a bomb exploded in a disco in Berlin, Germany, killing two U.S. servicemen. Claiming that Libyan agents were involved in the bombing, the Reagan administration now had "a smoking gun" against Libya. Expecting retaliatory strikes, American media organizations beefed up their presence in the Libyan capital, Tripoli, and were ideally situated to report live when the bombing raids on Tripoli and Benghazi began on April 14. More importantly, media opinion was strongly in favor of the bombings although the victims were predominantly Libyan civilians. As the *New York Times* editorialized one day after the raids, "Even the most scrupulous citizen can only approve and applaud the American attack on Libya." Another *Times* editorial noted that with the bombing America sent the message, "The tiger bites."[4] News organizations also reported extensively about the overwhelming congressional support for President Reagan's decision. Not surprisingly, Ronald Reagan's general public approval rating increased from a solid 62 percent before the bombing to 67 percent thereafter, while 70 percent or more Americans approved the bombing raids (see table 10.1). In the absence of oppositional voices among influential officials inside and outside the administration, the Congress, and within the media, the president's agenda was reflected in the news and in a public very supportive of Ronald Reagan.

Table 10.1.
Presidential Approval and Military Counterterrorism

Reagan Bombing of Libya 1986			Clinton Missile Strikes Afghanistan and Sudan 1998		
Date	General Approval	Action-Related Approval	Date	General Approval	Action-Related Approval
April 11–14	62%		August 6	70%	
April 15	strikes		August 7	strikes	
April 17–18	67%		August 11	67%	
April 24–28		72%	August 17	68%	
April 30–May 1	68%		August 19–20		71%

Before and after the announcement of the commencement of air strikes against ISIS a number of opinion surveys asked respondents whether they approved of President Obama's actions in Iraq, and majorities disapproved. However, when respondents were asked whether they approved or disapproved of the airstrikes against ISIS without the question mentioning Obama, very solid majorities supported those strikes.

Table 10.2.
Presidential Approval and Military Counterterrorism

Obama Raid Killing bin Laden 2011			Obama Start of Airstrikes against ISIS 2014		
Date	General Approval	Action-Related Approval	Date	General Approval	Action-Related Approval
April 25–27	47%		August 4–7	40%	
May 1	Raid		August 8	Start Air Strikes	
May 2–3	57%	85%	August 10–12	42%	
May 5–8	54%		August 17–20	43%	None directly on Presidential approval
May 20		85%			

1998 Missile Strikes against Targets in Afghanistan and Sudan: Two weeks after terrorists drove car bombs into U.S. embassy compounds in Kenya and Tanzania, causing hundreds of deaths, the U.S. military targeted al-Qaeda training camps in Afghanistan and what was described as a "chemical weapons related facility" in Sudan with seventy-nine Tomahawk missiles. The counterterrorism strikes were launched three days after President Clinton had publicly admitted an affair with White House intern Monica Lewinsky. Opinion leaders, especially the president's adversaries in Congress, claimed that Clinton had ordered the strikes in order to draw attention away from his sex scandal. Not only were those political attacks covered by the news media, reporters, too, expressed skepticism about the president's motives. Characteristic for the media's stance was an exchange during a press conference at the Pentagon. One reporter asked Secretary of Defense William Cohen whether he was familiar with the *Wag the Dog* movie in which an American president cooks up an imaginary war to deflect interest away from his sexual encounter with a teenage girl. "Some Americans are going to say this [the missile strikes] bears a striking resemblance to *Wag the Dog*," one reporter said. "How do you respond?" Cohen replied that "the only motivation driving this action today was our absolute obligation to protect the American people from terrorist activities."[5]

Along the lines of Brody and Shapiro's findings, the mass-mediated disagreement among opinion leaders was reflected in the news and not lost on the public. As table 10.1 shows, President Clinton's general approval decreased slightly whereas his decision to strike back at terrorists and their supporters had solid public support.

Hunting Down Osama bin Laden: On May 1, 2011, shortly before midnight—it was already May 2 in Pakistan—President Obama stunned the nation and the world with the following televised announcement: "Good evening. Tonight, I can report to the American people and to the world that the United States has conducted an operation that killed Osama bin Laden, the leader of al-Qaeda, and a terrorist who's responsible for the murder of thousands of innocent men, women, and children."[6] As the *New York Times* reported the next day, the president "drew praise from unlikely quarters on Monday for pursuing a risky and clandestine mission to kill Osama bin Laden, a successful operation that interrupted the withering Republican criticism about his foreign policy, world view and his grasp of the office." Former vice president Dick Cheney declared, "The administration clearly deserves credit for the success of the operation." New York's former mayor, Rudolph W. Giuliani, said, "I admire the courage of the president."[7]

A huge majority of the American public, 85 percent, expressed approval for President Obama's handling of the raid on bin Laden's secret compound and general approval for his performance as president jumped ten percentage points from 47 percent before the al-Qaeda leader's death to 57 percent thereafter (see table 10.2). This was reason enough for Republican media figures and opinion makers to wonder whether these approvals would translate into support for Obama in the 2012 presidential election. Before long, these circles made and repeated the claim that President George W. Bush deserved credit for the undoing of bin Laden. Their point was that the intelligence community would not have found the hideaway in Pakistan without exposing captured terrorists to "enhanced interrogation techniques." As Lanny Davis, a Fox News contributor, told Bill O'Reilly, "I wrote today that we have to give credit to

George Bush and those that used these techniques for getting information that directly or indirectly led to the death of Usama bin Laden. I don't think there's any way to deny that."[8] It was telling that President Obama's general approval dropped three percentage points in the second post-raid poll. Two weeks after bin Laden's demise Fox News commissioned a survey that asked respondents, "Do you think President Obama has been personally taking too much credit for the killing of bin Laden, the right amount of credit, or not enough credit?" A majority of Americans (53 percent) thought that Obama had taken the right amount of credit, 31 percent said he had taken too much and 12 percent too little credit, with 4 percent not voicing an opinion.

The commando mission against bin Laden became more of an issue during the 2012 presidential campaign. Just before the first anniversary of the raid and before Massachusetts Governor Mitt Romney won the Republican Party's nomination, the Obama campaign aired an ad that strongly implied that the presumptive GOP candidate would not have given the green light for the operation, using Romney's own words against him. Romney fired back with the claim that "the decision to go after bin Laden was a clear one and that 'even Jimmy Carter would' have made the call."[9] In the end, it is impossible to figure out whether and to what degree the media's reporting on the bin Laden coup may have factored into President Obama's reelection. As Table 10.2 shows, the start of airstrikes against ISIS in 2014, ordered by Barack Obama, did not result in a public approval gain for the president. For some, these actions were too little too late; for others they were likely to fail as military measures in Iraq and Afghanistan.

Mass-Mediated Counterterrorism in the Post–9/11 Years

Nothing reinforces people's fear of terrorist strikes more than heavily covered threat warnings issued by government officials on the one hand and by known terrorists on the other in the wake of major attacks. The months and years after 9/11 were a case in point. Besides around-the-clock coverage in television, radio, and the print media that highlighted the horrors of the attacks and the likelihood of more terrorism, there were many reports of threat warnings issued by administration officials and al-Qaeda leaders. Appearing before a Joint Session of Congress eight days after 9/11, President George W. Bush spoke about the threat against America. "Our nation has been put on notice: We are not immune from attack," he said. He told the nation, "I know many citizens have fears tonight and I ask you to be calm and resolute, even in the face of a continuing threat." Pointing to the enormity of what had "just passed," the president said that it was "natural to wonder if America's future is one of fear" before promising that "this country will define our times, not be defined by them."[10]

In the same speech, Bush announced the appointment of Tom Ridge to head up the Office of Homeland Security. First as head of that office and later as secretary of the newly created Department of Homeland Security, the former governor of Pennsylvania became a key figure in what he himself characterized as "the politics of terrorism" but what was more precisely a politics of counterter-rorism.[11] In this role, he and his staff disagreed repeatedly with other admin-istration officials' eagerness to issue public terror alerts indicating that attacks were likely or even imminent. Central in such discussions was a color-coded terrorism alert system with five levels that Ridge introduced in early 2002 to the public. While confusing to the public, it was exploited by certain adminis-tration officials as a useful prop in a threat manipulation scheme.

Before Memorial Day 2003, for example, Ridge and Attorney General John Ashcroft held press conferences on the same day. In response to questions about threats and security, Ridge told reporters that there was no reason to heighten the alert level. A few hours later, Ashcroft warned publicly of an imminent, ma-jor attack on the United States by al-Qaeda. President Bush was not pleased with Ridge's assessment; in their next regular meeting in the Oval Office he told the Secretary of Homeland Security that he wanted a united front (Ridge 2009, 228). Obviously, besides President Bush some of Tom Ridge's colleagues understood the usefulness of threat alerts in America's "war against terrorism."

When it comes to analyzing intelligence, reasonable people can differ about the meaning of often-sketchy information and the credibility of sources. But in discussing threat assessments on the part of those who fight terrorism, Albert Bandura took note of the likelihood that such judgments can be influenced by the desire to justify counterterrorism policies. As Bandura (2004, 129) put it:

> Lethal countermeasures are readily justified in response to grave threats that inflict extensive human pain or that endanger the very survival of the society. However, the criterion of "grave threat," although fine in principle, is shifty in specific cir-cumstances. Like most human judgments, gauging the gravity of threats involves some subjectivity. . . . Assessment of gravity prescribes the choice of options, but choice of violent options often shapes evaluation of gravity itself.

Not surprisingly, Secretary of Defense Donald Rumsfeld was a strong advo-cate of raising the threat level at any opportunity. Inside the Pentagon, Rums-feld made no bones about his motives. In his so-called snowflakes memos to his staff, the secretary "wrote of the need to 'keep elevating the threat' . . . and develop 'bumper sticker statements' to rally public support for an increasingly unpopular war" (Wright 2007, 1).

As Brigitte Nacos, Yaeli Bloch-Elkon, and Robert Shapiro (2011) document-ed, the news media were something like a supporting cast in the selling of the administration's formal terrorism threat alerts und the more frequent informal threat warnings. True to the media's tendency to highlight disconcerting news, the three leading TV networks, ABC, CBS, and NBC broadcast all twenty-three announcements of increases in the national, regional, or local terrorism alert levels and all of them were reported as lead stories at the top of newscasts. But the three networks reported decreases in threat levels much less prominently, airing only 13 percent of such announcements as lead stories and 87 percent further down in their broadcasts. When the Bush administration raised the nationwide terrorism alert, the networks devoted an average of five minutes and twenty seconds to such reports; when the terror alerts were lowered, the average news segment lasted only one minute and thirty-four seconds. The difference was even more pronounced for regional or local alerts: The average airtime for raised threat levels in these cases was two minutes and fifty-six seconds versus only twenty seconds for segments reporting on the lowering of the official alert level. When the three networks aired reports about threat advisories that did not involve changes in the color-code scheme, the average length of these stories was still fully two minutes and twenty seconds. In addition, the frequent threats from bin Laden and other al-Qaeda leaders received prominent and extensive coverage as well.

John Mueller (2006, 26) warned that "the harm of terrorism mostly arises from the fear and from the often hasty, ill-considered, and overwrought reaction (or overreaction) it characteristically, *and often calculatedly* [emphasis added], inspires in its victims." The media bought into the administration's threat scheme and became the government's helpers in keeping the American public's fear of more terrorist attacks alive (Nacos, Bloch-Elkon, and Shapiro 2011, chapter 2). Nisbet and Shanahan (2004) found in the post–9/11 period that people who paid "high level" attention to television news about national affairs and the war on terrorism were far more convinced that another terrorist attack would occur within the next twelve months than were "low level" and "moderate level" news consumers. Based on their experiments and survey analyses, Jennifer Merolla and Elizabeth Zechmeister (2009) demonstrated how perceptions of threat trigger authoritarian attitudes, lead to intolerance toward disliked groups, increase social distrust, curtail support of civil liberties, increase the likelihood of support for leaders dealing with the threat at hand, and affect opinions toward foreign policies. This is precisely what happened in the post–9/11 years, when the drumbeat of threat alerts and warnings by the administration and compliance by most opinion leaders inside and outside the media gave President Bush and his aides carte blanche for their extreme counterterrorism policies from the USA PATRIOT Act's curbing of civil liberties to the invasion of Iraq and human rights violations in the treatment of terrorists or suspected terrorists (see also chapter 9).

For the months and years immediately following 9/11, both the indexing and the propaganda model explain the mainstream media's pertinent reporting. Indeed, during that period "officials in Washington—especially President Bush and members of his administration—were able to set the media agenda when that was their intention" (Nacos, Bloch-Elkon, and Shapiro 2011, 183). When administration officials held news briefings, gave interviews, delivered speeches, and found plenty of other occasions to go public, TV networks and other media provided them with ample opportunity to sell their agenda.

When, on the other hand, the White House and other administration officials did not make strong efforts to promote certain counterterrorism measures, the news reflected this low-level engagement and offered other sources access, albeit without the prominence and frequency granted to top

Table 10.3
News Messages by Domestic Sources in TV Networks' Post–9/11 Terrorism Coverage

	Threat	Civil Liberties	Build-Up Iraq	Prevention	Preparedness
President/ Administration	21%	18%	26%	8%	5%
Members of Congress	5%	12%	1%	7%	5%
Experts	16%	10%	6%	22%	20%
Local/State Officials	8%	4%	—	5%	8%
Other Domestic	9%	23%	6%	6%	17%
Public/Public Opinion	9%	7%	—	15%	3%
Media	33%	26%	35%	36%	43%

Source: Nacos, Bloch-Elkon, and Shapiro 2011.

% = percentage of total sources (Note: because foreign sources are not included in the table, the listed sources do not add up to 100 percent in all cases).

Washingtonians. A systematic study of post–9/11 news about terrorist threat alerts and warnings, civil liberty policies, the selling of the Iraq War, terrorism prevention in the homeland, and preparedness for terrorist strikes showed the following (see table 10.3): The president and high administration officials were crafty in using the media to publicize the terrorist threat and the need to invade Iraq in order to prevent terrorist attacks. In both cases, the TV networks "indexed" the news mostly within the narrow range of Washington opinion leaders as far as domestic sources were concerned. The administration was least active with respect to prevention of terrorism at home and preparedness for other terrorist emergencies. As a result, there was only a moderate amount of news about those important but rather complex and not particularly dramatic policy areas. Finally, the administration's public engagement in issues arising from civil liberty restrictions in the name of security was less intensive compared to the hype surrounding the build-up to the Iraq War and the overblown messages about terrorist threat warnings but more rigorous compared to the modest selling and reporting of prevention and preparedness (Nacos, Bloch-Elkon, and Shapiro 2011, chapter 7).

Ever since 9/11, presidents, high administration officials, and the intelligence community left no doubt that the terrorist threat remained. Yet, they did not launch campaigns to urge the public to make sensible preparedness arrangements and seek information about their communities' emergency preparations. The newsrooms of leading media organizations were not interested either. Thus, in the three years from January 1, 2010 to December 31, 2013, the *Washington Post* published ninety-eight stories and the *New York Times* eighty-four about or mentioning both terrorism and preparedness; during the same period, the CBS *Evening News* aired six, and CNN's *The Situation Room* ten such segments. An analysis of those stories revealed that only a fraction of them were exclusively about the state of preparedness in the United States or some particular measures to prepare emergency responders and/or the general public for terrorist strikes. Yet another example that the news media, not all the time but to a large extent, follow the government's agenda: What is high on that agenda will be reported prominently; what is low will not be reported much or at all. As a result, a solid majority of Americans consider their communities' terrorism preparedness "inadequate" or are "unsure."[12]

After they examined some of the Bush administration's most drastic post–9/11 measures taken in the name of counterterrorism, Bennett, Lawrence and Livingston (2007, 137) concluded that "the administration assumed it could bend mass perception of reality even against massive evidence to the contrary, with only occasional challenges from the press and dissident sources." Indeed, the mass-mediated politics of counterterrorism policy was a case of news "indexed to power" (ibid., 174) that also met the propaganda model's criteria of a power elite using the media to manufacture consent (Herman and Chomsky 2002).

Eventually, major news organizations recovered their footing, in the cases of the *Washington Post* and the *New York Times* admitting their failures. But neither a mea culpa nor the return to professional journalists' self-proclaimed ethics codes could turn back the clock and undo the damage inflicted abroad and at home. Instead, the immediate post–9/11 era demonstrated that in crisis times the press must bark like a watchdog and not cozy up to the power elite like a lapdog.

Notes

1.   The video of the conversation is available on YouTube, accessed June 20, 2015, http://search.yahoo.com/search?p=Rather+on+Letterman+and+9%2F11&toggle=1& cop=mss&ei=UTF-8&fr=yfp-t-701.

2.   The statement is available at ASNE, accessed May 18, 2014, http://asne.org/content.asp?pl=24&sl=171&contentid=171.

3.   Quoted by David C. Martin and John Walcott, *Best Laid Plans: The Inside Story of America's War Against Terrorism* (New York: Harper & Row, 1988), 43.

4.   "The Terrorist and His Sentence," *New York Times*, April 15, 1986, A30; "The Bombs of April," *New York Times*, April 16, 1986, A26.

5.   News briefing by William Cohen, Secretary of Defense, August 20, 1998, according to FDCH Political Transcripts.

6.   "Obama's Remarks on Bin Laden's Killing," *New York Times*, May 2, 2011, accessed May 5, 2014, http://www.nytimes.com/2011/05/02/world/middleeast/02obama-text.html?pagewanted=all&_r=0.

7.   Jeff Zeleny and Jim Rutenberg, "Obama Finds Praise, Even from Republicans," *New York Times*, May 2, 2011, accessed May 5, 2014, http://www.nytimes.com/2011/05/03/us/politics/03obama.html.

8. The O'Reilly Factor, Fox News, May 5, 2011, retrieved from the Lexis/Nexis electronic archives, May 4, 2014.

9. "Romney: 'Even Jimmy Carter' Would Have Ordered bin Laden Attack," CNN, April 30, 2012, accessed May 6, 2014, http://www.cnn.com/2012/04/30/politics/campaign-wrap/index.html.

10. From President George W. Bush's speech before a joint session of Congress, September 20, 2011, accessed May 6, 2014, http://georgewbush-whitehouse.archives.gov/news/releases/2001/09/20010920-8.html.

11. The U.S. Department of Homeland Security was established on November 25, 2002, by the Homeland Security Act of 2002. In his memoir, Tom Ridge writes extensively about the politics of terrorism and counterterrorism inside and outside the Bush administration, especially in chapter 6 ("The Politics of Terrorism, Part I") and chapter 14 ("The Politics of Terrorism, Part II). Tom Ridge, *The Test of Our Times: America under Siege . . . and How We Can Be Safe Again* (New York: St. Martin's, 2009).

12. According to a 2011 poll commissioned by the Mailman School at Columbia University and conducted by the Marist Institute for Public Opinion. In early 2014, this was the last available poll about terrorism preparedness.

11

Responding to Terrorist Crises

Dealing with the Mass Media

On June 17, 2015, twenty-one-year-old white supremacy extremist Dylann Storm Roof killed nine African Americans during bible studies at the Emanuel AME Church in Charleston, South Carolina in an unspeakable act of home-grown terrorism. According to a survivor, the perpetrator said, "You rape our women and you're taking over our country. And you have to go."

The next day, President Barack Obama told the nation, "There is something particularly heartbreaking about the death happening in a place in which we seek solace and we seek peace, in a place of worship.

"Mother Emanuel is, in fact, more than a church. This is a place of worship that was founded by African Americans seeking liberty. This is a church that was burned to the ground because its worshipers worked to end slavery. When there were laws banning all-black church gatherings, they conducted services in secret. When there was a nonviolent movement to bring our country closer in line with our highest ideals, some of our brightest leaders spoke and led marches from this church's steps. This is a sacred place in the history of Charleston and in the history of America. . . .

"Until the investigation is complete, I'm necessarily constrained in terms of talking about the details of the case. But I don't need to be constrained about the emotions that tragedies like this raise. I've had to make statements like this too many times. Communities like this have had to endure tragedies like this too many times.

"We don't have all the facts, but we do know that, once again, innocent people were killed in part because someone who wanted to inflict harm had no trouble getting their hands on a gun. Now is the time for mourning and for healing. But let's be clear: At some point, we as a country will have to reckon with the fact that this type of mass violence does not happen in other advanced countries. It doesn't *happen in other places with this kind of frequency. And it is in our power to do something about it.*

"I say that recognizing the politics in this town foreclose a lot of those avenues right now. But it would be wrong for us not to acknowledge it. And at some point it's going to be important for the American people to come to grips with it, and for us to be able to shift how we think about the issue of gun violence collectively....

"The good news is I am confident that the outpouring of unity and strength and fellowship and love across Charleston today, from all races, from all faiths, from all places of worship indicates the degree to which those old vestiges of hatred can be overcome."¹

~

When man-made or natural disasters of extraordinary proportions occur, Americans look to local, state, and national officials to manage swift emergency responses and use mass media to inform the public. In the Charleston case, the local emergency response community was first in line to deal with the crisis with Police Chief Greg Mullen and Mayor Joseph P. Riley at the helm. In the hours after the attack, both men held several news briefings for a rapidly growing crowd of reporters. The police chief utilized live broadcasts to reassure Charlestonians and to display images of the perpetrator and his car, which led to Roof's capture in neighboring North Carolina within hours. The mayor echoed the emotional state of citizens telling them how difficult it was to come to grips with the tragedy. "To walk into a church and shoot someone is out of pure hatred," he said."² A day after the attack, South Carolina's Governor Nikki R. Haley visited Charleston, meeting with and consoling the victims' families. It was a model case of excellent responses by the professionals of the emergency response community on the one hand and political leaders on all levels of government on the other.

~

While more recently, the number of terrorist plots and actual attacks on U.S. soil increased, many of the more serious cases of anti-American terrorism occurred abroad. When terrorists target Americans and/or American facilities abroad, foreign response professionals and foreign governments, not U.S. authorities, are in charge of dealing with and managing these crises, whether they concern hijackings, other hostage situations, or hit-and-run incidents, such as facility attacks, bombings, or suicide missions. From the American point of view, when a terrorist incident takes place in the jurisdiction of hostile or indifferent governments, particular problems arise. Besides excluding U.S. response professionals, law enforcement specialists, and political crisis managers (or limiting their roles), these overseas cases tend to magnify the messages of foreign news sources. The reason is obvious: When anti-American terrorism occurs abroad, public officials, terrorists, supporters of terrorists, and other actors in those countries and regions are closest to what happened, why it happened, and what is done or not done in a particular situation. As a result, these foreign actors, far more than American officials, are the preferred news sources.

Detailed content analyses of news reporting during and after major anti-American incidents outside the United States have shown that the coverage of official sources in the most heavily covered "golden triangle" of Washington's foreign and national security news beats (White House, Department of State, and Department of Defense) tends to pale in terms of frequency and length of reporting and in terms of prominence of placement in comparison to foreign actors (Nacos 1996b, chapter 2). Just as important, in the domestic sphere, the traditionally most authoritative and most extensively covered foreign policy sources (e.g., American government officials), are less attractive to the media than are the U.S. victims of terrorism, whether survivors of hit-and-run attacks, hostages, or the families, friends, and neighbors of such victims. In other words, when anti-American terrorists strike abroad, the American authorities lose their media advantage over other American sources and over foreign sources, an advantage that is typical in other types of foreign crises that affect Americans and U.S. interests (Cook 1994; Nacos 1996b). As a result, terrorists, their supporters, and government officials abroad, especially when the latter have hostile or ambivalent sentiments toward the United States, are in excellent positions to exploit the media in order to convey their self-serving messages to the American and international public and to their domestic audiences as well. The official Washington, the president and his advisers included, is often left to rely on the mass media, notably television, for news of the latest developments concerning terrorist incidents abroad. For the White House as well as the Departments of State and Defense, television news, especially that provided by all-news channels such as CNN, is, even in normal times, equally as informative as, or even more revealing than the information received by American diplomats stationed abroad. The reason is not that reporters are smarter and quicker than American diplomats or intelligence agencies, but rather that terrorists themselves, indigenous government officials, and other foreign sources at incident sites often single out the mass media to disseminate their information.

Former Pentagon official and terrorism expert Noel Koch revealed that, when faced with terrorist situations, "one of the first things we do is tune in CNN" (Martin and Walcott 1988, 191). Top officials in other departments and agencies came to similar conclusions. Even when they had open phone lines to a particular U.S. Embassy, they learned more from watching television networks than from listening to their colleagues abroad or reading the intelligence dispatches of the National Security Agency (NSA). As Oliver North, who served on the National Security Council staff during the Reagan presidency, put it, "CNN runs ten minutes ahead of NSA" (Martin and Walcott 1988, 191). Thus, besides being unable to take the lead in responding to overseas terrorist incidents or in the management of such crises abroad, the U.S. government also loses its otherwise well-documented media advantage to foreign and domestic actors. This is not an enviable situation at times, when terrorists and other actors abroad try hard to use their media access in order to frighten and threaten Americans and when Washington's crisis managers need to communicate calmness, confidence, and an aura of control to a shell-shocked, fearful, or impatient domestic public.

Take the case of the American hostages in Syria who were held, tortured, and eventually executed by the Islamic State. In spite of the superiority of the U.S. military, a failed rescue by Special Forces commandos demonstrated the impotence of even the mightiest military power to free its citizens from comparably weak terrorist groups. Some family members mourning the victims of ISIS and similar groups were critical of President Obama and his administration for not doing more to free their loved ones. Some wanted negotiations with the hostage holders, others the government's okay to use private funds to pay ransom. While there were no indications that the U.S. government would change its official policy of making no deals with terrorists, the Obama administration worked with the families to establish a model for future, much improved communications between administration decision makers and the families of hostages. Moreover, the president himself expressed support for allowing private citizens to negotiate with and pay ransom to terrorists without fear of prosecution.

The situation is very different when terrorism, whether of the domestic or international variety, is committed on American soil. While no one would wish for terrorism inside U.S. borders rather than abroad, from the perspective of those who must respond to this sort of political violence, strikes inside the United States are at least more manageable than comparable incidents abroad: When terrorists act inside the United States, American political leaders, American response experts, and American law enforcement agencies are in charge, and, frankly, they are in a far better position to deal with the crisis at hand.

One important reason for this advantage is that in any kind of emergency situation within the country, whether natural or man-made, American response professionals are the most authoritative sources of information, and thus they are the most sought out by the media. This is an ideal position from which to convey important information to the public at large and to communicate with the victims, with the victims' families, friends, and neighbors, with the perpetrators and their supporters, and, last but not least, with political decision makers in various jurisdictions. In short, under these circumstances, those who respond to a terrorist event have the opportunity to manage information and influence the public in what they believe is the best solution for resolving an emergency situation of this kind and/or dealing with the aftermath of such an incident.

If this gives the impression that reacting to terrorism at home is little more than routine work for seasoned response professionals as far as their handling of public information and news media are concerned, this is certainly not the intent of this point and would not square with reality. It did not take the World

Trade Center and Pentagon attacks on September 11, 2001, and the subsequent bioterrorism in the form of anthrax spores, to recognize the difficulties of media-related parts in managing terrorist crises. Even in the domestic setting, political leaders and emergency response professionals deal typically with media representatives and organizations that have vastly different interests and priorities than have those who are responsible for handling these crises directly.

At this point, it is necessary to remind the reader of terrorism's fundamental publicity goals as outlined in chapter 2. Because terrorism is a means to communicate messages to the public and to governmental decision makers, terrorists, on the one hand, and crisis managers and response professionals, on the other, compete for media attention. There is probably no better example than that of Timothy McVeigh and the Oklahoma City bombing to demonstrate that news coverage is the precondition for advancing terrorists' substantive goals. Even before McVeigh finally revealed the media-centered plan behind the 1995 Oklahoma City bombing, it was perfectly clear that the news had carried his intended messages. Without McVeigh or his accomplice, Terry Nichols, saying a word in the aftermath of the devastating blow that left 168 persons dead and many more injured, the news ran with the clues he left: By igniting the bomb on the second anniversary of the FBI's raid on the Branch Davidian sect's compound in Waco, Texas, during which cult leader David Koresh and eighty of his followers died, McVeigh made sure that the mass media would dig into his and like-minded people's causes and grievances against the federal government. More important, as the news devoted a great deal of attention to the incident at Waco and the sentiments of right-wing extremists opposed to the federal government's alleged abuse of power, the public was reminded daily of the Waco nightmare that many Americans had probably forgotten. The result was a dramatic change in public attitudes toward federal agents' actions during the Waco incident. Shortly after the Oklahoma City bombing in April 1995, nearly three in four Americans approved of the actions of the FBI in Waco, but three months later, after an intensive mass-mediated debate of Waco and Oklahoma City, two in four Americans disapproved of the way the FBI and other federal agencies handled the Waco situation. Similarly, while two in four Americans did not support a new round of congressional hearings on Waco shortly after the Oklahoma bombing, several weeks later, three of five supported additional hearings.

By triggering news coverage that revisited troublesome questions about the Waco raid, the Oklahoma City bomber achieved what legitimate political actions, such as petitions to political leaders and peaceful protests, had not accomplished: Although Congress had held hearings into the Waco incident in 1993 and exonerated the FBI, new hearings were conducted because of the Oklahoma City bombing, the heavy news coverage of the linkage between that bombing and Waco, and the turnaround in public opinion.[3] Following these developments closely, McVeigh was pleased that the FBI and Attorney General Janet Reno were treated much more harshly in the new round of congressional hearings than during the original inquiry. He was "thrilled" when the Clinton administration appointed John Danforth, former U.S. Senator from Missouri, to head up a special investigation into the Waco incident. Although McVeigh was neither happy with the Danforth report, which put the blame for the Waco inferno squarely on cult leader David Koresh, nor with the outcome of a civil trial in Texas, in which a jury exonerated the government agents involved, he was convinced that his act of terrorism was a success because he accomplished his goal of alerting the American public to what he called abuse of power on the part of the federal government and, more importantly, he initiated changes in the FBI's and other federal agencies' rules of engagement in confrontations like Waco.[4] It is ironic that McVeigh's accusations against the federal government and its agents were once again highlighted, when his execution was stayed by Attorney General John Ashcroft after it was revealed that thousands of pages of the FBI's investigation into the Oklahoma City bombing had not been made available to McVeigh's defense attorneys.

Terrorists know that political violence is a potent means to penetrate the strong links between the mass media, the general public, and the governmental realm—connections that I describe earlier with respect to "the triangle of political communication" (see chapter 2, figure 2.1). The act of terrorism is a master key for unlocking the door that grants access to the mass media. This means that crisis managers and response specialists compete with the perpetrators of political violence in that each side wants to have the loudest and most persuasive voice and messages. In this competition, terrorists seem to start out with a significant advantage because their violent deeds are a powerful message that commands the mass media's attention and thus that of their target audience(s). But response specialists and crisis managers (such as members of police and fire departments, emergency medical teams, National Guard, etc.), and political leaders (such as mayors, county executives, governors, and presidents) are nevertheless in excellent positions to dominate the news because they are part of one of the cornerstones in the "triangle of political communication" with formal and informal links and relationships in place before emergencies arise. Finally, terrorism's victims, their families and friends, and the public at large may also have their own ideas about how a particular incident should be handled that are different from the response specialists' at the scene and the crisis managers' in their command centers. This is likely to be the case during hostage situations, when the authorities may not want to give in to the demands of hostage holders, while hostages and their loved ones may press for the release of captives—at any price.

It is clear then that the interests of the mass media, terrorists, their victims, all kinds of societal groups (such as the relatives and friends of victims), as well as response specialists call for a delicate management of public information and media relations on the part of those who respond to and deal with terrorist crises. Recognizing that the news media and terrorism response specialists have very different objectives, one student of mass-mediated political violence stated,

The mass media aim to "scoop" their rivals with news stories that will grip and sustain the public's attention and hence increase their ratings and revenue. The police, on the other hand, are first and foremost concerned with the protection of life, the enforcement of the law and apprehending those guilty of committing crimes. . . . There have been many examples where the efforts of the police have been directly threatened by the behaviour [*sic*] of sections of the media (Wilkinson 2001, 181).

Actually, the best examples of news reports interfering with rescue efforts or other activities by the authorities did not concern simply actions by the police but by other response professionals, such as hostage rescue commandos, as well. While the idea of divergent objectives of the media and the terrorism response community is obvious, the relationship between the two sides is far more complex than one purely shaped by conflict and adversity.

For those who manage terrorist crises and are part of the emergency response teams, the most important thing to remember is this: The mass media can and do interfere with the plans and intentions of those who are in charge of handling terrorist crises. But the same reporters and news organizations can also be very helpful and, in fact, crucial in efforts to manage such incidents.

Trying to curb the press and thus one of the most fundamental civil liberties of democracies in general and the United States of America in particular—freedom of the press, freedom of expression—is counterproductive and likely to fail. In totalitarian or authoritarian states, this will work. But in liberal democracies, moves by public officials to censor reporting on terrorism would strengthen terrorists' accusations against overbearing governments and abuse of power. Thoughtful and well-planned media liaison, on the other hand, can harness the possible excesses of reporting and, in fact, allow a degree of information management. While each terrorist crisis has its own complex characteristics and therefore calls for particular responses, there are some basic rules of thumb, caveats, experiences, and practical examples to draw from. The following ten recommendations for terrorism response professionals and crisis managers are meant as guidelines for incidents on American soil, but certain aspects can also be instructive for dealing with anti-American terrorism abroad.

∼

Recommendation #1: Feed the beast—Providing the media with a steady flow of information is not an option but an absolute imperative during and after terrorist incidents.

In his book *Feeding the Beast: The White House versus the Press*, newsman Kenneth T. Walsh describes the contentious relationship between the White House and the media during Bill Clinton's presidency. According to the author, one of the Clintonites' biggest problems was their failure to "feed the beast," as the media are called by Washington insiders. The White House would have been well advised to listen to Jack DeVore, the longtime press secretary of former senator and treasury secretary Lloyd Bentsen, who said that "a press secretary's job was to manufacture a constant supply of doggie biscuits" for the press. Reporters would gleefully lick the hand that fed them, but if you ran out of treats or news, DeVore said, "the press would devour your arm and try for more" (Walsh 1996, 9).

Just as public officials in the White House, Congress, and in other institutions, those who respond and manage terrorist incidents must attend to the basic information needs of the news media and thus avoid frustration and hostility on the part of reporters and their home offices that could influence the news presentation and ultimately damage crisis respondents' reputation, public image, and credibility. Whether crisis managers like it or not, unless they feed the beast, unless they respond to the necessities of the fourth estate, unless they know about and try to accommodate the deadline cycle and the logistics of news production, they will lose their advantage as the most authoritative news sources. A media beast deprived of food in the form of information is likely to turn on those who are closest to the emergency, criticize the way the crisis is handled, and look elsewhere to still its appetite for information and new angles with which to tell the story. Often the result is that rumors, not facts, are reported and attributed to anonymous sources. In this respect, the coverage of terrorist incidents and crimes can pose the same problems for those dealing with such cases. For example, because law enforcement officials did not provide much information to the press following the murder of two popular professors at Dartmouth College in New Hampshire, some news organizations followed whatever lead they could possibly come up with—and were often forced to revise or repudiate their "exclusives."[5]

Far more damaging was the failure of officials in the George W. Bush administration to inform the American public accurately, competently, and with one voice about the anthrax bioterrorism threat that followed the kamikaze attacks on the World Trade Center and the Pentagon. As media observer Howard Kurtz noted, "After six weeks of generally sympathetic coverage, the anthrax-obsessed press is turning on the Bush administration. In a spate of stories and segments, top officials are being depicted as bumblers who failed to move aggressively against anthrax-tainted mail while offering shifting [public] explanations of the danger."[6] Kurtz quoted one White House correspondent complaining that administration officials "don't know what they're talking about."[7] It did not help the relationship between the anthrax crisis managers and the press when administration sources blamed people in the media for being at fault and "on the verge of [anthrax-related] panic."[8] To be sure, one way or another reporters will question all kinds of sources, but if crisis managers and emergency response professionals play ball with media representatives and react to their need for information, they maintain their vantage point from which to frame and shape crisis information and construct the predominant story line. Most of all, it is important that those who deal with the media have knowledge of the latest developments and accurate information. With this in mind, how can response professionals prepare for the worst-case scenario?

First, just as those people involved in preparedness planning think of contingencies for all kinds of scenarios in terms of negotiating with hostage holders, rescuing hostages, or treating injured victims, it is important that they also develop plans for press and public information if terrorists strike. And just as specialists simulate various tasks and requirements of the preparedness scenario, the response community is well advised to undergo its media planning during such exercises. Confronting a serious disaster, the leading elected officials must deal directly with the news media and must inform the public immediately. Depending on the seriousness of the situation and the incident site(s), this informer would be the president, governors, mayors, and/or county executives. But other top administration officials, as well as leaders in law enforcement and other parts of the emergency response community, also must be prepared to handle the public information task and media liaison duties.

For this reason, it is recommended that these organizations designate persons in all emergency agencies who are to take lead roles in these areas. Although the FBI is the principal agency in the realm of domestic terrorism and the Federal Emergency Management Agency (FEMA) is assigned the major response responsibility in domestic disaster situations, local police and fire departments are probably better prepared to handle many aspects of press liaison during a crisis than are regional and federal officials. This does not mean that the FBI, FEMA, and other agencies will not deal with the media. But during and immediately after major incidents occur, the designated leaders in the community of response professionals must step up to the plate very quickly and provide information—often to the elected official who will directly interact with reporters and, through the media, with the public. Since journalists tend to cover preparedness exercises, the media/public information plan can and should be tested during such simulations.

Second, terrorist incidents often involve nongovernmental and governmental organizations, for example, the bombing of corporate headquarters or the hijacking or bombing of commercial airliners. In such cases, private corporations as well as public agencies are involved in crisis response measures—including media and public information. Is the commercial airline, whose plane has been targeted, or the bank, whose office has been struck, in charge of media and public information? Or does this role fall on public officials in the response community? These questions should be entertained and answered before actual terrorist situations occur so that the private and the public organizations and leaders are prepared to coordinate and cooperate and thus avoid confusion, miscues, and misinformation. In the wake of a terrorist strike, emergency response professionals need to work with nongovernmental organizations—especially in the area of public information.

Third, in the real world, the working press approaches and questions anyone at or near emergency sites that may possibly have some information. For this reason, it is not enough that officials in key positions are familiar with the opportunities and pitfalls of dealing with the news media. Ideally, every person in the response community should have some rudimentary understanding of what to do and what not to do when approached, interviewed, and pumped for information by reporters. The police officer who secures emergency sites, the fire fighter who operates equipment in rescue attempts, the emergency medical team that transports victims to hospitals, and the physician who works in the emergency room have firsthand experiences, observations, concerns, hopes, and conclusions that reporters want and should hear. All of these emergency professionals are privy to firsthand information, impressions, feelings, speculations, and rumors that could cause harm to hostages, innocent bystanders, emergency workers, and the law enforcement process if they are revealed to the press or to the general public—and thus to terrorists and their supporters as well. Doris Graber has pointed out that reporters and public officials alike sometimes "spin their own prejudices into a web of scenarios that puts blame for the disaster on socially outcast groups" (Graber 1997, 141). In the hours and days after the Oklahoma City bombing, for example, the mainstream media reported about an "Arab-looking" man as a possible suspect while so-called experts espoused a "Middle East connection" when questioned by reporters. As a result, innocent Arab Americans in Oklahoma and elsewhere became the targets of physical attacks and insults, while an equally innocent Arab American was held and questioned by the FBI as a suspect. It is not clear where this particular rumor originated. But the example should serve as a warning to response professionals not to become involved in rumor mongering because of the potentially catastrophic consequences. Indeed, when aware of rumors, officials are well advised to caution the media and the public not to spread and subscribe to unsubstantiated information. Local response personnel in places that are otherwise far removed from the major media markets are especially vulnerable when the national media descends onto a terrorism site. This is understandable but potentially harmful, according to one expert in the field who noted two decades ago,

> The lights, the cameras, the media's competitiveness, the pressure of deadlines, and other demands of a harried press corps can overwhelm untrained police officers attempting to deal with the media and can feed easily into the unfolding situation at hand (Miller 1982, 81).

Since this observation was made, the press has become far more competitive and aggressive in a media landscape that is increasingly shaped by a large number of all-news radio and television channels that thrive on breaking news stories with live broadcasts. As a result, not only small town police personnel and other emergency respondents but their colleagues in far larger jurisdictions are challenged by an onslaught of the media during major crises.

∾

Recommendation #2: Crisis managers and response professionals must understand that the media, especially television and radio, are the most effective means to reassure and calm an unsettled public.

When terrorists strike, they kill, hurt, and frighten their immediate victims in order to get the attention of and influence the general public and governmental decision makers. As they strike innocent persons and demonstrate the impotence of the targeted government to protect its citizens, terrorists spread fear and anxiety in their target audience and can even cause panic in the threatened society. While political instability is an unlikely consequence of terror in the American setting, terrorists certainly endeavor to make citizens wonder whether their government and its officials are fit to prevent terrorism in the first place, or at least effectively respond to acts of political violence. For these reasons, crisis managers must utilize the news media in order to project the image of professional, resolute, and competent leadership, even in the most difficult of circumstances. If an event has catastrophic dimensions, crisis managers and response professionals probably have more pressing problems than appearing before microphones and cameras, but they still need to find some way to disseminate information to the news media if only to let the populace know that something is being done, that the political leaders and the response community are on top of the crisis. In this respect, terrorist crises are like other disasters—hurricanes, earthquakes, floods, or riots.

When people are affected by a crisis, or hear about a particular disaster, they turn to the news media, especially radio and television, for information. It is certainly true that nowadays the websites of major news organizations and social media are major sources of information in general and during crises in particular. But for the time being, the traditional media seems first in line when it comes to reporting.

When electric power fails, many still rely on battery-powered electronic media, especially radio. Under no other circumstances are the ratings for TV and radio stations as high as during crises. As one media scholar noted,

> Information about crisis, even if it is bad news, relieves disquieting uncertainty and calms people. This mere activity of watching or listening to familiar reporters and commentators reassures people and keeps them occupied. It gives them a sense of vicarious participation, of "doing something."
>
> News stories [also] serve to reassure people that their grief and fear are shared (Graber 1997, 143).

Following the 1993 World Trade Center bombing in New York's Wall Street area, local newscasters urged people trapped inside the twin towers to remain calm and reassured them; they took phone calls from some of the people unable to leave the stricken building and thereby reassured the public as well. No doubt, the local media provided an important public service and followed the social responsibility ideal of the media in an exemplary way. The media played a similar role during a long hostage ordeal in which heavily armed members of the Hanafi Muslim sect held scores of hostages in three buildings in the center of Washington, D.C., for a prolonged period. One observer concluded that "the media benefited the police because their reporting kept citizens from becoming overly concerned, and because news reports assured citizens that the police had the situation well in hand" (Miller 1982, 82).

But while it is true that citizens feel better simply because they receive information via the news and see the faces and hear the voice of familiar news anchors and reporters, crisis managers are nevertheless counseled to use the media, not only indirectly but directly as well. By appearing in news conferences and granting interviews as soon as possible, crisis managers can best exploit the extraordinary public attention in order to get their messages across, to demonstrate their composure, and to convince citizens to keep their cool and trust that the authorities will do everything possible to protect and assist them.

By seizing the opportunity to "go public" in the early stage of a crisis, public officials are in an excellent position to frame the dimensions of the incident, the quality of their own responses, and thus the public perceptions of both. These first perceptions of how the public and private sector and the political leadership responded to the emergency will shape the public debate that is likely to follow once the most critical phase of the crisis has passed.

There is no better model for crisis managers than Rudy Giuliani, who was the shining light during New York's and America's darkest hours, days, and weeks following the terror attacks on the World Trade Center and the Pentagon. While President George W. Bush was obviously ill advised when he did not immediately head back to Washington from his visit to Florida and therefore was slow in assuming the role of national crisis manager, Mayor Giuliani impressed people in the New York metropolitan area and Americans everywhere with his cool, competent, hands-on leadership as he used the mass media skillfully to communicate with the public regularly. By showing that he and the emergency response specialists wasted no time and effort in dealing with the crisis at hand, the mayor had a calming effect on a city and country jarred by an unprecedented catastrophe. While he was actively involved in the emergency response, he knew instinctively that he had to address citizens in the metropolitan area at once. Two hours and six minutes after the first plane hit the World Trade Center's North Tower, Giuliani was live on New York 1, an all-news cable TV channel, urging calm. To this end, Giuliani said:

> The first thing I'd like to do is to take this opportunity to tell everyone to remain calm and to the extent they can, to evacuate lower Manhattan. We've been in contact with the White House and asked them to secure the space around the city. They've been doing that for at least the last hour, hour and a half. I've spoken with the governor several times and I agree that the [local primary] election today should be canceled.[9]

But while the mayor reassured fellow citizens that everything humanly possible was being done, he did not hide the incredible horror in Manhattan's downtown but described what he had seen and felt:

I was there shortly after it happened and saw people jumping out of the World Trade Center. It's a horrible, horrible situation, and all that I can tell them is that every resource that we have is attempting to rescue as many people as possible. And the end result is going to be some horrendous number of lives lost. I don't think we know yet, but right now we have to just focus on saving as many people as possible.[10]

Some three and one-half hours later, the mayor held his first news conference that was broadcast by the local, national, and international media. "We will strive now very hard to save as many people as possible," he said, "and to send a message that the City of New York and the United States of America is much stronger than any group of barbaric terrorists."[11]

Giuliani displayed strong and tireless leadership under unthinkably grim circumstances and, at the same time, compassion and grief, not only in these initial public communications but in the many press briefings that followed in the next hours, days, weeks, and months as well. He and others on the crisis management team made exemplary use of the mass media to inform the public as fully as possible about the situation and to direct people in the metropolitan areas as to what they should and should not do. This was a momentous task given that tens of thousands of people in the New York metropolitan area were directly affected by the terror—either because they were in the hit buildings or were relatives, friends, or colleagues of these victims—and were desperate for information. In addition, most people who lived or worked in New York City looked for and received information about public and private transportation, school and business closings, etc., from the media In short, no prewritten blueprint for this kind of emergency response could have prescribed a more perfect utilization of the mass media than the "going public" patterns that came naturally to Mayor Rudy Giuliani.

Once back in the White House, President George W. Bush, too, addressed the American public regularly and effectively. In less than four weeks following the events of 9/11, he made more than fifty public statements designed to convey the reassuring picture of an effective crisis manager.

∼

Recommendation #3: The emergency response community must utilize the mass media as vital instruments for enhancing and coordinating their actual emergency efforts—especially when telling the public what to do and what not to do.

It has been argued that in times of major domestic emergencies, radio and television become "vital arms of government" because they offer officials literally unlimited access to communicate with the public, with emergency specialists, and with other government authorities (Graber 1997, 135). While officials can be especially effective by personally appealing to their various audiences, they also can convey their needs, concerns, and warnings indirectly through reporters and other media personnel. In the hours and days following the

Oklahoma City bombing, for example, local television, radio, and the press were superb in serving the public interest not merely by informing their audiences of the bombing, its consequences, and the response activities, but also by functioning as conduits between emergency response specialists and the public in the affected city and beyond. In publicizing and repeating officials' appeals to citizens not to enter the disaster area and not to interfere with rescue efforts, but to donate blood for the injured in specified places, or to contribute warm clothing for rescue workers, the media assisted crisis managers a great deal. Moreover, as the national media reported on what response specialists described as difficult rescue efforts, emergency specialists around the country responded by offering to travel to the wounded city and assist exhausted rescue workers who had worked nonstop for days and nights.

Following the first World Trade Center bombing in 1993, TV and radio stations repeatedly broadcast important information released by public officials and spokespersons for private companies. For example, the employees of firms affected by the explosions were told not to report to work that evening and the next day(s). Motorists learned which streets were closed for all traffic; all citizens were informed of important emergency phone numbers.

Undoubtedly, during the most serious cases of terrorism on U.S. soil so far, crisis managers and emergency specialists utilized the mass media for their purposes in various ways. But the information disseminated by the media typically comes from all kinds of sources and is easily contradictory and confusing. For this reason, it is advisable to coordinate the release of information designed to enhance response efforts and, if possible, speak with one voice to the media and the public.

Again, Mayor Giuliani and others in his 9/11 crisis team were flawless in keeping the public abreast of the step-by-step rescue efforts and in telling New Yorkers how they could help or could hinder these difficult efforts. But despite all of their competence and skills in dealing with the news media, even these crisis managers could not prevent some news reports that were based on rumors. For example, several days after the collapse of the World Trade Center, the media reported that a group of missing firefighters had been found alive in the rubble. As it turned out, the report, raising the hopes of many families, was erroneous.

Finally, it is important that response professionals avoid the jargon that is common and appropriate when they communicate with other specialists in their field. Unlike beat reporters who are familiar with the work and the language of law enforcement officials and others in the emergency response community, general reporters and most citizens are not. Statements in news conferences and answers to reporters' questions must be given in the plain language that everyone understands. Using abbreviations is fine, when everyone knows the full meaning, but these abbreviations can annoy people who do not know what is meant and have to ask for further explanations.

～

Recommendation #4: Trained personnel in close proximity to response professionals must monitor the mass media around the clock for accuracy in crisis-related news and, during hostage situations, for news items that could endanger the lives of hostages and law enforcement officers and/or hamper efforts to end a standoff.

The response community must prepare for reliable personnel inside emergency command centers to monitor the mass media throughout the most critical phases of a crisis in order to ensure that publicized information is correct and that appeals for assistance of one kind or another are made only when prepared and backed up by organizational moves to facilitate responding citizens (for example, a vast number of blood donors descending on hospitals or schools or churches, or emergency workers coming from afar to assist in rescue tasks, or people massing medical facilities to receive antidotes for released biological or chemical agents). To do this job well, monitors must be close to crisis managers. If publicized information is wrong or contradictory, if rumors are elevated to the level of hard news, if appeals to help have resulted in sufficient offers, if a stricken population is misdirected with respect to treatment facilities, then the media must be contacted immediately so that mistakes are corrected or changing circumstances are reflected in the news. Given the all-out competition between news organizations, the pressure to present breaking news, the determination to report some new angle although a terrorist situation has not changed, and the tendency to sensationalize even genuinely dramatic situations, the hastily reported and often unverified news is likely to contain inaccuracies, mistakes, and problematic features. Hostage situations are particularly prone to suffer from crisis reporting, especially live broadcasts, which lack the safeguards otherwise built into the news process with roles for editors, news directors, and even legal advisers. At worst, the press publicizes information that has the potential to interfere with efforts to resolve a crisis and that endangers the lives of hostages, rescuers, and other actors. Since terrorists seek publicity when they strike, it is not surprising that they are eager to follow the news about their particular deeds. After igniting the potent bomb at the Alfred P. Murrah Federal Building, driving away, and being arrested for driving a car without license plates, Timothy McVeigh watched television while he was processed in an office in the Noble County Sheriff's Department. After the blast, he had not bothered to return to the Murrah Building to survey the damage he had caused. Hours later, he got his chance:

> McVeigh pretended to pay little attention to the television, but he was watching and listening to every word. This was the first opportunity to see what his bomb had done to the Murrah Building. His initial reaction was disappointment. Damn, he thought, the whole building didn't come down. But McVeigh says how even that [*sic*] revelation had a silver lining for him: with part of the Murrah Building still standing, in its ruined state, the American public would be left with its carcass, standing as a symbol. (Michel and Herbeck 2001, 245)

In McVeigh's case, his next stop was a county jail cell where he had no access to the news media. In other cases, terrorists follow the news continuously for clues of whether their deeds had the intended effects or, especially during hostage situations, to learn about actions and reactions of crisis response specialists and other actors in their target audience. After Corey Moore, an African American ex-Marine, took two white persons hostage in the city hall of Warrensville Heights, Ohio, to protest the treatment of black people in the United States, he eventually released one of his captives in exchange for a television set in order to monitor the news of the incident and to check whether hostage negotiators were being truthful or deceiving him.[12]

During the 1977 Hanafi Muslim incident in Washington, D.C., during which one person was killed, several people injured, and more than one hundred taken hostage in three different buildings, eleven people were able to hide in one part of one of the buildings and evade capture. At one point, a basket with food was lifted by rope to a window of the room where these people were hiding. A camera operator filmed the lifting of the basket, and a local station broadcast the video. It is believed that members of the Hanafi group who were not involved in the hostage taking, or supporters of the sect, monitored television news, notified the captors by phone, and set off a search by the heavily armed Hanafis for the missing people. By monitoring the news, the police knew of the sudden problem and prepared for a rescue effort that eventually freed the group of eleven from their hiding place—before the Hanafis got to them.

These and similar examples underline the importance of monitoring incident news around the clock by crisis command centers and reacting promptly to exploit new opportunities for crisis resolution, law enforcement, etc., or to prevent potentially harmful consequences of publicized information.

∾

Recommendation #5: Response specialists must keep in mind that most journalists and news organizations cooperate with the authorities faced with truly serious incidents. In this cooperative mode, the media can be instrumental in resolving these types of crises.

While reporters are chasing exclusives in order to scoop the competition, many of them are not inclined to disregard that they could endanger the victims of terrorism, especially hostages, and the members of rescue teams by reporting indiscriminately and revealing tactical information. During the Iran hostage crisis, for example, some reporters were aware that a few members of the U.S. embassy staff in Tehran had fled before the takeover and had found shelter in Canada's embassy. During the hijacking of TWA Flight 847 in 1985, some American journalists learned that another member of the U.S. military was aboard the hijacked airliner besides Navy diver Robert Stethem, who was brutally murdered by the terrorists simply because he was part of the American armed forces. In both cases, these facts were not publicized because responsible journalists did not want to jeopardize the welfare, or even the lives, of fellow Americans. In the changed media world of the twenty-first century, with heightened competition, such information is less likely to be withheld than in the past. Accordingly, when faced with terrorist incidents, leaking sensitive information to the press or disclosing this sort of intelligence confidentially are not options that response professionals should consider.

But in some situations, law enforcement officials and other response professionals may consider asking media organizations for assistance and cooperation. The most obvious cases arise when terrorists demand that the media in general, or specific news organizations, publicize their manifestos, statements, or communiqués in exchange for ending a hostage ordeal or ceasing deadly terrorist campaigns. Although the official position of the U.S. government is that its officials will not negotiate with terrorists and will not give in to their demands, in reality response professionals do negotiate and do accommodate terrorist objectives—especially in cases of domestic terrorism and with respect to terrorists' publicity requests.

In this respect, cases of mass-mediated terrorism are treated like incidents arising from criminal hostage situations. For example, in late January 2001, the last two of seven Texas prison escapees agreed to surrender peacefully to law enforcement officers in Colorado Springs, Colorado, after an opportunity to vent their grievances during a telephone interview with Eric Singer, a local television anchor. Law enforcement officers did not object to the live broadcast but in fact assisted in arranging the interview during which the escaped prisoners complained about the conditions in the Texas penitentiary system. It was far more controversial when the *Washington Post* and the *New York Times*, at the request of Attorney General Janet Reno and the FBI, published a thirty-five-thousand-word manifesto authored by the then still elusive "Unabomber," Theodore Kaczynski, in September 1995. By publicizing the tract against the ills of technology and consumerism five days before the author's deadline, the publishers justified their action with the desire to prevent the threatened mailing of yet another deadly letter bomb by a terrorist who had already killed three people and injured many more via explosive mailings. This was not the first time that law enforcement and other agencies asked the media to publish terrorist statements. In fact, in 1976, at the urging of the FBI and the FAA, four U.S. newspapers published the statements of Croatian nationals during a lengthy hijacking and bombing incident. Assured that their pleas for Croatia's independence had been published and had reached the American and international public, the hijackers surrendered in Paris.

While law enforcement specialists, hostages and their families, and news organizations justify their concessions to terrorists with the argument that they are trying to protect the victims, or potential victims, neither law enforcement nor media organizations should agree easily to these kinds of compromises. Obviously, resolving a terrorist crisis or removing a terrorist threat (and thereby sparing hostages' lives and suffering) must always be the primary consideration of response professionals. But response professionals must never forget that giving in to terrorists with respect to their media-centered goals could well encourage members of the same or different groups to resort to more political violence for the sake of media and public attention.

~

Recommendation #6: Although representatives of the news media will demand access to the site of a terrorist act, response professionals have the right and the responsibility to limit or deny access if the presence of media representatives threatens the safety of victims and response personnel or inhibits rescue efforts, negotiations, or other means to resolve the emergency.

Even in instances when political leaders acting as crisis managers and response professionals cooperate with the media, members of the fourth estate are likely to insist on access to the site of terrorism and reject restrictions in the name of the First Amendment and the constitutional guarantee of freedom of the press. The fourth estate tends to construe the First Amendment as the public's assurance of the right to be informed by a press that is free of governmental interference. Thus, the media will argue, in order to inform the public fully, the working press has an access right. However, the Supreme Court and lower courts have not backed such an absolute right to access. In *Branzburg v. Hayes*,[13] the court held that the Constitution does not guarantee the news media special access to information that is not available to the public at large. "Newsmen have no constitutional right of access to the scenes of crime or disaster when the general public is excluded," the court ruled. Earlier, in *Zemel v. Rusk*,[14] a unanimous Supreme Court ruled that the "right to speak and publish does not carry with it the unrestrained right to gather information." While the denial of unauthorized entry to the White House inhibits citizens' ability to gather information on the way the country is governed, the court wrote, "that does not make entry into the White House a First Amendment right." In yet another decision, *Los Angeles Free Press, Inc. v. City of Los Angeles*, the Court of Appeals of California ruled,

> Restrictions on the right of access to particular places at particular times are consistent with other reasonable restrictions on liberty based upon the police power, and these restrictions remain valid even though the ability of the press to gather news and express views on a particular subject may be incidentally hampered.[15]

The point here is not to encourage law enforcement officials and other response professionals to automatically deny media representatives access to incident sites whenever terrorism occurs. It should be clear from the previous recommendations that such a policy and practice would backfire because it would surely create an adversarial relationship with the fourth estate, risk the response community's status as primary news source, interfere with crisis managers' need to inform the public, and diminish their chances of cooperating with media organizations. But when the presence of the media interferes with the work of rescuers, negotiators, or other response professionals, law enforcement officers have the right to limit, or deny, media access. One way to deal with the onslaught of large numbers of newsmen and women would be to restrict access to the immediate incident site to those reporters who cover the police, fire, and emergency beats on a regular basis and possess press credentials issued by local police departments. Indeed, a Federal Appeals Court in California ruled precisely along these lines when it held that "regular coverage of police and fire news provides a reasonable basis for classification of persons who seek the privilege of crossing police lines."[16]

Ideally, response professionals would like to deal with media representatives who regularly cover their beats and are knowledgeable in these particular fields. But in reality, beat specialists may not be the only ones who cover major terrorist incidents and may even be replaced by star reporters and prominent anchors, typically generalists who lack the special expertise of beat reporters. In other words, while the police and other response agencies tend to deal mostly with beat reporters in their day-to-day work, they must be prepared to face generalists and members of the national media elite when terrorists commit major acts of mass-mediated violence. Denying access to generalists from local news networks and from prominent national media organizations, including star reporters and anchors, is probably not a realistic option for response professionals. If they can resist the star appeal of nationally known news personnel, most political leaders in their jurisdiction are less likely to do so at a time that assures them of great media exposure. These facts make the issue of access one of the most difficult problems for the response community and one that needs to be solved with the specifics of each case in mind.

Past observations and recommendations by experts remain valuable to this day. I still agree with suggestions that police departments should be proactive in this respect. For example, Abraham H.Miller (1982, 83–84) recommended the following,

> Police agencies, as a matter of course, should develop clear guidelines governing the news media's access to the scene of terrorist incidents and clear rules governing police lines and press identification passes. The media should be made aware of these guidelines and conditions before terrorist incidents and similar events occur. This step seeks to avoid the arguments and recriminations that can develop between individual reporters and police officers during the rush and confusion of violent incidents. Police departments, if they have the organizational capacity, should have contingency plans for dealing with events likely to draw national news media attention, particularly extensive television coverage.

While there is always a chance that members of the public will hurry to terrorism sites, the celebrity cult surrounding television news anchors and correspondents is likely to draw even more citizens to the scene. As a result, police officers will be harder pressed to provide effective crowd control that is often essential for recovery, rescue, and negotiation efforts.

~

Recommendation #7: As a general rule, crisis managers should not go the "prior restraints" route. In almost all terrorist emergencies, curbing press freedom is not an option. However, in extraordinary cases, when information—if revealed— would result in a "clear and present danger" for human life or the national interest in very specific and most serious ways, response professionals must sometimes consider this extreme and highly controversial step.

Suppose that a reporter has learned that a hostage rescue mission is in the making. Suppose that terrorists have killed several hostages after seeing news reports of a previous attempt that was eventually aborted. Suppose that the reporter has told his producer and editor about his scoop and has thus triggered debates inside his news organization as to whether or not to publicize the news. Suppose that crisis managers fear that the information will be publicized—sooner or later. Now, if there is a clear and present danger that additional hostages— or one single hostage—will die if the news of another rescue attempt is broadcast or published, response professionals and political leaders must consider calling a judge for a restraining order. And they have a good chance of obtaining it. This is not a likely scenario, but it is not an impossible one either. In the past, hostage situations have lasted for many months or years. In the first decade of the twenty-first century, the Abu Sayyaf in the Philippines, a terrorist and separatist group, held hostages for many months on several occasions, threatened numerous times that rescue efforts by the Filipino Army would cause the execution of hostages, and actualized these threats more than once. One can easily imagine other horror scenarios. Suppose that the CIA and/or other agencies have learned that a terrorist group plans a biological, chemical, or nuclear attack on an American city or region. Suppose that the intelligence has a few credible but also less convincing elements. Suppose that, as a precaution, measures to prevent a strike or, if that fails, respond to such an assault are put in place secretly. Suppose that the secret is leaked to a journalist who tries to verify the scoop as his news organization ponders the question of whether or not to publicize the information. It is not farfetched to assume that the news of an imminent attack with weapons of mass destruction would result in hysteria, panic, unorganized mass flight, or loss of life. Here, a case could be made for prior restraint and preventing the alarming news from being publicized.

For all the emphasis on freedom of expression and freedom of the press, even in the United States with its unique First Amendment rights, these fundamental and most precious liberties are not absolute. Nobody expressed this veracity better than Justice Oliver Wendell Holmes when he wrote for a unanimous Supreme Court,

> The most stringent protection of free speech would not protect a man in falsely shouting fire in a theatre and causing a panic. It does not even protect a man from an injunction against uttering words that may have all the effects of force. . . . The question in every case is whether the words used are used in such circumstances and are of such nature as to create a clear and present danger that will bring about the substantive evils that Congress has a right to prevent.[17]

In *Schenck v. United States*, however, Holmes and his brethren and the lower courts looked at a case after the fact: The controversial material had been published and those who published it had been indicted and found guilty of conspiracy to violate the Espionage Act of 1917. More than fifty years later, in *New York Times Company v. United States*, which arose out of the Pentagon Papers case, the Supreme Court ruled six to three against the government and its efforts to prevent the *New York Times* (and the *Washington Post*) from publishing internal government documents about the Vietnam War. In other words, this was an issue of prior restraint because the Nixon administration had asked the courts for an injunction directing the *Times* and the *Post* not to publish classified material. But it is noteworthy that only two of the justices in the majority, Hugo Black and William O. Douglas, insisted that the First Amendment does not allow prior restraint in any circumstance. The seven other justices, albeit to varying degrees, recognized exceptions to the stringent meaning of freedom of expression and freedom of the press in the American context. Justice Potter Stewart, for example, wrote that prior restraint was permissible under the U.S. Constitution if disclosure would "surely result in direct, immediate, and irreparable damage to our Nation or its people."[18]

While those rare and exceptional cases in which the dissemination of information represents a clear and imminent danger to people are most likely during wars, one can argue that terrorism is in this sense a type of warfare. To this end, one prominent legal scholar applied the "clear and present danger" doctrine and other landmark rulings specifically to the terrorist situation and concluded,

> Despite the strong presumption of unconstitutionality, prior restraint may be constitutionally permissible where specific harm of a grave nature would surely result from media dissemination of certain information. Although general reporting of terrorism would lack the contextual immediacy required to justify suppression, the same may not be true during contemporaneous coverage of ongoing incidents, particularly in hostage situations. Numerous scenarios are imaginable in which prior restraints may be justified to save lives. (Bassiouni 1981, 40)

Again, only in extreme situations when there is no doubt that the pending publication of certain information will lead to irreparable harm—most likely to hostages and law enforcement and other response professionals—is the prior restraint route a potential option for those who manage and respond to terrorist acts.

~

Recommendation #8: Encouraging media guidelines for reporting terrorist incidents may be prudent; however, trusting that news organizations will follow their guidelines is not.

Following the above-mentioned Hanafi hostage drama in 1977, the outspo-
ken Patrick Buchanan charged that "American TV has become patsy, promoter
and paymaster for political terrorists—their preferred vehicle of communication."[19] Buchanan was not the only one who criticized media organizations
for the excessive amount and, more importantly, the kind of coverage they
devoted to the incident. Critics inside and outside the media were especially
concerned about live interviews with the hostage holders inside the occupied
buildings and their sympathizers outside. As they offered the Hanafis a public
forum to air their grievances, media organizations all over the country and
abroad seemed to give sect members an incentive not to negotiate a quick end
to the situation but to exploit this opportunity for unlimited publicity. According to one observer,

> What did Khaalis [leader of the Hanafi sect] obtain for his efforts? Media expo-
> sure, in otherwise unreachable proportions. There was continuous live televi-
> sion coverage; domination of virtually the entire first section of the *Washington
> Post* for two days; and transatlantic phone interviews. The event transformed
> the Hanafi Muslims from a little-known group, even within Washington, to the
> focal point of national and international media coverage (Miller 1980, 83).

Nobody was more aware of this sudden fame than Hanafi leader Hamass
Abdul Khaalis, who became very selective during the hostage drama as to the
news organizations with which he would communicate. He turned down radio
and TV stations with limited audiences, telling them that they were not worth
talking to. At one time, he declined to give an interview with a Texas radio
reporter after learning that his station had only twenty thousand watts, informing the reporter that he would not talk to radio stations with less than fifty
thousand watts (Jaehning 1978, 723). Moreover, by revealing on the air details
about law enforcement officers' actual moves and anticipated actions, news
organizations provided up-to-date information to the Hanafis that may have
hampered early efforts to resolve the crisis and endangered the well-being of
innocent bystanders and response professionals. One result of the Hanafi incident was that several news organizations, among them wire services, daily
newspapers, and TV and radio networks, developed internal guidelines for
reporting terrorist situations. Among the first media organizations to enact
such codes was United Press International. Its guidelines were representative
for these kinds of blueprints, pledging not to jeopardize lives, not to become
part of an unfolding terrorist incident, and not to participate in negotiations.
But these guidelines were, and still are, altogether broad, leaving ample room
to circumvent the specific prohibitions with phrases such as, "In all cases we
will apply the rule of common sense" or "We will judge each story on its own
and if a story is newsworthy cover it despite the danger of contagion" (Miller
1982, 146–47). In the more than three decades since the first guidelines for
terrorism coverage were adopted, far more dramatic, far lengthier, and far
deadlier terrorism has plagued the United States abroad and at home. Neither

formal guidelines nor informal newsroom agreements on how to handle the coverage of terrorist incidents has eradicated excessive and potentially harmful reporting. If anything, the growing competition in the media market and the trend from hard news to infotainment news has led to more aggressiveness in pursuing the sensational, dramatic, tragic, and frightening aspects of news in general and in the area of terrorism incidents in particular. Even in news organizations with the best intentions to adhere to self-imposed guidelines, these codes of behavior and reporting fly out of the window in the face of major incidents, when the competitive juices flow especially energetically in the struggle for ratings, circulation, and, most of all, corporate profit imperatives.

Nevertheless, thoughtful media professionals have developed far more detailed and stringent guidelines. Bob Steel of the Poynter Institute provides an excellent example of unambiguous prescriptions for responsible reporting of terrorist incidents, hostage situations, and similar incidents. Unlike the provisions in most guidelines of this kind, Steel's fifteen points are precise and not watered down by general statements that result in loopholes.[20] If news organizations would follow these sorts of guidelines, they would be far less likely to become unwitting accomplices in terrorist schemes. It certainly makes sense to encourage news organizations to consider and discuss how to cover, or not to cover, terrorist situations regardless of whether the results are formal guidelines or simply a better understanding of the problems surrounding this sort of coverage. Over time, such practices and measures could affect terrorism coverage for the better. But unless all news organizations sign on to what critics will call self-censorship, the competitive tendencies will prevail and prevent meaningful changes.

~

Recommendation #9: By showing their human face in dealing with terrorism's victims and their loved ones, members of the response community will help others—and themselves.

When terrorists strike, response specialists must deal with victims as well as with their families, friends, neighbors, and the larger public. On one level, crisis managers and everyone else involved in dealing with an act of terror are expected to be cool, rational, and detached enough to effectively handle whatever has to be done. On another level, however, the same people are expected to be sensitive to the feelings of the immediately affected people and responsive to their needs. In no other area of the emergency response field are both gratitude and resentment more easily and more vehemently expressed than in the real or perceived treatment of victims and their families. The visuals of exhausted emergency workers who dug victims out of the rubble of the Murrah Federal Building in Oklahoma City, the compelling pictures of grief-stricken rescuers carrying dead children from the scene of unspeakable terror, the sensible words of officials speaking for the police and fire departments and other organizations added up to a mass-mediated composite of a crisis response community with a human face that was comforting to the injured, to the families of victims, and to the nation. The unspoken message here was that of men and women who went beyond the call of duty in their difficult work and were at all times a part of a community in shock and pain. Because of the scope of the 9/11 terrorism, the heroics of the rescuers were even more visible. Although losing hundreds of their colleagues when the World Trade Center collapsed, members of New York's fire and police departments worked relentlessly around the clock in efforts to save lives, even when there was no longer any hope. These rescuers' selfless efforts, witnessed by New Yorkers and Americans in the hours, days, weeks, and months after the 9/11 terror, changed the perceptions of the men and women in New York's fire and police departments. Perhaps nothing expressed this genuine admiration more than Halloween 2001, when many boys and girls dressed up as firefighters and police officers, and Christmas of that year, when children wished for fire engines and police cars from Santa. And there were other groups that conveyed this spirit of absolute compassion—the teams of FEMA, the iron workers, the members of the National Guard, and even the search dogs that pushed on in spite of their badly cut feet. In a way, New York's darkest hour became its finest; New York became a community that closed ranks behind the shining example of emergency response specialists who revealed the human face behind their first-rate professionalism.

Fourteen years later, the same spirit of community and unity characterized the sentiments in Charleston, South Carolina, in the wake of the horrific act of domestic terrorism that took the lives of nine members of the Emanuel AME Church. Religious and political leaders, emergency response professionals, and rank-and-file citizens all came together displaying determination to overcome hate and violence.

But there have also been instances when victims of terrorism, their families, and even the public at large may not see the human face of response professionals, and this causes them to react critically. Following the catastrophic bombing of PanAm Flight 103 over Lockerbie, Scotland, for example, both the airline and the U.S. State Department were harshly criticized by the victims' families for not providing prompt information and assistance to those who wanted to travel to the crash site. Most of all, even years after the incident, families of the Flight 103 victims complained bitterly about the insensitivity of the State Department personnel that they encountered. Eventually, the Department of State conceded that there was a need "to build a more integrated approach . . . sensitizing our people to dealing with such tragedies, and the need for compassionate follow-through. . . . [W]e can never forget that we are participating in a life-shattering event for these families, and that we must proceed with utmost care."[21]

All organizations, public and private, need to realize that terrorism, like other crises, calls for both professional and human response. To show compassion by deed for the victims of terrorism and their loved ones is certainly the most important imperative here, but to translate this reality into a media reality is another. Certainly, the victims of terrorism and/or their loved ones will be thankful when they encounter compassionate response professionals.

But beyond this, it is also important that crisis managers and those who speak for the emergency response community project this compassionate and comforting image via the media to a traumatized public. Public perception is not shaped by reality but by the pseudo-reality reflected in the mass media.

～

Recommendation #10: Last but not least, terrorism response professionals can circumvent the traditional news media and communicate directly with each other and, more importantly, with the public by using the Internet.

Terrorism response professionals would not have to think about how to handle media relations, that is, how to assure factual reporting or how to react to potentially damaging incident-related media revelations, if they could circumvent the fourth estate and directly communicate with the public. But while the traditional print and electronic media are alive and well and still the dominant mode of transmitting news and public information, the digital media offer emergency and terrorist response communities excellent means to inform, warn, and instruct the public during and after incidents without going through the traditional news media.

Today, many cities, counties, and towns communicate with their residents via e-mail, text, or phone messages about emergencies whether man-made terrorist and criminal events or natural occurrences, such as hurricanes, floods, wildfires.

When television and radio stations are knocked off the air, part of the citizenry may still be able to access the Internet via battery-powered computers. This scenario is not as obscure as it might seem at first. When a terrorist bomb exploded in the garage of the World Trade Center in 1993 and rocked the building's twin towers mightily, it knocked out most of New York's broadcast transmitters on the top of the towers. As a result, only WCBS, which maintained a back-up system on the Empire State Building, was able to broadcast over local airwaves. Otherwise, television coverage was available only for those who had access to cable channels. But whether or not the traditional media function is normal, terrorist response professionals will be most successful in getting their own messages across to the public if they utilize their websites. It may well be that the vast majority of Americans will first turn to television and radio when terrorists strike, and that others will prefer the websites of their favorite news organizations to inform themselves, but if law enforcement and other response agencies inform the public of their own sites, chances are that many citizens will access these sites for the most authoritative emergency information. Such Internet sites need to be updated often and diligently and are additional means to provide media organizations around the country and the world with new and archived press releases, statements, warnings, clarifications, etc. Finally, the Internet provides an ideal means for response professionals to communicate with each other, especially when geographically far apart. While the traditional media has been helpful in the past in alerting emergency specialists to the needs of a particular incident, the Internet can serve as a more specialized means of communication between response professionals in ways that the traditional news media cannot. Here, for sure, the jargon of specialists is perfectly fine and makes for shorter and quicker communication, action, and cooperation.

The Media's Responsibility

While this chapter addresses questions of public information and media relations during terrorist crises from the perspectives of public officials and emergency response specialists, implicit in this discussion is also the kind of stance that the news media should take in such situations. To be sure, the media have a responsibility to fully inform citizens of important events and developments. Governmental power—especially authority in extraordinary situations—needs monitoring and robust checks to prevent abuse of power. If there are mistakes or abuses, the media must ensure that they are revealed. But the media must also remember their responsibility to the public interest and public good as first articulated in the Canons of Journalism in the 1920s and reemphasized in updates of these professional guidelines for the fourth estate. A responsible press must not only insist on factual and full information but must also recognize in extraordinary cases that certain revelations in the news could have devastating consequences for rescue personnel and the victims of terrorism.

Notes

1. White House, accessed June 19, 2015, https://www.whitehouse.gov/blog/2015/06/18/latest-president-obama-delivers-statement-shooting-charleston.

2. Jason Horowitz, Nick Corosaniti, and Ashleu Southall, "Nine Killed in Shooting at Black Church in Charleston," *New York Times*, June 17, 2015, accessed, June 19, 2015, http://www.nytimes.com/2015/06/18/us/church-attacked-in-charleston-south-carolina.html.

3. For more on media coverage, changes in public opinion, and new congressional hearings with respect to Waco, see Brigitte L. Nacos, *Terrorism and the Media: From the Iran Hostage Crisis to the Oklahoma City Bombing* (New York: Columbia University Press, 1996), preface to the paperback edition.

4. Interview with Lou Michel, April 9, 2001.

5. After the *Boston Globe* published a story that, according to anonymous official sources, the killings were crimes of passion, the New Hampshire Attorney General reacted with a press release and the categorical statement that "investigators do not

hold the belief attributed to them." For more on this topic, see Jim Fox, "Small Town, Big Story," *Brill's Content* (June 2001): 70–71.

6. Howard Kurtz, "For Every Cool Head, a Thousand Overheated Muffins," *Washington Post*, October 29, 2001, C1.

7. Ibid.

8. Ibid.

9. Quoted here from Andrew Kirtzman, "Mayor Dodges Death and Calms the City," *New York Daily News*, October 21, 2001.

10. Ibid.

11. Ibid.

12. The incident in 1977 ended when President Jimmy Carter agreed to speak to Corey Moore by phone if he released his remaining hostage unharmed and if he surrendered to police. Moore laid down his weapons and surrendered after he heard the president on television promising to keep his end of the arrangement.

13. 408 U.S. 665; 1972.

14. 381 U.S. 1; 1965.

15. Cal. App. 3d 448; 1970.

16. Ibid.

17. *Schenck v. United States*, 1919 (249 U.S. 47).

18. *New York Times Company v. United States*, 1971 (403 U.S. 713).

19. This remark was attributed to Buchanan in *TV Guide*, March 26, 1977, A5.

20. Bob Steel, "Guidelines for Covering Hostage-Taking, Crises, Prison Uprisings, Terrorist Actions," Poynter Institute, July 1999, accessed 1 April 2002, http://www .poynter.org/dj/tips/ethics/guidelines.htm.

21. Cited in the "Report of the President's Commission on Aviation Security and Terrorism," Washington, DC: U.S. Government Printing Office, May 15, 1990, 102.

12

Conclusion

Final Thoughts on Mass-Mediated Terrorism

AFTER THE DEPARTMENT OF HOMELAND SECURITY (DHS) distributed an intelligence report about the growing threat of violent right-wing extremism to police departments and other law enforcement agencies in early 2009, then DHS Secretary Janet Napolitano was harshly criticized by conservative politicians and interest groups.[1] Critics were outraged because the report, which had been worked on during the Bush administration, mentioned disillusioned veterans as potential recruits. To the extent that the mainstream and online media paid attention to the report, they focused on the partisan controversy but not on the content of the intelligence findings.

In the following years, while transnational terrorism and threats thereof were hyped in the news, there was little or no media attention to right-wing antigovernment, white supremacy, militia type organizations. There was no scarcity of information. Organizations like the Anti-Defamation League and the Southern Poverty Law Center kept tabs on hate groups of all varieties and the political violence—terrorism—perpetrated by their followers. The New America foundation kept records of post–9/11 terrorist acts on American soil committed by right-wing extremists on the one hand and jihadists on the other hand with the statistics showing throughout that right-wing terrorists killed more persons than did jihadists.[2] All of these results of research and investigations were available on the websites of the above organizations.

It took the killing of nine members of the Emanuel African Methodist Episcopal Church in Charleston, South Carolina, by a white supremacist in June 2015 for some of the leading news organizations to finally pay attention to this threat. On June 24, 2015, the *New York Times* published and prominently placed a story under the headline, "Homegrown Extremists Tied to Deadlier Toll Than Jihadists in U.S. Since 9/11" with the following lead:

In the 14 years since Al Qaeda carried out attacks on New York and the Pentagon, extremists have regularly executed smaller lethal assaults in the United States, explaining their motives in online manifestoes or social media rants.

But the breakdown of extremist ideologies behind those attacks may come as a surprise. Since Sept. 11, 2001, nearly twice as many people have been killed by white supremacists, antigovernment fanatics and other non-Muslim extremists than by radical Muslims: 48 have been killed by extremists who are not Muslim, compared with 26 by self-proclaimed jihadists, according to a count by New America, a Washington research center.[3]

Contrary to the reporter's assumption, the higher death toll by right-wing terrorists would and should not have come as a surprise, had his newspaper and other media devoted to this threat merely a fraction of the attention, space, and airtime they gave to jihadist terrorism. It was the over-coverage of jihadist violence and the under-coverage or non-coverage of right-wing violence that led to perceptions removed from reality. Public officials were part of the problem as well. After Janet Napolitano was attacked for issuing the aforementioned intelligence report on right-extremist violence—she did not dare to call it "terrorism"—experts in the counterterrorism community were careful not to make the same "mistake" of pointing out that the jihadist threat was not the only one in the homeland.

This is a perfect example of the mainstream media's power to set not only the media agenda but the public and elite agendas as well; this case demonstrates furthermore the ability of the media to frame the news simply by reporting more, less, or not at all on developments, events, or threats of violence.

Another outfall of the attack against Charleston parishioners was a mass-mediated debate about the proper characterization of the massacre and its perpetrator. Whereas some called the white supremacist killer a deranged person, psychopath, drug addict, or criminal with no ideological agenda, others considered him a terrorist with a segregationist white supremacy agenda. Hillary Clinton spoke of "racist terrorism." There was no agreement but this was nevertheless an exceptional case in that the definitional differences were discussed with some political leaders, criminal justice experts, reporters, and anchors who called right extremist violence an act of terrorism just as jihadist violence is commonly characterized with the t-word. Twenty years earlier, the Oklahoma City bombing was understood as American terrorism but there was no mass-mediated debate as unfolded after the Charleston shootings. Only time will tell whether this was the beginning of finding common ground on the perennial definitional issues in the realm of non-state political violence.

Finally, a word of prudence: While the threat of terrorism at home and abroad looks like an increasingly serious threat, especially in view of terrorist organizations, such as ISIS, Boko Haram, and al-Shabaab that control large territorial chunks, it is also true that so far terrorism is not an existential threat. Far more Americans die every year in car accidents and from heart attacks than as result of terrorist strikes. When major news organizations present day-in and day-out breaking news about the Islamic State and other terrorist threats, news consumers can come away easily with unrealistic assessments of the nature of those threats.

Notes

1. Department of Homeland Security, "Rightwing Extremism," accessed June 24, 2015, http://fas.org/irp/eprint/rightwing.pdf.

2. The New America Foundation's statistics on homegrown terrorism continue to be updated. "Homegrown Extremism 2001–2015," accessed June 24, 2015, http://securitydata.newamerica.net/extremists/analysis.html.

3. *New York Times*, accessed June 24, 2015, http://www.nytimes.com/2015/06/25/us/tally-of-attacks-in-us-challenges-perceptions-of-top-terror-threat.html.

Bibliography

Adams, James. 2001. "Virtual Defense." *Foreign Affairs* 80.3 (May/June): 98–112.

Adams, William C., ed. 1981. *Television Coverage of the Middle East*. Norwood, NJ: Ablex Press.

Alali, A. Odasuo, and Kenoye Kelvin Eke, eds. 1991. *Media Coverage of Terrorism: Methods of Diffusion*. Newbury Park, CA: Sage.

Alford, Matthew. 2010a. *Reel Power: Hollywood Cinema and American Supremacy*. London: Pluto Press.

———. 2010b. "Why Not a Propaganda Model for Hollywood?" In *Screens of Terror: Representations of War and Terrorism in Film and Television since 9/11*, edited by Philip Hammond. Bury St Edmunds: Arima Publishing.

Alger, Dean. 1998. *Megamedia: How Giant Corporations Dominate Mass Media, Distort Competition, and Endanger Democracy*. Lanham, MD: Rowman & Littlefield.

Allison, Graham T., Owen R. Coté, Steven E. Miller, and Richard A Falkenrath. 1996. *Avoiding Nuclear Anarchy*. Cambridge, MA: MIT Press.

Altheide, David L. 1982. "Three-in-One News: Network Coverage of Iran." *Journalism Quarterly* 59:482–86.

———. 1987. "Format and Symbols in TV Coverage of Terrorism in the United States and Great Britain." *International Studies Quarterly* 31:161–76.

———. 2007. "The Mass Media and Terrorism." *Discourse & Communication* 1 (3).

Arquilla, John, and Theodore Karasik. 1999. "Chechnya: A Glimpse of Future Conflict?" *Studies in Conflict and Terrorism* 22:207–29.

Arquilla, John, and David Ronfeldt. 1999. "The Advent of Netwar: Analytical Background." *Studies in Conflict and Terrorism* 22:193–206.

Arquilla, John, David Ronfeldt, and Michele Zanini. 1999. "Networks, Netwar, and Information Age Terrorism." In *Countering the New Terrorism*, edited by Ian O. Lesser et al. Santa Monica, CA: RAND), 39–84.

Avrich, Paul. 1991. *Sacco and Vanzetti: The Anarchist Background*. Princeton, NJ: Princeton University Press.

Bagdikian, Benjamin. 2000. *The Media Monopoly*. 6th ed. Boston: Beacon.

Baker, Gerard. 1999. "Starbucks Wars: The Seattle Riots Demonstrate the Failure of Mainstream US Politics to Provide an Outlet for Protest." *Financial Times*, December 4, 10.

Bandura, Albert. 2004. "The Role of Selective Moral Disengagement in Terrorism and Counterterrorism." In *Understanding Terrorism: Psychological Roots*, edited by Fathali M. Mogahaddam and Anthony J. Marsella, 121–50. Washington, DC: American Psychological Association Press.

Barber, Benjamin R. 1995. *Jihad vs. McWorld: How Globalism and Tribalism are Reshaping the World*. New York: Ballantine.

Bassiouni, M. Cherif. 1981. "Terrorism, Law Enforcement, and the Mass Media: Perspectives, Problems, Proposals." *Journal of Criminal Law & Criminology* 72 (1): 1–51.

Baudrillard, Jean. 1993. *The Transparency of Evil*. London: Verso.

Bell, Kerryn E. 2009. "Gender and Gangs: A Quantitative Comparison." *Crime and Delinquency* 55 (3): 363–87.

Bennett, W. Lance. 1990. "Towards a Theory of Press-State Relations in the United States." *Journal of Communication* 40 (Spring): 103–25.

———. 2001. *News: The Politics of Illusion*. New York: Longman.

Bennet, W. Lance, Regina G. Lawrence, and Steven Livingston. 2007. *When the Press Fails: Political Power and the News Media from Iraq to Katrina*. Chicago: University of Chicago Press.

Bennett, W. Lance, and David L. Paletz, eds. 1994. *Taken By Storm: The Media, Public Opinion, and U.S. Foreign Policy in the Gulf War*. Chicago: University of Chicago Press.

Berkowitz, Leonard, and Jacqueline Macaulay. 1971. "The Contagion of Criminal Violence." *Sociometry* 34 (2): 238–60.

Bernstein, Richard. 2004. "Tape, Probably Bin Laden's, Offers Truce to Europe." *New York Times*, April 16.

Bessner, Daniel, and Michael Stauch. 2010. "Karl Heinzen and the Intellectual Origins of Modern Terror." *Terrorism and Political Violence* 22 (2): 143–76.

Beyer, Lisa. 2001. "Roots of Rage." *TIME*, October 1, 44–47.

Bhuiyan, Natascha. 2014. "ISIS: The Propaganda Jihad." Unpublished research paper.

Birke, Sarah. "How ISIS Rules." 2015. *New York Review of Books* LXII (2): 26–28.

Bloom, Mia. 2005. *Dying to Kill: The Allure of Suicide Terror*. New York: Columbia University Press.

Bok, Sissela. 1998. *Mayhem: Violence as Public Entertainment*. Reading, MA: Perseus.

Boyer, Peter J. 1988. *Who Killed CBS? The Undoing of America's Number One News Network*. New York: Random House.

Braden, Maria. 1996. *Women Politicians and the Media*. Lexington: University of Kentucky Press.

Brody, Richard A. 1991. *Assessing the President: The Media, Elite Opinion, and Public Support*. Stanford, CA: Stanford University Press.

Brody, Richard A., and Catherine E. Shapiro. 1989. "A Reconsideration of the Rally Phenomenon in Public Opinion." In *Political Behavior Annual*, vol. 2, edited by Samuel Long. Boulder, CO: Westview.

Bryant, Jennings, and Dolf Zillmann, eds. 1986. *Perspectives on Media Effects*. Hillsdale, NJ: Laurence Erlbaum.

Carr, David. 2014. "With Videos of Killings, ISIS Sends Medieval Message by Modern Method." *New York Times*, September 8. http://www.nytimes.com/2014/09/08/business/media/with-videos-of-killings-isis-hones-social-media-as-a-weapon.html?ref=world&_r=0.

Castells, Manuel. 2009. *Communication Power*. New York: Oxford University Press.

Catton, William R. Jr. 1978. "Militants and the Media: Partners in Terrorism?" *Indiana Law Journal* 53:703–15.

Chase, Alston. 2000. "Harvard and the Unabomber." *Atlantic Monthly* 285.6 (June): 41–65.

Chomsky, Noam. 1988. *The Culture of Terrorism*. Boston: South End Press.

Conway, Maura, and Lisa McInerney. 2012. "What's Love Got To Do With It? Framing 'JihadJane' in the US Press." *Media, War & Conflict* 1 (5): 6–21.

Cook, Timothy E. 1994. "Domesticating a Crisis: Washington Newsbeats and Network News after the Iraqi Invasion of Kuwait." In *Taken by Storm: The Media, Public Opinion, and U.S. Foreign Policy in the Gulf War*, edited by W. Lance Bennett and David L. Paletz. Chicago: University of Chicago Press.

Cotter, John M. 1999. "Sounds of Hate: White Power Rock and Roll and the Neo-Nazi Skinhead Subculture." *Terrorism and Political Violence* 11.2 (Summer): 111–40.

Crelinsten, Ronald D. 1997. "Television and Terrorism: Implications for Crisis Management and Policy-Making." *Terrorism and Political Violence* 9.4 (Winter): 8–32.

Crenshaw, Martha. 1983a. "Introduction: Reflection on the Effects of Terrorism," in *Terrorism, Legitimacy, and Power: The Consequences of Political Violence*, edited by Martha Crenshaw. Middletown, CT: Wesleyan University Press.

———, ed. 1983b. *Terrorism, Legitimacy, and Power: The Consequences of Political Violence*. Middletown, CT: Wesleyan University Press.

———, ed. 1995. *Terrorism in Context*. University Park: Pennsylvania State University Press.

———. 2006. "The American Debate over 'New' vs. 'Old' Terrorism." Unpublished paper.

Creswell, Robyn, and Bernard Haykel. 2015. "Battle Lines: Want to Understand the Jihadis? Read Their Poetry." *The New Yorker*, June 8 & 15.

Dahlen, Eric R., Ryan C. Martin, Katie Ragan, and Myndi M. Kuhlman. 2004. "Boredom Proneness in Anger and Aggression: Effects of Impulsiveness and Sensation Seeking." *Personality and Individual Differences* 37:1615–27.

Danitz, Tiffany, and Warren P. Strobel. 1999. "The Internet's Impact on Activism: The Case of Burma." *Studies in Conflict and Terrorism* 22:257–69.

Davis, Mike. 2007. *Buda's Wagon: A Brief History of the Car Bomb*. London: Verso.

Deese, David A. 1994. "Making American Foreign Policy in the 1990s." In *The New Politics of American Foreign Policy*, edited by David A. Deese. New York: St. Martin's.

Delli Carpini, Michael X., and Bruce A. Williams. 1987. "Television and Terrorism: Patterns of Presentation and Occurrence, 1969 to 1980." *Western Political Quarterly* 40 (1): 45–64.

———.1994. "Methods, Metaphors, and Media Research: The Uses of Television in Political Conversation." *Communication Research* 21 (6): 782–812.

———. 2001."Let Us Infotain You: Politics in the New Media Environment." In *Mediated Politics: Communication in the Future of Democracy*, edited by W. Lance Bennett and Robert Entman. New York: Cambridge.

Dempsey, James X. 2000. "Counterterrorism and the Constitution." *Current History* (April): 164–68.

Denson, Bryan. 2001. "Eco-Terrorist Group Prolific: The Earth Liberation Front's Attacks Rack up Extensive Damages." *The Oregonian*, January 11.

Denson, Bryan, and James Long. 1999. "Eco-Terrorism Sweeps the American West." *The Oregonian*, September 26.

Dickey, Christopher, and Gretel C. Kovach. 2002. "Married to Jihad." *Newsweek*, January 14, 48.

Downing, John. 2008. "Social Movement Theories and Alternative Media: An Evaluation and Critique." *Communication, Culture & Critique* 1:40–42.

Drew, Christopher. 1995. "Japanese Sect Tried to Buy U.S. Arms Technology, Senator Says." *New York Times*, October 31, A4.

———. 1999. "Ideologues Drive the Violence." *The Oregonian*, September 27.

Driscoll, Margarette. 2015. "My ISIS Boyfriend: A Reporter's Undercover Life with a Terrorist. *New York Post*, March 7.

Edelman, Murray. 1977. *Political Language: Words that Succeed and Policies that Fail.* New York: Academic Press.

———. 1988. *Constructing the Political Spectacle.* Chicago: University of Chicago Press.

Edelstein, David. 2006. "Now Playing at Your Local Multiplex: Torture Porn. Why Has America Gone Nuts for Blood, Guts, and Sadism?" *New York Magazine*, accessed May 19, 2014. http://nymag.com/movies/features/15622.

Edwards, George C. 1983. *The Public Presidency.* New York: St. Martin's.

Elter, Andreas. 2008. *Propaganda der Tat: Die RAF und die Medien.* Frankfurt: Edition Suhrkamp.

Entman, Robert M. 1996. "Reporting Environmental Policy Debate: The Real Media Biases." *Harvard International Journal of Press/Politics* 1 (3): 77–92.

Entman, Robert M., and Andrew Rojecki. 2000. *The Black Image in the White Mind: Media and Race in America.* Chicago: University of Chicago Press.

Ewen, Stuart. 1996. *PR! A Social History of Spin.* New York: Basic.

Fallows, James. 1996. *Breaking the News: How the Media Undermine American Democracy.* New York: Pantheon.

Fanon, Frantz. 1963. *The Wretched of the Earth.* New York: Grove Weidenfeld.

Ferguson, Niall. 2001. "Clashing Civilizations or Mad Mullahs: The United States between Formal and Informal Empire." In *The Age of Terror: America and the World after September 11*, edited by Strobe Talbot and Nayan Chanda, 113–41. New York: Basic.

Finkel, Michael. 2000. "The Child Martyrs of Karni Crossing." *New York Times Magazine*, December 24.

Forest, James J. F. 2012. "Criminals and Terrorists: An Introduction to the Special Issue." *Terrorism and Political Violence* 24 (2): 171–79.

Frank, Michael C. 2010. "Alien Terrorists: Public Discourse on 9/11 and the American Science Fiction Film." In *Screens of Terror: Representations of War and Terrorism in Film and Television since 9/11*, edited by Philip Hammond. Bury St Edmunds: Arima Publishing.

Franz, Barbara. 2015. *Immigrant Youth, Hip Hop, and Online Games: Alternative Approaches to the Inclusion of Working-Class and Second Generation Migrant Teens.* Lanham, MD: Lexington Books.

Friedman, Thomas L. 2002. "No Mere Terrorist." *New York Times*, March 24, sect. 4, 15.

Gabler, Neal. 1998. *Life the Movie: How Entertainment Conquered Reality.* New York: Knopf.

Galvin, Deborah M. 1983. "The Female Terrorist: A Socio-Psychological Perspective." *Behavioral Science and the Law* 1:19–32.

Gans, Herbert J. 1980. *Deciding What's News.* New York: Vintage.

Geranios, Nicholas K. 1999. "Anarchists Occupy Building to Protest WTO." Associated Press, December 3.

Gerbner, George, and L. Gross. 1976. "Living with Television: The Violence Profile." *Journal of Communication* 26 (2): 173–99.

Golestan, Mehrak. 2004. "Dirty Kuffar," *Index on Censorship* 33 (3): 8–10.

Gordon, Avishag. 1997. "Terrorism on the Internet: Discovering the Unsought." *Terrorism and Political Violence* 9.4 (Winter): 159–65.

Graber, Doris. 1997. *Mass Media and American Politics.* Washington, DC: Congressional Quarterly Press.

Green, James. 2006. *Death in the Haymarket: A Story of Chicago, the First Labor Movement and the Bombing that Divided Gilded Age America.* New York: Pantheon.

Greenberg, Joel. 1996. "Rabin Assassin's Testimony: 'My Goal Was to Paralyze Him.'" *New York Times*, January 24.

Guelke, Adrian. 1998. "Wars of Fear: Coming to Grips with Terrorism." *Harvard International Review* (Fall): 44–47.

Gunter, Barrie. 2008. "Media Violence: Is There a Case for Causality?" *American Behavioral Scientist* 51 (8): 1061–1122.

Hallin, Daniel L. 1986. *The "Uncensored War": The Media and Vietnam.* New York: Oxford University Press.

Harmon, Christopher C. 2000. *Terrorism Today.* London: Frank Cass.

Hendrickson, Ryan C. 2000. "American War Powers and Terrorism: The Case of Osama bin Laden." *Studies in Conflict & Terrorism* 23.3 (July–September): 161–74.

Herman, Edward, and Gerry O'Sullivan. 1989. *The Terrorism Industry: The Experts and Institutions That Shape Our View of Terror.* New York: Pantheon.

Herman, Edward S., and Noam Chomsky. 2002. *Manufacturing the News: The Political Economy of the Press.* New York: Pantheon.

Herrmann, Mareike. 2008. "Not One of those Screaming Girls: Representing Female Fans in 1990s' Germany." *Women's Studies in Communication* 31 (1): 79–103.

Hickey, Neil. 1998. "Money Lust: How Pressure for Profit is Perverting Journalism." *Columbia Journalism Review* (July–August).

Highfield, Tim, Stephen Harrington, and Axel Bruns. 2013. "Twitter as a Technology for Audiencing and Fandom." *Information, Communication & Society* 16 (3): 315–39.

Hoffman, Bruce. 1995. "'Holy Terror': The Implications of Terrorism Motivated by a Religious Imperative." *Studies in Conflict & Terrorism* 18.4 (October–December).

———. 1997. "Why Terrorists Don't Claim Credit." *Terrorism and Political Violence* 9.1 (Spring): 1–6.

———. 1998. *Inside Terrorism*. New York: Columbia University Press.

———. 1999. "Terrorism Trends and Prospects." In *Countering the New Terrorism*, edited by Ian O. Lesser et al., 7–38. Santa Monica, CA: RAND.

Hollihan, Thomas A. 2001.*Uncivil Wars: Political Campaigns in the Media Age*. Boston: Bedford/St.Martin's.

Horton, Donald, and R. Richard Wohl. 1956. "Mass Communication and Para-Social Interaction: Observations on Intimacy at a Distance." *Psychiatry* 19 (3): 215–29.

Hoskin, Andrew, and Ben O'Laughlin. 2007. *Television and Terror: Conflicting Times and the Crisis of News Discourse*. Houndmills, Basingstoke: Palgrave Macmillan.

Hugick, Larry, and Alec M. Gallup. 1991. "Rally Events and Presidential Approval." *Gallup Poll Monthly*, June.

Iyengar, Shanto. 1991. *Is Anyone Responsible? How Television Frames Political Issues*. Chicago: University of Chicago Press.

Iyengar, Shanto, and Donald R. Kinder. 1987. *News That Matters*. Chicago: University of Chicago Press.

Jacobs, Lawrence R., and Robert Y. Shapiro. 2000. *Politicians Don't Pander: Political Manipulation and the Loss of Democratic Responsiveness*. Chicago: University of Chicago Press.

Jaehning, Walter B. 1978. "Journalists and Terrorism: Captives of the Libertarian Tradition." *Indiana Law Review* 53:717–44.

James, Caryn. 2001. "The Oklahoma City Bomber's Final Hours Are Hardly Television News's Finest," *New York Times*, June 12, A26.

Jenkins, Brian M. 1974. "International Terrorism: A New Kind of Warfare." The RAND Paper Series. Santa Monica, CA: RAND Corporation.

———. 1981. "The Psychological Implications of Media-Covered Terrorism." Paper issued by the RAND Corporation.

———. 1987. "Der internationale Terrorismus." *Aus Politik und Zeitgeschichte*.

Jenkins, Henry. 2006. *Fans, Bloggers, and Gamers: Exploring Participatory Culture*. New York: New York University Press.

Johnson, Larry C. 2001. "The Declining Terrorist Threat." *New York Times*, July 10, A19.

Kamin, Sam. 2007. "How the War on Terrorism May Affect Domestic Interrogations: The 24 Effect." *Chapman Law Review*, accessed May 18, 2014. http://www.chapmanlawreview.com/archives/1312.

Kaplan, Jeffrey. 1995. "Violence in North America." *Terrorism and Political Violence* 7 (1): 44–95.

Katz, Daniel, et al. 1954. *Public Opinion and Propaganda*. New York: Dryden Press.

Kegley, Charles Jr. 1990. *International Terrorism: Characteristics, Causes, Controls*. New York: St. Martin's.

Kellerman, Barbara. 1984. *The Political Presidency: Practice of Leadership*. New York: Oxford University Press.

Keohane, Robert O., and Joseph S. Nye Jr. 1998. "Power and Interdependence in the Information Age." *Foreign Affairs* 77.5 (September/October): 81–94.

Kernell, Samuel. 1985. *Going Public: New Strategies of Presidential Leadership*. 3rd ed. Washington, DC: Congressional Quarterly Press.

Kingston, Susan. 1995. "Terrorism, the Media, and the Northern Ireland Conflict." *Studies in Conflict and Terrorism* 18.

Kitman, Marvin. 2001. "The Nation's Painful Video Vigil." *Newsday*, September 23.

Kupperman, Robert, and Jeff Kamen. 1989. *Final Warning: Averting Disaster in the New Age of Terrorism*. New York: Doubleday.

Kurtz, Howard. 2001. "Media Hype May No Longer Be Necessary." *Washington Post*, September 16.

Kuzma, Lynn M. 2000. "Trends: Terrorism in the United States." *Public Opinion Quarterly* 64.1 (Spring): 90–105.

Laqueur, Walter. 1987. *The Age of Terrorism*. Boston: Little, Brown.

———. 1999. *The New Terrorism: Fanaticism and the Arms of Mass Destruction*. New York: Oxford University Press.

———. 2003. *No End to War: Terrorism in the Twenty-First Century*. New York: Continuum.

Lemann, Nicholas. 2001. "The Quiet Man." *The New Yorker* (May 7): 56–71.

Lesser, Ian O. 1999. "Changing Terrorism in a Changing World." In *Countering the New Terrorism*, edited by Ian O. Lesser, Bruce Hoffman, John Arquilla, David Ronfeldt, Michele Zanini, and Brian Jenkins, 1–5. Santa Monica, CA: RAND.

Linsky, Martin. 1986. *Impact: How the Press Affects Federal Policy Making*. New York: Norton.

Lippmann, Walter. 1997 [1922]. *Public Opinion*. New York: Free Press.

Livingston, Stephen. 1994. *The Terrorism Spectacle*. Boulder, CO: Westview.

MacArthur, John R. 1993. *Second Front: Censorship and Propaganda in the Gulf War*. Berkeley: University of California Press.

Macdonald, Andrew. 1996. *The Turner Diaries*. 2nd ed. New York: Barricade Books.

MacFarquhar, Neil. 2004. "Acting on Threat, Saudi Group Kills Captive American." *New York Times*, June 19.

Margalit, Avishai. 1995. "The Terror Master." *New York Review*, October 15.

Marsden, Paul, and Sharon Attia. 2005. "A Deadly Contagion?" *The Psychologist* 18 (3): 152–55.

Martin, David C., and John Walcott. 1988. *Best Laid Plans: The Inside Story of America's War Against Terrorism*. New York: Harper & Row.

Matusitz, Jonathan. *Symbolism in Terrorism: Motivation, Communication, and Behavior* (Lanham, MD: Rowman & Littlefield, 2014).

McElvoy, Anne. 1995. "The Trapping of a Tigress." *Times of London*, September 9.

McLuhan, Marshall. 1994 [1964]. *Understanding Media: The Extension of Man*. Cambridge, MA: MIT Press.

McMullan, Ronald K. 1993. "Ethnic Conflict in Russia: Implications for the United States." *Studies in Conflict and Terrorism* 16.3 (July–September): 201–18.

Merolla, Jennifer L., and Elizabeth J. Zechmeister. 2009. *Democracy at Risk: How Terrorist Threats Affect the Public*. Chicago: University of Chicago Press.

Michel, Lou, and Dan Herbeck. 2001. *American Terrorist: Timothy McVeigh & the Oklahoma City Bombing*. New York: Regan Books.

Midlarsky, Manus I., Martha Crenshaw, and Fumihiko Yoshida. 1980. "Why Violence Spreads: The Contagion of International Terrorism." *International Studies Quarterly* 24 (2): 262–98.

Miller, Abraham H. 1980. *Terrorism and Hostage Negotiations*. Boulder, CO: Westview.

———. 1982. *Terrorism, the Media and the Law*. Dobbs Ferry, NY: Transnational Publishers.

Miller, Martin A. 1995. "The Intellectual Origins of Modern Terrorism in Europe." In *Terrorism in Context*, edited by Martha Crenshaw. University Park: Pennsylvania State University Press.

Morgan, Robin. 2001. *The Demon Lover*. New York: Washington Square Press.

Mueller, John E. 1985. *War, Presidents and Public Opinion*. Lanham, MD: University Press of America.

———. 2006. *Overblown: How Politicians and the Terrorism Industry Inflate National Security Threats*. New York: Free Press.

Nacos, Brigitte L. 1990. *The Press, Presidents, and Crises*. New York: Columbia University Press.

———. 1994a. *Terrorism and the Media: From the Iran Hostage Crisis to the World Trade Center Bombing*. New York: Columbia University Press.

———. 1994b. "Presidential Leadership During the Persian Gulf War." *Presidential Studies Quarterly* 24.3 (Summer): 563–75.

———. 1996a. "After the Cold War: Terrorism Looms Larger as a Weapon of Dissent and Warfare." *Current World Leaders* 39.4 (August): 11–26.

———. 1996b. *Terrorism and the Media: From the Iran Hostage Crisis to the Oklahoma City Bombing*. New York: Columbia University Press.

———. 2000. "Accomplice or Witness? The Mass Media's Role in Terrorism." *Current History* 99 (April): 174–78.

———. 2003. "The Calculus behind 9-11: A Model for Future Terrorism? *Studies in Conflict & Terrorism* 26 (1): 1–16.

———. 2005. "The Portrayal of Female Terrorists in the Media: Similar Framing Patterns in the News Coverage of Women in Politics and in Terrorism." *Studies in Conflict and Terrorism* 28:435–51.

Nacos, Brigitte L., Yaeli Bloch-Elkon, and Robert Y. Shapiro. 2011. *Selling Fear: Counterterrorism, the Media, and Public Opinion*. Chicago: University of Chicago Press.

Nacos, Brigitte L., Robert Y. Shapiro, and Pierangelo Isernia, eds. 2000. *Decisionmaking in a Glass House: Mass Media, Public Opinion, and American and European Foreign Policy in the 21st Century.* Lanham, MD: Rowman & Littlefield.

Neustadt, Richard E. 1980. *Presidential Power: The Politics of Leadership from FDR to Carter.* New York: Macmillan.

New York Times. 1996. "Chechen Chief Threatens Attacks against Europe." February 7.

Nimmo, Dan, and James E. Combs. 1985. *Nightly Horrors: Crisis Coverage in Television Network News.* Knoxville: University of Tennessee Press.

Norris, Pippa. 1997. *Women, Media, and Politics.* New York: Oxford University Press.

Nunberg, Geoffrey. 2004. "The –Ism Schism; How Much Wallop Can a Simple Word Pack?" *New York Times,* Week in Review, June 11, 7.

Nye, Joseph S. Jr., and William A. Owens. 1996. "America's Information Edge." *Foreign Affairs* 75.2 (March–April): 20–36.

Ogun, Mehmet Nassid. 2012. "Terrorist Use of the Internet: Possible Suggestions to Prevent the Usage for Terrorist Purposes." *Journal of Applied Security Research* 7:203–17.

O'Sullivan, John. 1986. "Media Publicity Causes Terrorism." In *Terrorism: Opposing Viewpoints,* edited by Bonnie Szumski. St. Paul: Greenhaven.

Page, Benjamin I. 1996. *Who Deliberates? Mass Media in Modern Democracy.* Chicago: University of Chicago Press.

Page, Benjamin I., and Robert Y. Shapiro. 1989. "Educating and Manipulating the Public." In *Manipulating Public Opinion,* edited by Michael Margolis and Gary A. Mauser. Pacific Grove, CA: Brooks/Cole.

———. 1992. *The Rational Public.* Chicago: University of Chicago Press.

Paletz, David L., and Alex P. Schmid. 1992. *Terrorism and the Media.* Newbury Park, CA: Sage.

Panetta, Leon, and Jim Newton. 2014. *Worthy Fights: A Memoir of War and Peace.* New York: Penguin.

Parenti, Michael. 1992. *Make-Believe Media: The Politics of Entertainment.* New York: St. Martin's.

———. 2010. "Foreword." In *Reel Power: Hollywood Cinema and American Supremacy,* edited by Matthew Alford. London: Pluto Press.

Patterson, Thomas E. 1993. *Out of Order: How the Decline of the Political Parties and the Growing Power of the News Media Undermine the American Way of Electing Presidents.* New York: Knopf.

Picard, Robert G. 1986. "News Coverage as the Contagion of Terrorism: Dangerous Charges Backed by Dubious Science." Paper presented at the Annual Meeting of the Association for Education in Journalism and Mass Communication at Norman, OK, August.

———. 1991. "News Coverage as the Contagion." In *Media Coverage of Terrorism,* edited by A. Odasuo Alali and Kenoye Kelvin Eke. Newbury Park: Sage.

Pillar, Paul R. 2001. *Terrorism and U.S. Foreign Policy.* Washington, DC: Brookings.

Pluchinsky, Dennis A. 1997. "The Terrorism Puzzle: Missing Pieces and No Boxcover." *Terrorism and Political Violence* 9.1 (Spring): 7–10.

Postman, Neil. 1986. *Amusing Ourselves to Death: Public Discourse in the Age of Show Business*. New York: Penguin.

Pratkanis, Anthony, and Elliot Aronson. 1992. *Age of Propaganda*. New York: Freeman.

Ranstorp, Magnus, and Gus Xhudo. 1994. "A Threat to Europe? Middle East Ties with the Balkans and Their Impact upon Terrorist Activity throughout the Region." *Terrorism and Political Violence* 6.2 (Summer).

Rapoport, David C. 1997. "To Claim or Not to Claim; That is the Question—Always!" *Terrorism and Political Violence* 9.1 (Spring): 11–17.

——. 2004. "The Four Waves of Modern Terrorism." In *Attacking Terrorism: Elements of a Grand Strategy*, edited by Audrey Cronin and James Ludes. Washington, DC: Georgetown University Press.

Reeve, Simon. 1999. *The New Jackals: Ramzi Yousef, Osama bin Laden and the Future of Terrorism*. Boston: Northeastern University Press.

Reeves, Jimmy, Mark Rogers, and Michael Epstein. 1996. "Rewriting Popularity: The Cult Files." In *Deny All Knowledge: Reading the X Files*, edited by David Lavery, Angela Hague, and Marla Cartwright. Syracuse, NY: Syracuse University Press.

Reich, Walter, ed. 1990. *Origins of Terrorism: Psychologies, Ideologies, Theologies, States of Mind*. New York: Cambridge University Press.

Reuter, Christoph. 2004. *My Life is a Weapon: A Modern History of Suicide Bombing*. Princeton, NJ: Princeton University Press.

Richardson, Louise. 1999. "Terrorists as Transnational Actors." *Terrorism and Political Violence* 11 (4): 209–19.

Ridge, Tom. 2009. *The Test of Our Times: America under Siege . . . and How We Can Be Safe Again*. New York: St. Martin's.

Riley, John. 2000. "Sorting It All Out." *Newsday*, November 1, A45, A61.

Ronfeldt, David. 1999. "Netwar across the Spectrum of Conflict: An Introductory Comment." *Studies in Conflict and Terrorism* 22:189–92.

Rose, Gideon. 1999. "It Could Happen Here: Facing the New Terrorism." *Foreign Affairs* (March–April), accessed June 2, 2007. http://www.foreignaffairs .org/19990301fareviewessay1030/gideon-rose/it-could-happen-here-facing-the -new-terrorism.html.

Rose, Richard. 1991. *The Postmodern President*. 2nd ed. Chatham, NJ: Chatham House.

Rubenstein, Richard E. 1987. *Alchemists of Revolution: Terrorism in the Modern World*. New York: Basic.

Rubin, Bernard. 1985. *When Information Counts: Grading the Media*. Lexington, MA: Lexington Books.

Rubin, B., and J. C. Rubin. 2002. *Anti-American Terrorism and the Middle East*. New York: Oxford University Press.

Sageman, Marc. 2004. Understanding Terror Networks. Philadelphia: University of Pennsylvania Press.

——. 2008. *Leaderless Jihad*. Philadelphia: University of Pennsylvania Press.

Said, Edward W. 1981. *Covering Islam: How the Media and the Experts Determine How We See The Rest Of The World*. New York: Pantheon.

Scheuer, Jeffrey. 1999. *The Sound Bite Society: Television and the American Mind.* New York: Four Walls Eight Windows.

Schlesinger, Philip, Graham Murdock, and Philip Elliott. 1984. *Televising Terrorism: Political Violence in Popular Culture.* New York: Charles Scribner's Sons.

Schmid, Alex P., and Janny de Graaf. 1980. "Insurgent Terrorism and the Western News Media: An Exploratory Analysis with a Dutch Case Study." Center for the Study of Social Conflicts, Dutch State University, Leiden, The Netherlands.

——. 1982. *Violence as Communication: Insurgent Terrorism and the Western News Media.* Beverly Hills, CA: Sage Publications.

Sedgwick, Mark. 2004. "Al Qaeda and the Nature of Religious Terrorism." *Terrorism and Political Violence* 16 (4): 795–814.

——. 2007. "Inspiration and the Origins of Global Waves of Terrorism. *Studies in Conflict & Terrorism* 30 (2): 97–112.

Seib, Philip. 2001. *Going Live: Getting the News Right in a Real-Time, Online World.* Lanham, MD: Rowman & Littlefield.

Shanahan, James, and Michael Morgan. 1999. *Television and its Viewers: Cultivation Theory and Research.* New York: Cambridge University Press.

Shaw, Tony. 2015. *Cinematic Terror: A Global History of Terrorism on Film* (New York: Bloomsbury).

Shiper, David K. 1998. "Blacks in the Newsroom." *Columbia Journalism Review* (May–June).

Simon, Steven, and Daniel Benjamin. 2001. "The Terror." *Survival* 43.4 (Winter): 5–18.

Sontag, Deborah. 2000. "Israel Acknowledges Hunting Down Arab Militants." *New York Times*, December 22, A12.

Spencer, Alexander. 2006. "Questioning the Concept of 'New Terrorism.'" *Peace Conflict & Development* 8 (January): 1–33.

Steffensmeier, Darrell, and Emilie Allan. 1996. "Gender and Crime: Toward a Gendered Theory of Female Offending." *Annual Review of Sociology* 22 (1996): 459–87.

Stern, Jessica. 1999. *The Ultimate Terrorist.* Cambridge, MA: Harvard University Press.

——. 2000. "Pakistan's Jihad Culture." *Foreign Affairs* (November–December).

Stern, Kenneth S. 1996. *A Force Upon the Plain: The American Militia Movement and the Politics of Hate.* New York: Simon & Schuster.

Stever, Gayle S. 2009. "Parasocial and Social Interaction with Celebrities: Classification of Media Fans." *Journal of Media Psychology* 14 (3). http://web.calstatela.edu/faculty/sfischo.

Tarrow, Sidney. 2011. *Power in Movement: Social Movements and Contentious Politics.* 3d ed. New York: Cambridge University Press.

Thorup, Mikkel. 2008. "The Anarchist and the Partisan—Two Types of Terror in the History of Irregular Warfare." *Terrorism and Political Violence* 20 (3): 333–55.

Tilly, Charles, and Sidney Tarrow. 2007. *Contentious Politics.* New York: Oxford University Press.

Tilly, Charles, and Lesley J. Wood. 2009. *Social Movements 1768–2008.* 2nd ed. Boulder, CO: Paradigm.

Tremlett, Giles. 2002. "ETA Brings Women Fighters to the Fore." *The Guardian* (London), August 27.

Tulis, Jeffrey K. 1987. *The Rhetorical Presidency.* Princeton, NJ: Princeton University Press.

Van Atta, Dale. 1998. "Carbombs & Cameras: The Need for Responsible Media Coverage of Terrorism." *Harvard International Review* (Fall): 66–70.

Verhovek, Sam Howe, and Joseph Kahn. 1999. "Talks and Turmoil: Street Rage; Dark Parallels with Anarchist Outbreak in Oregon." *New York Times*, December 3, A12.

Vetter, Harold J., and Gary R. Perlstein. 1991. *Perspectives on Terrorism.* Pacific Grove, CA: Brooks/Cole.

Victor, Barbara. 2003. *Army of Roses: Inside the World of Palestinian Women Suicide Bombers.* New York: Rodale.

Walsh, Kenneth T. 1996. *Feeding the Beast: The White House versus the Press.* New York: Random House.

Walter, Christopher. 2002. "Twisted by Anger, She Turned to Terror." *Times of London*, January 31.

Weimann, Gabriel. 2006. *Terror on the Internet: The New Arena, the New Challenges.* Washington, DC: United States Institute of Peace.

Weimann, Gabriel, and Conrad Winn. 1994. *The Theater of Terror: Mass Media and International Terrorism.* New York: Longman.

Whine, Michael. 1999a. "Cyberspace—A New Medium for Communication, Command, and Control by Extremists." *Studies in Conflict and Terrorism* 22:231–45.

———. 1999b. "Islamist Organizations on the Internet." *Terrorism and Political Violence* 11.1 (Spring): 123–32.

Whiting, Sophie A. 2012. "The Discourse of Defence: 'Dissident' Irish Republican Newspapers and the 'Propaganda War.'" *Terrorism and Political Violence* 24 (3).

Whitlock, Craig. 2004. "From Bin Laden, Different Style, Same Message," *New York Times*, November 25.

Wieviorka, Michel. 1993. *The Making of Terrorism.* Chicago: University of Chicago Press.

Wilcox, Philip C. 2001. "The Terror." *New York Review of Books*, October 18.

Wilkinson, Paul. 1997. "The Media and Terror: A Reassessment." *Terrorism and Political Violence* 9 (Summer): 132–34.

———. 2001. *Terrorism versus Democracy: The Liberal State Response.* London: Frank Cass.

Wolfsfeld, Gadi. 2001. "The News Media and the Second Intifada." *Harvard International Journal of Press/Politics* 6 (4): 113–18.

Wright, Robin. 2007. "From the Desk of Donald Rumsfeld . . ." *Washington Post*, November 1.

Yankelovich, Daniel. 1991. *Coming to Public Judgment.* Syracuse, NY: Syracuse University Press.

Yoo, John. 2006. *War by Other Means.* New York: Atlantic Monthly Press.

Young, Marissa. 2015. "Inside ISIS: How the Islamic State is using Media to Capture World Attention." Unpublished seminar paper, Columbia University.

Zaller, John R. 1992. *The Nature and Origins of Mass Opinion.* New York: Cambridge University Press.

Zanini, Michele. 1999. "Middle Eastern Terrorism and Netwar." *Studies in Conflict and Terrorism* 22:247–56.

Zoroya, Greg. 2002. "Her Decision to Be a Suicide Bomber." *USA TODAY,* April 22, A1. Retrieved from the ProQuest archive on November 1, 2003.

Index